To Lynne Allen
Love, Melissa Forney

THE
ASTONISHING JOURNEY
OF
TEDDY BODAIN

Professional Resources by Melissa Forney

Dynamite Writing Ideas

The Writing Menu

Razzle Dazzle Writing

Primary Pizzazz Writing

Writing Superstars: How to Score More Than Ever Before

Pizzazz: Songs for the Writing Classroom

Melissa Forney's Picture Speller for Young Writers

Melissa Forney's Word Wall Words

The Astonishing Journey of Teddy Bodain, TEACHER EDITION

Teddy Bodain's Adventure Quest (Language Arts Workbook)

Melissa Forney's Writing Camp

Fiction by Melissa Forney

No Regard Beauregard and the Golden Rule

A Medal for Murphy

Oonawassee Summer

To Shape a Life

The Astonishing Journey of Teddy Bodain

THE ASTONISHING JOURNEY OF TEDDY BODAIN

Written by Melissa Forney

Illustrated by Dave Olson

The Astonishing Journey of Teddy Bodain
by Melissa Forney

Book Design: Vickie Raines Spurgin
Illustrations: Dave Olson
Editors: Rebecca Rossi and Naomi Ingram
Proofreader: Tiffany Morgan

Printed in USA
Printing No. 10 9 8 7 6 5 4 3 2 1
Library of Congress Cataloging-in-Publication Data
Forney, Melissa 1952-
        The Astonishing Journey of Teddy Bodain/Melissa Forney.
                p.cm. — (Teddy Bodain)
        Summary: An eleven-year-old girl crosses primitive Florida
by covered wagon in the year 1892. She is separated from her parents
in a yellow fever epidemic and has to survive on her own.

ISBN: 978-0-9790094-4-0
Library of Congress Control Number: 2008904290

Published by:

Buttery Moon Multimedia, Inc.
2487 S. Volusia Avenue
Suite 107
Orange City, FL 32763
Phone: 800-500-8176
Phone: 386-532-3600
Fax: 386-532-3800
www.butterymoonmultimedia.com

Dedication

To Carolyn Kinslow
who lights the world with humor
and bubbles over with laughter.
MJF

To my wife, Barbara
who hangs in there with me
and shares all of life's joys.
DWO

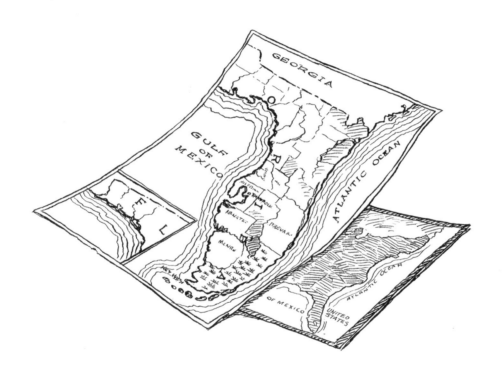

Contents

Acknowledgments

I would like to thank the following people for their help in composing questions and writing prompts and for their careful reading of my manuscript: Dr. Rick Forney, Rebecca Rossi, Maureen O'Neill, Victoria Greening, Jan Rule, and Rebecca Reynolds. Along with Katie Rule and Debbie Goguen, you form a cohesive, thoughtful, caring staff. I value your help, as I could never do it alone.

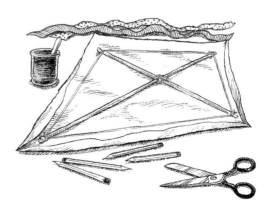

Notes to Teachers from the Author

I have walked the same road you are walking. I am a writing teacher and was in the classroom for many years. My specialty is teaching primary and intermediate children how to tap into their imaginations and use their natural creativity. What fun! Some of my best moments have been spent collaborating with kids. Their natural curiosity and zaniness are catnip to an author.

I also write writing books for teachers. For many years teachers have asked, "Hey, why don't you write a book that starts on day one and tells us exactly what to teach each day?" That would be nearly impossible, I thought, because kids all over this country study different topics and come from different backgrounds. They have had a variety of experiences and have a veritable smorgasbord of interests. And of course, you can't generalize about kids: no two are alike. Ask any mother. She'll tell you.

Still, I know teachers everywhere have to teach writing and language arts skills because of increased pressure for kids to score well on state and national testing. Many of the teachers I work with want to pull out their hair because their current writing curriculum produces "cookie-cutter writing" that is both boring and repetitive. So I thought, there must be some way to combine an adventurous story that kids would love, along with writing assignments, vocabulary, reading questions, grammar questions, and so forth.

And so, after some dreaming and scheming, Teddy Bodain was born.

The Astonishing Journey of Teddy Bodain is an outdoor historical novel, set in the year 1892. Teddy's adventure is meant to START ON THE FIRST DAY OF SCHOOL, or as soon as possible after your year starts. The novel, told through the letters of a ten-year-old girl, has been serialized to be read every day for 130 days of school. This means that, in most places, you would start in August and finish sometime in March.

Teddy's letters have a corresponding language arts lesson on the back of each day. Each day's lesson covers one of the following topics:

reading and vocabulary	writing skill questions
narrative writing	reading short response
expository writing	reading extended response
grammar	persuasive writing

This means there are 16+ lessons for each of these topics. Let's hope you are doing cartwheels right now! It's not easy to come up with language arts lessons that make kids beg for more. I've tried to use all of my powers, so the story would be thrilling, and your students would hardly know they were learning new skills on every page. Try it, sometime, and see if it ages you like it has me.

Almost all of the corresponding lessons that teach these language arts skills are included in my books, *Razzle Dazzle Writing* and *Writing Superstars: How to Score More Than Ever Before*. Both books are results based and have been used in thousands of classrooms with gratifying success, I am happy to report. References for specific skills and lessons are in the back of this book.

You will read *The Astonishing Journey of Teddy Bodain* each day with your students. You have permission from Buttery Moon Multimedia Inc. to copy the lessons as you need them. The student novel is now available for purchase so that your students may follow along as you read the letters aloud.

You will teach writing-skill lessons from *Writing Superstars* and *Razzle Dazzle Writing* or any other balanced literacy resource. And finally, you and your students will use the lessons that correspond with each day's letter as the application.

MODEL:	Read one letter from *The Astonishing Journey of Teddy Bodain*.
TEACH:	Teach lessons from *Writing Superstars* and *Razzle Dazzle Writing*.
APPLICATION:	Complete the lesson that corresponds with each day's letter.

March 7, 1892

Dear Martha,

We left two weeks ago today, but so much has happened, it seems like we've been gone forever. I still can't believe we are part of a wagon train. Everywhere I look are covered wagons, up front and behind. Did you ever dream I would be on a wagon train? That sounds like something we would read about in a dime novel!

I wish you and your family could have come with us. It's different for you. Your pap owns his own land. Mama hated to leave Mississippi, but owning land means everything to her and Pap. This is their chance. The worst part for me was leaving you. I'll miss Mississippi, but—Florida! What will it be like? The chance to have a new adventure.

I had to get used to riding all day in the wagon. Mama and I ride on the wooden seat up behind Jester and Jingo. That's right, the same mules Pap plowed the fields with. They are the prettiest team on the train. Some folks already have their oxen, but most are driving mules. Pap said we'll have to trade our mules in for oxen when we reach Dothan, Alabama.

I like being up high on the wagon seat. It's incredible! You can see everything from up there. But the wagon bounces and lurches when one of the mules steps in a rut. I get sore after a while, especially on my sitting-down place. Ha ha!

You saw our wagon before we left Salter's Grove, but that was before we covered it with the huge canvas. The first day out we stopped early, so Mama and I spread the canvas out on the grass and painted it with linseed oil. Linseed oil makes it waterproof. Pap stretched it up over the wooden stays, and he and Mama and I lashed it all around, as tight as a drum. Of course, the wagon is not as roomy as our cabin, but it will have to be our home for the journey. Pap says he's hoping we'll be on our land in four months, even though it is 1,000 miles away. That sounds like the longest trip imaginable.

We don't have all our supplies yet. We'll stop to buy everything when we cross Alabama and arrive in Dothan. Mama brought food from home to last till then. That way, the wagon is not so heavy for the mules to pull. Pap wants them to be in good shape, so he can get top dollar when he trades for oxen.

You would be so proud of Jester and Jingo, especially Jester. He's so handsome. I know they're the same old mules we had on the farm, but they look like royal horses when they pull this fine wagon. A boy my age, whose wagon is ahead of ours by about ten wagons, walked by yesterday. He yelled, "Them's fine mules!"

I shouted back, "The finest on this train!" Mama pinched me. She said the kids will think I'm stuck up if I talk like that. She is always trying to hush me.

Martha, how am I going to make it on this journey without you? I promise to write every day or as often as I can. Will you write me, too? For now, you can send your letters to: Miss Theodosia Bodain, C/O Postmaster, General Delivery, Dothan, Alabama.

It will be weeks till I get there, but I will look forward to hearing from you. Martha, you are my best friend forever!

Love,
Teddy

Reading Multiple Choice Questions for the Letter of March 7, 1892
Circle the letter of the correct answer.

1. Where is Teddy's wagon train headed?
   A. from Alabama to Florida
   B. from Mississippi to Alabama
   C. from Mississippi to Florida
   D. from Florida to Georgia

2. Who are Jester and Jingo?
   A. oxen
   B. horses
   C. alligators
   D. mules

3. Why are Pap and Mama moving?
   A. to go swimming in the ocean
   B. to own their own land
   C. to ride in a covered wagon
   D. to visit their relatives

4. What will Pap trade the mules for?
   A. wagon
   B. sheep
   C. oxen
   D. house

5. Who is Teddy writing to?
   A. Martha
   B. Helen
   C. Grace
   D. Audrey

6. What did a boy yell at Teddy?
   A. "Come see me."
   B. "Them's fine mules!"
   C. "Ready, set, go!"
   D. "There's trouble up ahead."

7. Read the following sentence from the story.
   She is always trying to hush me!
   What does the word *hush* mean?
   A. quiet
   B. obey
   C. hurry
   D. listen

March 8, 1892

Dear Martha,

This morning, as we were driving the wagon, Mama said, "Oh, look, Teddy! There's a cardinal. See his bright red color? Seeing a redbird means good luck."

Mama and her birds. She used to tell me that when the cardinals start singing, as the sun comes up, it sounds like they're saying, "Good morning! Good morning!"

The people in the wagon in front of us are the Carters. They're older than Pap and Mama. Their son and his wife, Emily, and their baby have the wagon in front of them. All the Carters shared supper together with us last night. The men built the fire and watered the teams. Mama and Mrs. Carter made black-eyed peas, ham, and cornbread. Emily and I bathed her baby and Dylan in a tub. Her baby, Lucy, is a year old. Even though Dylan is almost two, they had a good time together splashing in the water.

After we bathed the babies, we washed their diapers, rinsed them, and Emily helped me twist out all the water. You know how I hate that part. She strung a line between our wagons, and we hung the diapers out to dry overnight. I have to wash diapers every night, so Dylan will have fresh ones for the next day. Sometimes, Mama swaps chores with me. She lets me wash the supper dishes, and she does the diapers.

My favorite time of day is after supper when all the chores are done. We sit outside by the fire. We can see the fires of all the other families stretched along the train. We can hear folks playing the fiddle or the mandolin. Pap plays his harmonica sometimes. Mr. Carter, his son, Martin, and Pap talk about the trip and tell stories. Mama and Emily rock their babies by the fire while Mrs. Carter bundles her healing herbs. I'm just supposed to listen. Mama says children should be seen and not heard. But even so, I like listening to the stories and watching the babies fall asleep.

At night, Mama and I sleep in the wagon with Baby Dylan between us. We have a soft pallet on the floor. Mama made it out of old blankets and goose down. I always put Veronica beside me on the pillow. I still can't believe you gave her to me, Martha. She is the best going-away present ever, and she is the most beautiful thing I've ever owned. I will keep her forever.

This afternoon, Mama used her paints to paint some little flowers along the back of our wagon. They're bright and cheerful and make our wagon look different from anyone else's. Mama is so smart.

It's still cold, especially after the sun goes down. I'm glad we have the featherbed to keep us warm. Pap sleeps outside under the wagon. I don't know how he stands it. Mama heats big rocks in the campfire, and when they're piping hot, she wraps them in felt. She tucks them in Pap's sacking to keep his feet warm. Then, she covers him with several quilts on top of the sacking. Pap says he sleeps nice and cozy.

Pap and the other men sleeping under their wagons watch for rustlers and varmints. I wonder what we'll have to watch for in Florida. Folks say Florida is a wilderness.

Great buckets of butterbeans!

Oh, remember that kid who is from the wagon ten wagons ahead of us? He came by today, when we were rolling, and asked, "You play marbles?"

I said, "Better than any boy!" It's a good thing Mama didn't hear me.

He said, "Alright then. How about tomorrow?"

Wait till I whup him good! I'll show that kid who's boss.

Love,
Teddy

Name_____ Date_____

Reading Multiple Choice Questions for the Letter of March 8, 1892
Read and answer the writing prompt below.

Narrative Prompt: Teddy had to leave her friends and her life in Mississippi behind. Think about something important you've had to leave behind. It could be one of your possessions. It could be a friend or a family member. It could be a teacher who was especially kind. It could even be a place. Now write the story of what happened and what you had to leave behind. Add details and examples, so we can understand how you felt. Use an additional piece of paper if you need more room to write. When you've finished, read your story to yourself. Ask yourself, are there any important details I've left out? If so, add them in. Now share your story with another writer.

_____

_____

_____

_____

_____

_____

_____

_____

_____

_____

_____

_____

_____

_____

_____

March 9, 1892

Dear Martha,

I lost my best shooter and 12 of my favorite marbles. Vexation!

That kid I told you about, Travis, showed me a thing or two about playing marbles. We played Ring Taw, and he was good! He said he'd give them back because this was the first time we'd played together, but I said, "No, we said 'keepsies,' and you won fair and square." So my marble sock is half empty. I wasn't too mad about it 'cause we had fun. I'm planning to win them back, anyway.

Guess what? I counted the kids on the wagon train. There are 56 children from 24 families. That's not counting the babies. Those are the kids who are at least three years old and older. I met another girl my age, Minnie Good. Everyone likes her because she's GOOD. Get it? I like her, too, but you will always be my best friend.

Martha, I have the best news to tell you. Miss Cassie Melman, six wagons back, is riding with the wagon train even though she's a single lady. She was a teacher in Mississippi and has agreed to have school for us children several times a week, whenever we can. Isn't that terrific?

I hope she has some good books. You know how I am with books.

Miss Melman is pretty and wears her hair up under a straw hat. She also wears long, white, starched skirts. I think she looks so smart and stylish. I told Mama all about it, and she said, "Let's see how long Miss Cassie Melman can keep those white, starched skirts clean."

We're starting school tomorrow afternoon. How in the world will we have school on a wagon train? I wonder.

I forgot to tell you that we brought Girlie with us. You know Mama wouldn't leave Mississippi without her. She's tied to the back of our wagon on a loose line and walks along when we're rolling. Mama milks her first thing each morning. I milk her at night. When we pass meadows of what Mama calls "good grass," she tells me to run cut a basketful for Girlie. She says, "I don't want her getting into milkweed or onion grass." Mama puts the extra grass in a huge bag and hangs it from the side of the wagon. If we camp by a field of clover or good grass, Pap stakes Girlie out with the mules, and she can eat to her heart's content. If not, Mama feeds her the sweet, dried grass from the bag. I think anyone who produces milk for an entire family deserves the best grass the Good Lord can provide, don't you?

We made pancakes this morning for breakfast. I skimmed the cream from Girlie's milk, poured it in a glass canning jar, added a pinch of salt, and shook it until it turned to butter. We're camped right by a spring. The water's cold, so I washed the ball of butter in the cold water to get the whey out. Mama said it was the best butter she'd ever tasted. I told Mama her pancakes were the best I'd ever tasted.

Pap said, "I have the two best cooks on the train."

The candle has burned low and will soon go out. Mama saves the stubs for me, so I can write after she blows out the lantern. She is trying to save our oil until we get to Dothan. I melt the ends of the stubs and stick them together, so I have one tall candle. It's not pretty, but it works.

I can hear Pap snoring. Mama and Dylan have been asleep for a while now.

I better get some shut-eye.

Love,
Teddy

Name_____ Date_____

Reading Short Response Questions for the Letter of March 9, 1892
Read the example. Now read and answer the questions below it.
Be sure to use complete sentences to answer the questions.

1. How do we know Girlie is important to Mama?

   Mama wouldn't leave Mississippi without Girlie. She makes sure

   Girlie gets "good grass." Mama asks Teddy to cut sweet grass, and put

   it in a special bag. If there is no good grass to eat, Mama feeds her the

   sweet, good grass from the bag. I know Girlie must be important to Mama

   because she makes sure she milks Girlie first thing in the morning.

   _____

   _____

2. Why does Pap say, **"I have the two best cooks on the train,"** to Mama and Teddy?

   _____

   _____

   _____

   _____

   _____

   _____

   _____

3. What are some things you know about Miss Cassie Melman?

   _____

   _____

   _____

   _____

   _____

March 10, 1892

Dear Martha,

We had school today. During the afternoon break, Miss Melman met with those of us who are 11 to 14 years old. I know what you're thinking. My birthday isn't until June, but it's so close, she said I could join the older group.

Miss Melman reminds me of Miss Pedigrew at Salter's Grove School. She tells wonderful stories. She's originally from Charleston, South Carolina, and took piano lessons from the time she was a child. Martha, she has a piano on the wagon train! I know it seems hard to believe. Way, way back at the end of the train there are two extra wagons. Folks hired drivers and their wagons to take extra belongings and furniture to Florida.

Miss Melman took us to the very end of the train and showed us her piano. She told us she tipped the men who loaded the wagon to put her piano in last by the back opening. That way, she can sit on the little stool and play it anytime she wants. When she's not playing, she keeps it covered with three quilts and an oilcloth. It's a deep red wood. Mahogany, she calls it. Mama would love to own a piano like that. She always wanted to learn to play. I guess that's why she sings so much.

I told Mama about the piano. I thought she'd be happy about it, but she said, "What will Miss Cassie Melman do in Florida with a piano and starched, white skirts?" Then, for a while, she wouldn't talk to anyone. I can't figure her out sometimes.

Anyway, let me get back to the school part. Miss Melman will have school with several groups of kids each week. One of the men drives her wagon, and that frees her up to teach. Sometimes, we will meet during a rest period when we stop to let the animals rest. Sometimes, we will stop early, so we can have school for longer periods of time.

The kids who don't know their letters, or how to read very well, are in the beginner group. I'm in the intermediate group. Minnie Good is in my group, too. So is Travis Lark, the boy who beat me out of my marbles. They're both 11. I'm the youngest, but I'm still the best reader. The only thing is, our teacher, Miss Melman, uses my real name, Theodosia, not Teddy. I told Mama. She said, "You tell Miss Fancy Pants she can call you Teddy like everyone else." I had to grit my teeth when Mama said that. Why does Mama say things like that? Great buckets of butterbeans!

During our class, we reviewed the alphabet, the vowels, and consonants with hornbooks. Surprise! Miss Melman has a trunk full of BRAND NEW hornbooks because she is on her way to Florida to teach at The Sheridan School for Girls. Since they're new, the horn coverings are very clear with no scratches or curled-up corners. Remember the ones at Salter's Grove School? I still have a scar on my arm where a piece of old horn had curled away from the nail.

Anyway, Miss Melman said that she will read two books to us while we are on our journey: Alice in Wonderland, for the girls, and Tom Sawyer, for the boys. I am so happy about that. It will make the trip go faster.

After school was over, Travis and I played marbles again. I knuckled down as best as I could, but Travis won the lag and got to start. He picked off ten more of my marbles. I'm down to six. I lost my peewee and two of the cat's eyes I won from your brother.

Vexation!

Love,
Teddy

Name_____ Date_____

Expository Writing Prompt for the Letter of March 10, 1892
Read and answer the writing prompt below.

Expository Prompt: Going to school on a wagon train in 1892 was very different from the way we go to school today. Think about some of the differences. Now explain those differences. Be sure to include details and examples, so we'll be able to form a "mind movie" of just what you mean. Remember your paper needs a beginning, a middle, and an ending. If you need more space, continue on another sheet of paper. After you write, read your piece to yourself. Think of ways to improve, and add those improvements to your writing. Now share your expository piece with another writer. Help each other improve.

_____

_____

_____

_____

_____

_____

_____

_____

_____

_____

_____

_____

_____

_____

_____

_____

_____

_____

_____

_____

March 11, 1892

Dear Martha,

Today is Saturday, but we are on the move, just like usual. The sky is as blue as a cornflower. Sometimes, Mama and I look at the clouds and try to say what the shapes look like. But not today. There's not a cloud in the sky.

I spent most of today walking or riding with Pap. Mama was happy to sit up on the wagon seat by herself and let me play. The train moves slowly—the pace of mules walking—so I'm allowed to go anywhere I like, as long as I keep up and don't lag behind the last wagon. I feel as free as a bird!

For a while, Pap let me ride with him on Gabriel. As one of the men who "pushes" the train, Pap has to get up early and build a fire or stoke the coals from last night's fire, so Mama or I can cook breakfast. Then, he wakes the families along the caravan and meets with Captain Walsh about the route for the day. They look at maps and decide how far we'll go and where we'll make camp for the night.

After that, when we shove off, Pap rides along beside the wagons and makes sure everything is in working order. That's when he lets me ride with him. I sit right behind Pap on Gabe's back and hold on to his waist. When I want to get down, I slide off the back end, over Gabe's rump. The only bad part is I feel bowlegged for a while when I get down. Yep, that's me: Bowlegged Teddy.

I walked for a while with Minnie Good and her sister, Hallie. They both have cornhusk dolls they made before the trip. I carried Veronica. Minnie thinks she is elegant. Hallie especially loves her hair. When I told them it was your very own real hair, cut by your mother and glued onto Veronica's china head, they wanted to touch it to feel how real it is.

While we were walking, Travis Lark galloped up with big news. He's one of the messenger boys. He rides his horse, Dixie, all up and down the train delivering messages to the pushers or taking notes to different families. He said Captain Walsh announced that tonight we will camp just outside of Meridian, and we'll stay until Monday! Do you know what that means? We will get to see the biggest city in Mississippi! Minnie and Hallie and I talked all about it. Meridian has a huge railway station, wide city streets with lots of stores, and a Grand Opera House. Emily Carter has been there and showed me a stack of postcards.

Miss Emily is nice. She has some fashion catalogues, and she gave them to me, Minnie, and Hallie. We rip out pictures of people and glue them to cardboard. Then, we cut them out and cut stands for their feet, so they'll stand up on their own. The next thing we do is cut out all sorts of clothes from the catalogue pages and leave little paper tabs on them when we cut them out. Then, we fold them over, like paper dolls. Minnie and Hallie and I LOVE cutting out our paper dolls, and we each have whole families of them. We have dozens and dozens of outfits for them, too.

Miss Emily said maybe later on she'll teach me how to make my own real doll clothes for Veronica. I can already sew and mend, but I've never actually cut out doll clothes and sewn them up. That will be lots of fun. Then, I can make Veronica matching outfits to mine.

As soon as I found out we're stopping at Meridian, I ran home to tell Mama. Of course, she lit up like a Christmas tree. Mama has always wanted to see Meridian. Who knows what all we will see and do?

Love,
Teddy

Name_____ Date_____

Reading Extended Response Questions for the Letter of March 11, 1892
Read the example. Now read and answer the questions below it.
Be sure to use complete sentences, reasons, and details to answer the questions.

1. Explain some things Teddy does to have fun during the day on the wagon train.

The wagon train moves very slowly, so the trip might be long and boring.
Teddy spends part of the day riding with Pap on his horse, Gabriel. That
way she gets to see what Pap's day is like and some of the chores he has
to do. Teddy likes to carry her doll, Veronica, while she walks beside
the wagons with her friends, Minnie and Hallie. She likes to show off
Veronica a little because she is more elegant than a cornhusk doll. She
and her friends also have a ball by making paper dolls from catalog
pictures. They cut out people, glue them to cardboard, and find pictures of
clothes they can dress them with.

2. Why did Travis Lark gallop up to Teddy, Minnie, and Hallie? What did this mean for the girls?

_____

_____

_____

_____

_____

_____

_____

_____

_____

_____

_____

March 12, 1892

Dear Martha,

We are camped at Meridian, Mississippi. Today is the day! We are going into town as soon as Mama finishes putting up her hair and Pap shines his boots. Everyone is excited about seeing this grand town and all the sights. I'm about to jump out of my shoes if they don't hurry up!

Mama and I spent last evening taking baths, washing our hair, and laying out our outfits. Mama set the washtub right beside our wagon on the far side. She hung quilts around it for privacy while I heated buckets of water over the campfire. Pap hauled more buckets of fresh water for rinsing.

It felt great to take a bath. The mules and wagons churn up a lot of dust each day, and it gets in our clothes and shoes and hair. The water felt warm and soothing. I used a cake of soap and a sponge and scrubbed away the layers of sweat and dust. Mama washed my hair, and I brushed it dry near the fire.

Mama has been saving our good clothes in case we stop somewhere special. Well, Meridian is about as special as it gets. I'm wearing my new blue dress with the white pinafore. I braided my hair and tied blue bows on the ends.

I'm not the only excited one. We're all in a tizzy! Last night, we were so excited about our trip into Meridian, we forgot to eat! Just before bedtime, Pap said, "Grace, did we forget to eat supper?"

Mama looked shocked. Then, she said, "Dalton Bodain, I do believe you are right!" and we had a good laugh about it. She gathered some cornbread left over from midday, and we ate cornbread with honey and drank some of Girlie's milk. It was like having a picnic right here inside the wagon, just the four of us. It was just our family, having fun together.

Dylan said, "Tornbread." Isn't that cute? Tornbread. He says something new every day. He is so adorable in his outfit. He has a matching hat, and it makes him look like a little man.

Pap is calling. It's time to go into town. Martha, I wish you were going with me, but I'll write every detail in my next letter.

Love,
Teddy

Grammar Questions for the Letter of March 12, 1892
Circle the letter of the correct answer.

1. Which sentence has the correct use of commas?
   A. Mama and I spent last evening taking baths, washing our hair, and laying out our outfits.
   B. Mama and, I spent last evening, taking baths washing our hair and laying out our outfits.
   C. Mama and I spent last evening taking baths washing our hair and laying out our, outfits.
   D. Mama, and I spent last, evening taking baths washing our hair and laying out our outfits.

2. Where do the quotation marks go in the following dialogue?
   A. Dylan "said," Tornbread.
   B. Dylan said, "Tornbread."
   C. "Dylan said," Tornbread.
   D. Dylan said, Torn"bread."

3. What should go at the end of this sentence?
   Isn't that cute
   A. a period
   B. an exclamation point
   C. a quotation mark
   D. a question mark

4. In the following sentence, which word is incorrect?
   Last night, we was so excited about our trip into Meridian, we forgot to eat!
   A. night
   B. about
   C. was
   D. forgot

5. In the following sentence, which word is the verb, or action word?
   Pap hauled more buckets of fresh water for rinsing.
   A. hauled
   B. rinsing
   C. more
   D. water

6. In the following sentence, what punctuation mark would be the best ending?
   We're all in a tizzy
   A. a question mark
   B. a period
   C. quotation marks
   D. an exclamation point

March 13, 1892

Dear Martha,

Goodness gracious and great buckets of butterbeans! How can I ever explain all about Meridian? It was astounding! I will try to describe everything, so you can experience it with me.

Trains from all over Mississippi and Atlanta and other places arrive here in Meridian many times each day, blowing their steam whistles. Clouds of white steam shoot up into the air. When the conductor shouts, "All aboard!" you better scamper on that train because it's about to leave the station. We saw many travelers with fine trunks and stylish clothing.

Dylan sat on Pap's shoulders and waved. A girl wearing a sailor dress handed him a red balloon. He clapped his hands and said, "Loon!"

I have never seen so many bicycles in one place. They are every color of the rainbow and finely made. We first started seeing them on the walk into town, but there are many of them on the streets of Meridian, too. Men, women, and children ride bicycles—whole families. We saw a pretty girl and her beau on a bicycle built for two. I've seen women ride side-saddle, but here, many of them straddle their bikes with one foot on each side. No kidding! Most of the women who ride that way were wearing special bicycle bloomers. Not skirts—BLOOMERS! It was a funny sight. Can you picture a bunch of women in their bloomers, riding bicycles? Pap said, "What next?"

"Very practical," Mama said. "Why shouldn't women wear split skirts or bloomers? One day, women might wear trousers, like men. Skirts and dresses aren't always best for working or riding a horse or a bicycle." I hope someday I get to ride a bicycle wearing bloomers. Will you do it, too?

When we arrived in downtown Meridian, Mama said, "Dalton, I'd like to have our photograph taken while we're wearing our good clothes."

I expected Pap to throw his hat down, but he said, "Grace, I'd be right proud to have a photograph."

Mama said, "Good. I don't know when I've seen you look more handsome."

Pap said, "It's not every day that I get to walk hand in hand down the streets of Meridian with a gal as pretty as you."

Mama blushed!

We went to Mr. L.H. LeGrand's Photographic Studio and had our picture taken. The photographer got under a black drape that hung from his enormous camera. We had to stand very still, and that is hard to do with an almost two-year-old baby. But Mr. LeGrand let Dylan keep his balloon for the picture, and he settled down.

I sat next to Pap, Dylan sat on Pap's lap, and Mama stood behind Pap with her hand on his shoulder. Mama may not wear starched, white skirts like Miss Melman, but she was beautiful. When Mr. LeGrand took our photograph, he used flashing powder that flashed as bright as lightning. It startled us! We thought Dylan might cry, but he said, "Boom!"

We walked down Main Street and, Martha, there were more stores than you could shake a stick at. There were millinery stores with lovely new hats displayed in the windows. There were stores that sold clothing and sundries, drugstores, hardware stores, bookstores, butcher shops, a Christmas store, and a store that sold nothing but ice. The place where every woman wanted to go, however, was the Marks Rothenberg Department Store. It's the biggest store you could ever imagine, with floors and floors of stuff for sale. Absolutely everything. We even bought a sit-down lunch and root beer mugs at their fountain.

But that's not the best part! Wait till you hear this!

I'll have to tell you tomorrow. Mama told me to blow out the candle. She's told me twice, and she means business this time. Vexation!

Love,
Teddy

Writing Questions for the Letter of March 13, 1892
Circle the letter of the correct answer.

1. Read the following sentence from Teddy's letter:
   When the conductor shouts, "All aboard!" you better scamper on that train because it's about to leave the station.
   What is the word *scamper* an example of that is a good idea to use in our own writing?
   A. an expression
   B. a mini-story
   C. a strong verb
   D. a simile

2. Read the following sentence from Teddy's letter:
   There were stores that sold clothing and sundries, drugstores, hardware stores, bookstores, butcher shops, a Christmas store, and a store that sold nothing but ice.
   What does the author use that we should use in our own writing?
   A. descriptive writing
   B. specific examples
   C. persuasive writing
   D. juicy color words

3. Read the following sentence from Teddy's letter:
   He clapped his hands and said, "Loon!"
   What is this an example of that we should use in our own writing?
   A. a simile
   B. onomatopoeia
   C. dialogue
   D. an opinion

4. Read the following passage from Teddy's letter:
   We saw many travelers with fine trunks and stylish clothing. Dylan sat on Pap's shoulders and waved. A girl wearing a sailor dress handed him a red balloon.
   What is this an example of that we should use in our own writing?
   A. onomatopoeia that shows sound effects
   B. descriptive writing that allows our reader to picture what we are describing
   C. comparing two things using the words "like" or "as"
   D. dialogue

5. In Teddy's letter, Dylan uses the word, **"Boom!"** This word is dialogue, but what is it also an example of that we should use in our own writing?
   A. an adjective
   B. an opinion
   C. a simile
   D. onomatopoeia

March 14, 1892

Dear Martha,

Here's the continuation of "Teddy Bodain's Bodacious Trip into Meridian." Ha ha! When we went to see the Grand Opera House on 5th Street, people were gathered all over, admiring the beautiful, red building. Mama wanted to read the poster that tells what opera or operetta would be presented that day. We went to the lobby to read the poster, and there was Miss Cassie Melman.

She said, "Why, hello, Mrs. Bodain. I'm so happy to see you!"

Mama looked surprised. She said, "Oh?"

Miss Melman acted like she was telling Mama a secret. "I just met the piano player of the opera house. I told him I, too, play the piano. He was kind enough to give me three tickets to today's matinee. Three free tickets! Isn't that wonderful?"

Mama didn't act like it was wonderful. She said, kind of stiff-like, "How nice for you."

Miss Melman said, "Do you know what's playing?"

Mama said, "The poster says that today's operetta is The Pirates of Penzance."

Miss Melman clapped her hands. "Yes! I've always wanted to see it. I'm a big fan of Gilbert and Sullivan operettas. I saw The Mikado and H.M.S. Pinafore back in Charleston. They are just the happiest, most funny musicals. The Pirates of Penzance is supposed to be their finest work." Then, she said, "Would you please join me, Mrs. Bodain? We could go to the matinee performance together and use these tickets."

Mama looked at Pap. He smiled. "I think that's a fine idea."

Mama's face was all sunshine. She said, "I would be delighted to attend with you, Miss Melman. How kind of you to ask."

I'm ashamed to say it, but I thought I would die on the spot. I knew that Mama was going to ask me to watch Dylan, and I wouldn't get to go. I tried not to pout. I was happy for Mama but sad for me.

But dear Miss Melman said, "This is a once-in-a-lifetime opportunity. Mrs. Bodain, would you permit Theodosia to join us? I have another ticket. The three of us could go together."

I didn't beg, but my eyes were as big as saucers. I held my breath.

Mama looked toward Pap. She and I knew someone had to take care of Dylan. This was Pap's special day, too.

We knew he would want to go to the hardware store and the livestock stockade.

Pap didn't let us down. He said, "Why don't I take this big ol' boy with me, and we'll go to the hardware store like men, while you hens go to the musical." I wanted to dance for joy!

Mama said, "Theodosia, would you like to join us?" Great buckets of butterbeans! Mama called me Theodosia, right in front of Miss Melman.

I said, "Yes, Mama, thank you, and thank YOU, Miss Melman." I acted ladylike, but in my mind, I was jumping up and down and doing cartwheels on the sidewalk.

The Pirates of Penzance was INCREDIBLE. Tomorrow, I'll tell you all about it.

We are leaving Meridian this morning. Mama reminded me that now would be a good time to post all your letters. She is going to town one last time. I unknotted my handkerchief and gave her a penny for each letter. Remember the pennies we saved?

Love,
Teddy

Name_____ Date_____

Persuasive Writing Prompt for the Letter of March 14, 1892
Read and answer the prompt below.

Persuasive Prompt: Miss Melman invited Teddy to see the production of *The Pirates of Penzance*, a once-in-a-lifetime experience. If you had a choice, would you rather live during the time of pirates or now? Decide which you would prefer. Now convince us why your choice is BETTER than the other one. Use examples, reasons, comparisons, and great descriptions as you persuade us.

_____

_____

_____

_____

_____

_____

_____

_____

_____

_____

_____

_____

_____

_____

_____

_____

_____

_____

_____

_____

March 15, 1892

Dear Martha,

I wish you could have been with me for the performance of The Pirates of Penzance. The Grand Opera House was a sight. It had carved balconies, artistic silhouettes painted on the ceiling, gold-covered drama and comedy masks, velvet curtains, and plush, upholstered seats. It looked like something out of a picture postcard. I now know that the reason they call it "The Grand Opera House" is because it is very grand, indeed.

Miss Melman told us that the operetta would be funny, and she was not kidding. We spent the afternoon laughing. I never knew what I've been missing.

The story is about a man, Frederick, who has grown up as an apprentice to a group of pirates. The pirates like to think that they are fierce, but they are really a bunch of marshmallows.

Frederick has to work for the pirates until he turns 21 years of age, which he has. He tries to leave their company, but at the last minute, just before he is to marry the beautiful Mabel, the pirates inform him that he was born on leap year, February 29th, and that he has only had five birthdays. That means that in their eyes, he is only five years old, not 21. But in the end, it all turns out well, and Frederick gets to marry Mabel.

We laughed at so many things during the performance, my sides hurt. The pirates acted crazy and swung out over the audience on ropes. One pirate winked at me and dropped a beautiful pink rose in my lap. He was very handsome. I winked back, and Mama pinched me.

She whispered, "Don't be fresh."

Oh! Mama just doesn't understand me sometimes. I was just getting into the spirit of the play.

The women's costumes were made of the finest silks and satins in bright yellow, red, blue, coral, turquoise, and purple. They were exquisite and stylish. During the intermission, I heard Miss Melman and Mama discussing the styles and fabrics. I never knew Mama was interested in those kinds of things. Great day in the morning!

Another feature that was incredible was the orchestra. There were at least 25 musicians, all dressed in fine black evening clothes. I've heard Pap play the fiddle before, but this was nothing like that. During the second intermission, Miss Melman took me forward to look in the orchestra pit. She pointed out the cello, viola, oboe, clarinet, trumpet, French horn, flute, piccolo, and the kettle drums. There were others, but I forget what all they were. I've never seen so many instruments in one place.

The man who is the piano player came over to speak to Miss Melman.

He said, "I see you used your tickets. I'm glad to see you here."

Miss Melman introduced me as her student. The piano player said, "Well, Theodosia, what do you think of our production of The Pirates of Penzance?"

I said, "I think it's spectacular."

He said, "Then, please come backstage after the performance and meet the cast."

Mama was impressed that we were allowed to go backstage when the musical was over. I met the pirate who gave me the pink rose, the pirate who had winked at me. Mama was standing beside me.

He said, "I'm glad you brought your sister with you to meet the cast."

Mama blushed! I bet she secretly likes handsome pirates, too.

I want to be a singer when I grow up and star in a Gilbert and Sullivan operetta. I will never forget this day for as long as I live. The only thing that would have made it better is if you had been there, too.

Love,
Teddy

Reading Multiple Choice Questions for the Letter of March 15, 1892
Circle the letter of the correct answer.

1. What does Teddy say the Grand Opera House looks like?
   A. like a queen's palace
   B. like her old school
   C. like something out of a picture postcard
   D. like the theater of Shakespeare

2. What did Teddy do that made Mama pinch her?
   A. she winked at a pirate
   B. she pinched Miss Melman
   C. she talked during the performance
   D. she wouldn't sit still

3. What did the pirate drop in Teddy's lap?
   A. a looking glass
   B. a pink rose
   C. a yellow daisy
   D. a French horn

4. When asked what she thought of the production of *The Pirates of Penzance*, Teddy said that
   it was **"spectacular."**
   What does the word *spectacular* mean?
   A. terrific, fantastic, wonderful
   B. terrible, awful, horrible
   C. mysterious, curious, weird
   D. ordinary, boring, so-so

5. Miss Melman showed Teddy the cello, viola, oboe, clarinet, trumpet, French horn, flutes,
   piccolos, and the kettle drums.
   What are these things?
   A. pirate gear
   B. ship gear
   C. instruments in the orchestra
   D. good things to eat

6. Teddy's letter tells us Mama blushed.
   What does the word *blush* mean?
   A. Mama was cold
   B. Mama's face turned red
   C. Mama's toes tingled
   D. Mama was hot

March 16, 1892

Dear Martha,

So many good things have happened to me in the last three days, I can hardly take it all in. When Mama came back from town this morning, she had a package for me. Inside were three pencils, a pencil sharpener, an eraser, two tablets of paper, a box of envelopes, and four candles. I almost fell over. Three pencils, all at once! What a windfall.

She said, "It's an early birthday present. You've always got your nose in a letter, writing with nubs of pencils, and trying to see by stubby little candles." She put her hand under my chin and said, "I'm proud that you are a writer. Keep it up." Great buckets of butterbeans! Mama is proud of me.

Yesterday, Mama made a johnny cake for our lunch. She made an extra one, and she asked me to take it to Miss Melman. It was her way of saying thank you for sharing her tickets. Then today, Miss Melman walked along with the train and caught up with our wagon. She gathered her skirts and climbed right up on the seat with Mama. Mama smiled when she saw Miss Melman had come for a visit.

"I'm having to walk extra today because that johnny cake you made was so good, I ate every bite of it. Thank you kindly," Miss Melman said.

I was feeding Dylan right behind them in the wagon, so I could hear their talk. I wanted to be out there so bad, but I knew I had better stay right where I was. Mama left all her friends behind in Mississippi. It was nice that Miss Melman had come to call.

Mama said, "We had the best time at the opera house. I thank you again for inviting us."

Miss Melman said, "I've been thinking, Mrs. Bodain. I know you love music. Theodosia tells me you've always wanted to learn how to play the piano."

Tarnation. I didn't mean for her to go and tell Mama what I said.

But Mama said, "I've considered it, yes. But I never had a piano."

Miss Melman said, "Well, I've come to suggest a trade. I hate to admit it, Mrs. Bodain, but I have no cooking experience to speak of. Somehow, I've gotten by with not cooking all of my life. I lived at home, where we had a cook, and then I attended college, where we took our meals in a cafeteria. I've lived in boarding houses, where the food was provided. But now that I'm going to live on my own in Florida…."

Mama said, "You'll need to know how to cook."

Miss Melman said, "It's a bit embarrassing, I'm afraid. Would you teach me, Mrs. Bodain? Theodosia tells me you are a terrific cook. I can tell from the johnny cake you sent over that she's right."

Mama said. "That girl runs her mouth too much. But yes, I'll teach you."

Miss Melman sounded excited. "Then, I'll teach you to play the piano." Mama must have looked shocked, because Miss Melman said, "Yes, I will. You can learn on my piano in the last wagon. By the time we reach your new home in Florida, you'll be able to play most hymns and a few solo pieces."

Mama said, "Do you think so, Miss Melman?"

Miss Melman said, "I certainly do. And please call me Cassie."

Mama said, "It would give me something to look forward to. I get so tired of sitting up here on this seat all day, bouncing around, following the wagon in front. Maybe Teddy—Theodosia—would watch Dylan for me while we have lessons."

Martha, I couldn't help myself. I shouted, "I WILL!"

Mama called, "Are you back there listening to our talk?" But she wasn't mad. "We've got a trade," she told Miss Melman. "And please call me Grace."

I am so happy when a good thing happens for Mama.

Love,
Teddy

Name_____ Date_____

Narrative Writing Prompt for the Letter of March 16, 1892
Read and answer the following writing prompt.

Narrative Prompt: Teddy received a wonderful present from Mama. Think of a wonderful present you have received, OR you can make up an imaginary present. Think about the details of the gift: What did it look like? What made it wonderful? Why were you happy to receive it? Who gave it to you and why? After you've thought of these details, write the story. Write descriptively, so we can form "mind movies" of your experience. When you've finished, ask other students to help you improve. Share your stories aloud with each other.

_____

_____

_____

_____

_____

_____

_____

_____

_____

_____

_____

_____

_____

_____

_____

_____

_____

March 17, 1892

Dear Martha,

We have been on the road for 25 days. We left on February 22nd. That means we've traveled over 200 miles. I have never been so far from home before. Pap says our journey will be 1,000 miles. Our next big stop is Dothan, where we will buy most of our supplies.

Alabama is like one big pine forest. Everywhere you look are the tallest trees, towering overhead like giants. We have passed a lot of farms. The people come out to wave us on. I'm sure we make a curious sight, a train of big, covered wagons, and people and animals walking along beside it. I feel like we are on a great adventure. Folks must know we are homesteading, because sometimes they call out, "Where you headed?"

Captain Walsh calls, "Florida!"

Then, they yell, "Good luck!" or "Don't let the gators get you!"

One man shouted, "There's rich land down that-a-ways." I'm sure Pap was glad to hear that.

We spotted a cardinal this morning. Mama said, "A redbird! Good morning, Mr. Redbird!" She pointed to a brown bird who fluttered and landed on a bush near the cardinal. "That's his mate. See? She's brown, but she sings just as sweetly." I hope we have cardinals in Florida, or Mama is going to be very disappointed.

Today, we had school again. We had a spelling bee. We did really well, so as a reward, Miss Melman started reading Tom Sawyer. We flipped a coin to see whether we would read Alice in Wonderland or Tom Sawyer first. Well, the coin was "heads," so we started with Tom Sawyer. I was secretly glad, even though Miss Melman chose that book as the boys' book. She read aloud to us for almost an hour. I can already tell that it's going to be the best book ever.

She read the part about Tom having to whitewash Aunt Polly's fence as punishment for skipping school. He tricked the rest of his friends into whitewashing the fence for him. He acted like whitewashing was the best fun a kid could have. When his friends came by to watch him work, he went on and on about how much fun he was having. They actually paid him to let them take turns whitewashing his aunt's fence. When the fence was whitewashed (in record time!), Tom had a pocketful of money. He was so clever.

We moaned when Miss Melman stopped reading and said, "That's all for today."

Guess what? Travis Lark is teaching me how to use a slingshot. I've never owned one before, but Travis had an extra strip of rubber, and he cut a sling for me. I still think he feels bad for taking my marbles. This afternoon we stopped to let the animals drink at a wide stream. Travis told me to search for small, smooth stones to use as ammunition. I filled my pockets with them.

He cut a thin branch fork, shaped like the letter "y," from a hickory tree growing near the stream. He wound the strip of rubber around each of the forks of the "y." Man, can that thing shoot! Martha, hickory wood doesn't bend much, so it makes a perfect slingshot. I put a small stone in the center of the rubber sling, pulled it back, took aim, and let her fly. I can shoot far! We practiced the rest of the afternoon, shooting at targets along the way. I'm going to practice every day. I still don't have any aim.

Love,
Teddy

Name_____ Date_____

Reading Short Response Questions for the Letter of March 17, 1892
Read the example. Now read and answer the questions below it.
Be sure to use complete sentences to answer the questions.

1. What is the difference between a cardinal and his mate?

The cardinal is red, but his mate is brown. The cardinal is a male,

and his mate is a female. The cardinal usually leads the way. His mate

follows behind.

_____

_____

2. How did Tom Sawyer trick his friends?

_____

_____

_____

_____

3. Why do you think Miss Melman chose *Tom Sawyer* for the boys and *Alice in Wonderland* for the girls?

_____

_____

_____

_____

_____

4. How would a slingshot be useful in Teddy's day?

_____

_____

_____

_____

March 18, 1892

Dear Martha,

We had fresh fish for breakfast this morning. I've never tasted anything so good.

Last evening, we camped by a river. Pap and I went fishing. He cut two bamboo poles and strung them with line while I caught crickets. The fish were biting! As fast as I could bait my hook, there was a bluegill on the line.

Pap said, "Teddy, if you know how to fish with next to nothing, you'll never go hungry. See how I cut these poles? Bamboo grows all over. You just have to look for it growing near water. I keep a length of fishing line in my pocket, but you can use string or thread or whatever you have handy. I've caught a fish on my boot string before."

I said, "And it wasn't hard to catch crickets. I just swooped my hand through the tall grass and looked for whatever tried to hop away."

Pap said, "Most fish like to bite when the sun is just coming up or going down. They get hungry, just like we do, and a cricket looks mighty good. You can use anything for bait: worms, minnows, crickets."

I said, "Did you fish when you were a boy?"

Pap said, "All the time. Me and my dog, Darby. He went everywhere I went."

I thought about that. "I'd like to get a dog."

Pap said, "That's a fine idea." I thought it was a fine idea, too. Why hadn't I thought of it before?

I said, "Where would I get a dog? We're on the move all the time."

Pap said, "At the right time, a dog will find you."

We caught 13 bluegill. Pap strung them together by running the line through their gills. He slipped the fish back down in the river to keep them alive and tied the line to a big rock. I used a chalky rock to write BODAIN on the big rock, so folks from the train would know they were our fish if they came to the same spot. Pap went back early this morning to clean the fish with his knife.

"Always bury the heads and guts," he said. "Never leave a mess behind."

Now, this morning, I fried the fish over our campfire. Mama was feeding Dylan, but she told me what to do. I dipped the fish in cornmeal and fried them in our big black skillet in lard. When they were brown on one side, I turned them over on the other side. I made a pot of grits, and that was our breakfast. Mama said I did as good a job as any grown woman.

One thing about being in a wagon train: you have to do everything, or as much as you can, while the train is rolling or in the little time before we leave in the morning or before the sun goes down when we stop to camp. In the morning, Mama puts our clothes to soak in buckets of river water and hangs them on the side of the wagon. Then, in the afternoon, she scrubs them on a board, rinses them, and hangs them on a line Pap strings beside our wagon for the night.

It's my job to redd up the wagon each day. Once we get rolling, I shake out our featherbed and roll it up. I fold the blankets and Pap's quilts. Then, I sweep the floor and set up Dylan's playpen. Mama and Pap made it before we left. It's almost as big as the center of the wagon. Dylan can play with his blocks and toys while we are on the move. A wagon can be dangerous for a baby because the back is open, and he might tumble out. Sometimes, Miss Emily invites Dylan over, and he and Lucy play together in her playpen.

Dylan is getting so smart. He calls me "Taddy," and he can name some of the animals in my picture book. But one thing upsets me. He ALWAYS wants to play with Veronica. When he sees me take her out, he screams, "Ronnie! Ronnie!" and tries to reach her. She is too beautiful and delicate for a baby to play with.

Love,
Teddy

Expository Writing Prompt for the Letter of March 18, 1892
Read and answer the following writing prompt.

Expository Prompt: Teddy learns how to fish. This could be an important skill for her survival. Think of an important skill you have learned. If you can't think of one, you can make up a skill, and pretend you are now an expert. Now write an expository piece, and explain your skill. Remember to include lots of specific details and descriptive writing, so we can picture your skill and how to do it. Be sure your piece has a beginning, a middle, and an ending.

_____

_____

_____

_____

_____

_____

_____

_____

_____

_____

_____

_____

_____

_____

_____

_____

_____

_____

March 19, 1892

Dear Martha,

Something terrible happened today. Hallie Good, Minnie's little sister, had a terrible accident, something I just warned about in my last letter. Astonishing!

While the caravan was moving, she was sitting too near the back of their wagon and tumbled out to the ground. The fall broke her arm, and the wagon behind the Good's wagon had to turn quickly to keep from running her over.

Travis Lark rode to tell the pushers, and the whole train stopped. All the grownups came to look, even Captain Walsh.

Mama didn't want me to go, but I said, "Mama, I have to go! It's Hallie!" So she let me.

Hallie's arm was broken bad. This part will be hard to read, Martha. Mrs. Carter, our neighbor, and her husband had to set Hallie's arm. It was terribly painful. Hallie cried something awful. I wanted them to stop. They finally lined up her bones. That was a relief. Then, Mrs. Carter wrapped her arm with a long, rolled-up bandage. While she wrapped it, Mr. Carter heated a little pot of wax over the campfire. He used a paintbrush to paint Hallie's arm bandage all over with a thick coat of wax. While the wax was still soft, Mrs. Carter put a long, smooth, wooden splint alongside Hallie's arm.

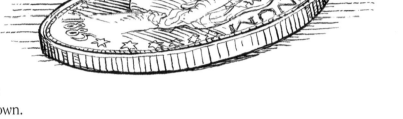

Then, she wrapped it again with another long bandage, and Mr. Carter painted it again with the wet wax. Soon, Hallie's arm was as snug as a bug in a rug.

Captain Walsh said, "You are a brave girl," and gave her a silver dollar. She's the only kid I know with a silver dollar. I hope she lets us look at it up close. I've never had a silver dollar of my own.

Now, Hallie has to wear a sling to keep her arm still. Mrs. Carter gave her a tincture to help with the pain. I hope I never break my arm, that's for sure.

Pap rode up in the wagon with me this afternoon. Mama went to take her first piano lesson, and I had to watch Dylan. I can't watch a baby who squirms all the time and drive the team, so Pap drove, and I held Dylan on my lap. I like it when Pap is driving our wagon. He whistles a lot and tells stories.

"Teddy," he said, "what do you think of our trip so far?"

I said, "I don't know. It's fun."

Pap said, "I see you writing all the time. What are you writing?"

I told him about writing to you. He said, "When I was a boy, I don't think I wrote a single letter. I didn't have anyone to write to. We didn't know our kinfolk. The only other Bodain I'd heard about was a cousin, Daniel Bodain, who lived near Micanopy, Florida. I would have liked to have known him."

I like it when Pap tells me about our family.

"My father died when I was about your age. I had to grow up quick. Be a man. Help my mama like my father had. I put new hinges on our cabin door. I learned to hunt and fish to put food on the table. I plowed the field and helped Mama bring in all the crops."

"How did you learn to do all that?" I asked.

"Just by doing. You can learn anything if you need to."

I told him about my slingshot. "That's a handy skill to have. Are you any good?"

I said, "Not yet, but I'm practicing." I want to get good at it. Maybe I can help Pap put food on the table.

Love,
Teddy

Name_____ Date_____

Reading Extended Response Questions for the Letter of March 19, 1892

Answer the questions below. Be sure to use complete sentences, reasons, and details.

1. Using details from the letter, explain how Mr. and Mrs. Carter set Hallie's broken arm. How did Hallie feel during and after the time her arm was being set? How do you know?

_____

_____

_____

_____

_____

_____

_____

_____

2. When Pap was a boy, his father died. He had to do things to help him **"grow up quick."** Explain what Pap did to grow up quick. How did he learn to do those things?

_____

_____

_____

_____

_____

_____

_____

_____

_____

_____

March 20, 1892

Dear Martha,

It rained all day today. It was miserable traveling in the rain. Mama put an oilcloth over us to keep us dry as we drove the team. Jester and Jingo were soaked. The road is full of puddles and mud, so we had to go slowly. A muddy road can mean danger for animals who are pulling a heavy load.

Baby Dylan cried all day. Mama thinks he's teething. I spent a long time rocking him and singing all his favorites. He loves for me to sing "The Little Green Frog Who Lives in the Bog."

When I went to get one of his books down from the shelf, he saw Veronica. You can imagine what happened then. He cried, "Ronnie! Ronnie!" I didn't want to, but I let him hold her while I rocked him, and he finally went to sleep. While he was sleeping, I put Veronica back up on the shelf. I don't want her to get wet and dirty on a day like this.

I sat by Mama on the wagon seat. "Am I selfish because I don't let Dylan play with Veronica?"

Mama said, "I think you're trying to take care of something that is precious to you. That's not being selfish. You're good to your brother."

That made me feel a little better. I love Dylan to pieces, but a baby could ruin a doll.

Today is Sunday, but we couldn't have preaching because it was too wet. Folks rode in the wagons instead of walking alongside. That made the train very slow because of the heavier load and because of the mud. At times, it seemed like we were hardly moving. Most of the time, folks get down and walk along. That makes the load lighter for those of us who have mules instead of oxen.

Mama and I were going out of our minds with boredom. We played games, naming all the birds we could think of and then all the different kinds of trees we could think of. We told riddles. Then, I got an idea. When Dylan was taking his nap, I got my copy of Little Women and read it aloud. Mama loved it.

She said, "I read Little Women when I was a girl, Teddy. Beth was always my favorite. She's the one who played the piano so beautifully."

There we were, under an oilcloth, in the rain, driving a team of mules, headed for Florida. But as I read, we both felt like we were actually in the story. Have you read it, Martha? The story is about four sisters: Jo, Amy, Beth, and Meg. Their father is a chaplain during The War Between the States. Jo is my favorite character because she loves to write so much (but sometimes she has a bad temper), and she's a tomboy and loves adventure, just like I do.

Now, I'm reading two books at once: Tom Sawyer, which Miss Melman is reading aloud to us, and Little Women, which I am reading aloud to Mama. So today wasn't a total loss with all the rain. Mama and I have a book to share.

Another good thing is that we caught rainwater in buckets. Pap and all the men filled their canteens. You never know when we might not have a stream or a river or a spring to camp near. Water is precious. We collect it wherever we can. Rainwater is like gold.

I have still been thinking of getting a dog. A dog would be a good companion. But we're on the move almost every day, driving from one place to the next.

How will a dog ever find me?

Love,
Teddy

Grammar Questions for the Letter of March 20, 1892
Circle the letter of the correct answer.

1. In the following sentence, which word is the subject?
   A muddy road can mean danger for animals that are pulling a heavy load.
   A. muddy
   B. animals
   C. road
   D. danger

2. Which sentence has the correct use of commas?
   A. I love Dylan to pieces, but a baby could ruin a doll.
   B. I love Dylan to pieces but, a baby could ruin a doll.
   C. I love Dylan, to pieces, but a baby could ruin a doll.
   D. I love Dylan to pieces but a baby, could ruin a doll.

3. Which example has the word spelled correctly?
   A. Beutifully
   B. Butifulley
   C. Beautifully
   D. Beautifuly

4. In the following sentence, which word is incorrect?
   Pap and all the men filled there canteens.
   A. men
   B. and
   C. canteens
   D. there

5. What punctuation mark should go at the end of this sentence?
   A dog would be a good companion
   A. a question mark
   B. a period
   C. a quotation mark
   D. a parenthesis

6. What is needed at the end of the following sentence?
   How will a dog ever find me
   A. a period
   B. a question mark
   C. a capital letter
   D. an exclamation point

March 22, 1892

Dear Martha,

Good news! The sun is shining. Jumping jubilation! Everything had to dry out: our clothes, our canvas, even Pap's feet. Captain Walsh stopped the train yesterday because we weren't making progress in such a downpour anyway. The wagon wheels were caked with mud. That made it too hard on the mules to pull the wagons.

Martha, Mama did something that was a wonder. Pap's feet were bothering him something awful. His boots were soaked through, and he'd been out in the driving rain trying to help folks settle their wagons in the downpour. Mama helped him get his boots off, but it was a chore. The leather was tight, and Pap's feet were swollen. Mama put some thick mud in the bottom of the washtub and hauled it up in the wagon.

She smoothed the mud flat and put a folded newspaper on top of the mud. Then, she stacked small pieces of fat lighter wood we had stored in a box under the seat of the wagon and lit a fire. She fixed a place for Pap to sit, so his feet were up over the washtub. In no time, Pap's feet were dry, and he was smiling.

He said, "My feet are dryer than seven acres of parched corn!"

Can you believe Mama made such a good fire right up in the wagon? I wish I was smart like her.

Today, she's drying Pap's boots, so he's wearing his old plowing boots. We're on the move again. Early this morning every man, woman, and child helped scrape mud from the wagon wheels. We had to scrape it off and sling it to the side, so the next family wouldn't drive through it again once we got going.

I haven't been able to write since Sunday. It was just too crazy with all this rain. We were crowded into the wagon, day and night. We kept warm by huddling together. Since we had nothing else to do, we played checkers. Pap beat us every game! I lit one of my candle stubs and read Little Women. Mama and I already knew the story, of course, but Pap had never heard it before.

The lightning crackled something awful. That scared Baby Dylan, and we took turns holding him and playing little games to keep him entertained. I felt sorry for most folk's mules and oxen. They had to stand out in the rain the entire time, but not Jester, Jingo, Gabriel, and Girlie. Pap strung a big oilcloth between our wagon and the Carters' wagon in front of us. He propped it up with poles, so our animals could be out of the rain.

Pap slept in the wagon with us because it was far too wet for him to sleep under the wagon. Before he went to bed, Mama rubbed his feet with lard. I was supposed to be asleep, but when they thought I wasn't listening, I heard Pap say, "Grace, I love you more than the moon is round."

Mama said, "Oh, go on."

Pap said, "I do. I can't help it. I love you more than the stars are bright."

Mama said, "Hush now. Teddy will hear."

Pap said, "So what if she hears? I love you, and I hope you love me, too."

Mama didn't say anything, so Pap said, "Well, do you?"

She still didn't say anything, so Pap said again, "Well, DO YOU?"

I could hear Mama laughing real quiet. Then, she whispered, "Well, what woman wouldn't love a man who keeps her milk cow out of the rain?"

Pap said, "Well, alright then."

Great buckets of butterbeans! Mama and Pap sound like sweethearts.

Love,
Teddy

Writing Questions for the Letter of March 22, 1892
Circle the letter of the correct answer.

1. Read the following sentence from Teddy's letter:
    He said, "My feet are dryer than seven acres of parched corn!"
    Pap's statement is an example of what kind of writing skill?
    A. strong verb
    B. transitional phrase
    C. comparison
    D. juicy color word

2. Read the following sentence from Teddy's letter:
    The leather was tight, and Pap's feet were swollen.
    This sentence is an example of what type of writing skill?
    A. descriptive writing
    B. persuasive writing
    C. onomatopoeia
    D. beginning, middle, and ending

3. Read the following phrase from Teddy's letter:
    Jumping jubilation!
    This phrase is an example of what type of writing skill?
    A. simile
    B. juicy color word
    C. dialogue
    D. voice

4. Read the following sentence from Teddy's letter:
    The lightning crackled something awful.
    The word *crackled* is an example of what type of writing skill that we should use in our own writing?
    A. simile
    B. adverb
    C. onomatopoeia
    D. specific emotion word

5. Read the following sentences:
    Great buckets of butterbeans! Mama and Pap sound like sweethearts.
    These sentences are examples of what type of writing skill that we should use in our writing projects?
    A. details that you can picture
    B. zinger
    C. grabber
    D. strong verbs

March 23, 1892

Dear Martha,

Tomorrow, we'll be in Dothan, Alabama, the last stop before Florida. We'll spend a few days in Dothan, so folks can buy supplies, trade in their mules, get haircuts, and so forth. I'm going to go straight to the post office to see if I have a letter from my best friend, Martha Lyndall!

Captain Walsh had a meeting with Pap and the other train pushers this morning. He said that we all should be on the lookout for rattlesnakes. Rattlesnakes can grow as thick as a man's arm, he said, and six feet long. They usually stay hidden under old logs or piles of pine needles, but after a heavy rain, they like to sun themselves. I hope no one stumbles onto a rattlesnake. Pap said if you come across one, the best thing to do is to back away. I don't want to tangle with a rattlesnake!

I've been practicing my slingshot. Minnie and Hallie asked Travis to make them one, so now we each have our own slingshot. Travis points out targets along the way, and we practice hitting them. That is, Minnie and I practice. Hallie can't use her broken arm for several more weeks, and you can't use a slingshot one-handed!

Yesterday, Travis said, "Teddy, you're getting pretty good with that thing. Have you shown your pap?" I want to get really good before I show Pap. Minnie's just getting started. Sometimes, she lets the stone fall out before she releases the sling. Sometimes, I do that, too.

I got to thinking. I'm a strange kind of tomboy. I like to play dolls with Minnie and Hallie, and I like to cook with Mama. On the other hand, I like driving the team, fishing, and using my slingshot. But then again, I like to go to musicals, like The Pirates of Penzance.

I asked Mama about it, and she said that I was a sponge and not to worry about it.

I said, "What do you mean by a sponge?"

Mama said, "You soak up knowledge everywhere you turn, Teddy. You are a most inquisitive girl."

Guess what? Miss Melman came over for a new cooking lesson today. The men had just shot a deer, so Pap brought home two pieces of venison, one for us and one for the Carters. Mama showed Miss Melman how to cut the meat into cubes, soak it in brine, and make a delicious stew.

Mama said, "Venison can be tough, so you have to soak it first to make it tender."

She showed Miss Melman how to set up the tripod over the fire and hang the pot just right, so it would come to a boil.

Mama said, "You want your pot to hang just over the flames, but you don't want them licking up the side of the pot." She saw how Miss Melman had hung the pot. "Cassie, you've got it just right. Your stew will cook but won't burn. I do believe you are catching on right quick-like."

While the stew was bubbling along, Mama and Miss Melman cut up potatoes, onions, carrots, and apples to add to the stew.

Miss Melman said, "Apples, Grace? I never would have thought to add apples."

Mama said, "Just wait till you taste it. They add a hint of sweetness that is oh, so good."

All the Carters joined us for supper. Mrs. Carter brought cornbread and cucumber salad. Miss Emily brought fresh water from the spring and boiled raisin pudding. We had a feast! Everyone complimented Miss Melman and Mama on the stew. Mama is a good teacher.

Love,
Teddy

Name_____ Date_____

Persuasive Writing Prompt for the Letter of March 23, 1892
Read and answer the following prompt:

Persuasive Prompt: In today's letter, Mama is teaching Miss Melman how to cook. Do you think it is better to learn to cook at Teddy's age or when you are older like Miss Melman? Give convincing arguments for the opinion you choose. Include in your argument the best way to learn to cook. Read your paper quietly to yourself and add any details and good writing skills that you might have missed. Share your paper with another writer in your class.

_____

_____

_____

_____

_____

_____

_____

_____

_____

_____

_____

_____

_____

_____

_____

_____

_____

_____

_____

_____

March 24, 1892

Dear Martha,

After a long day's drive, we have arrived in Dothan, Alabama! It's too dark to see much of anything, so I'll tell you all about it tomorrow.

We had school today. Miss Melman played a game with us where we had to know our multiplication tables and quickly give the answers. I was a little embarrassed because I'm not as good at arithmetic as I am at spelling, grammar, and writing. But Minnie was a whiz! She knew every answer!

Miss Melman said, "Minerva, you knew every single multiplication answer correctly. Our entire class is going to walk back to my piano, and I will play a beautiful piece of music in your honor." We all thought that was a terrific prize, although I was just a teensy bit jealous that it was Minnie and not me.

Travis Lark helped take the quilts and oilcloth off the piano, and the rest of us gathered just outside the back of the wagon. Minnie sat right near Miss Melman on a trunk that was being stored in the wagon.

Miss Melman said, "This is a very popular piano piece. It is called 'Narcissus,' which is also the name of a beautiful flower. The composer is Mr. Ethelbert Nevin."

I have never heard of a man being named Ethelbert before!

Miss Melman said, "Children, Ethelbert Nevin wrote his first song for the piano at the age of 13, not much older than some of you. This shows that you can do excellent work, even as a child. Minerva, because you have done excellent work in the area of mathematics, I am playing this song in your honor."

Well, it was about the most beautiful melody I've ever heard. Miss Melman is talented at playing the piano. I am happy that she is Mama's piano teacher. Now, all day, I've been saying the name, Ethelbert Nevin, over and over in my mind. What a name! Don't you think it is curious? I'm going to work on my multiplication tables, so maybe one day Miss Melman will play a special song for me.

Mama and Pap have been going over their list of things they will buy while we are in Dothan. We are all getting up early because Pap says there will be many chores to do over the next two days. When we work together, he says, "Many hands make light work."

Miss Emily is staying here with her baby, Lucy, tomorrow, and she offered to keep Dylan for Mama, so we could all go into Dothan together and make our purchases. Mama's face beamed! She usually has to take Dylan with her, and this will give Mama a chance to shop and make her purchases without worrying about a baby.

She said, "May I do a kindness for you in exchange? I am much obliged."

But Miss Emily said, "Now, I'm just being neighborly. Every woman enjoys shopping without toting a baby around on her hip."

Mama told me secretly that she will buy a present for Miss Emily. I am excited about helping Mama and Pap make their purchases. We will miss Dylan, but it will be nice to shop, just the three of us.

Love,
Teddy

Reading Multiple Choice Questions for the Letter of March 24, 1892
Circle the letter of the correct answer.

1. Where did Teddy say the wagon train had finally arrived?
   A. Birmingham, Alabama
   B. Pensacola, Florida
   C. Montgomery, Alabama
   D. Dothan, Alabama

2. Which subject did Teddy say she was not very good at?
   A. spelling
   B. arithmetic
   C. grammar
   D. writing

3. To which student did Miss Melman dedicate "Narcissus" by Ethelbert Nevin?
   A. Travis
   B. Teddy
   C. Minnie
   D. Jasper

4. How old was Ethelbert Nevin when he wrote his first song?
   A. 13
   B. 25
   C. 8
   D. 40

5. What did Teddy tell us Pap says when the whole family works together?
   A. "Whistle while you work."
   B. "All in a day's work."
   C. "Many hands make light work."
   D. "It is good to help the ones we love."

6. What is the name of Emily Carter's baby?
   A. Jenny
   B. Minnie
   C. Sarah
   D. Lucy

7. Why did Miss Melman tell the children about Ethelbert Nevin?
   A. She wanted to tell a good story, so the children would be entertained.
   B. He was an interesting man.
   C. She wanted them to know you can do excellent work, even as a child.
   D. She was in love with Ethelbert Nevin.

March 25, 1892

Dear Martha,

I am exhausted! Every bone in my body is weary. Today has been an incredible, exciting day with lots of adventures, but the best thing is that I GOT YOUR LETTERS!!!!

Early this morning, when it was still dark, Pap took out our family's money box. Some folks keep their money in Captain Walsh's wagon in a strongbox, but not Pap. When he had our wagon built, he had them build in a secret compartment under the wagon. If you didn't know about it, you would never guess it's there. He and Mama went over their list a million times.

I took Dylan up to Miss Emily Carter's wagon while he was still asleep. She slipped him into the pallet with Lucy and said, "He'll be fine. Have a wonderful day." Miss Emily is so nice.

Pap drove our wagon into Dothan and parked it at the livery stables for the day. When we make each of our purchases, they are delivered to our wagon at the livery, so we can haul them back to our campsite.

Our first stop was the general store. The store was big, but it was crowded with folks, both town folks from Dothan and folks from our wagon train. The best thing was that the post office was right there in the general store. I asked at the window if they had any mail for Theodosia Bodain, and the man said, "Yes, we do. Here are five letters from Salter's Grove, Mississippi." Great buckets of butterbeans! I was so happy I could have done backflips. I'm going to read one letter each day for the next five days!

At the general store, we bought supplies for our trip:

100 pounds of flour	50 pounds of cornmeal
50 pounds of salt	80 pounds of sugar
100 pounds of coffee	100 pounds of dried beans
40 pounds of salted bacon	8 pounds of oatmeal
25 pounds of dried beef	5 pounds of raisins
25 pounds of brown sugar	50 pound keg of pickles
5 pounds of pepper	50 pounds of dried apples
50 pounds of dried peaches	linseed oil
1 keg of axle grease	fresh vegetables
10 candles	lamp oil
5 pounds of pretzels	5 pounds of peppermint sticks
1,000 toothpicks	2 gallons of vinegar

While we waited for our store goods to be delivered, we had other chores to tend to. Pap got a shave and a haircut at the barber shop. Mama had a tooth pulled at the dentist's office. The cobbler put new soles on Pap's boots. Mama bought a book of piano music, 50 different kinds of flower and vegetable seeds to plant in Florida, and some liniment for sore muscles. We bought clothes: underwear, stockings, aprons, overalls, work dresses, flannel shirts, suspenders, and baby clothes for Dylan (he is growing like a weed).

We also bought Miss Emily a pound of lemon drops for keeping Dylan while we were gone. She told Mama, "You didn't need to get me a thing. He was a good boy and kept Lucy entertained. But lemon drops are my favorite!"

Now, I'm going to read your first letter. I've saved it for the last thing I do today.

All I can say is, Ethelbert Nevin!

Love,
Teddy

Name_____ Date_____

Narrative Writing Prompt for the Letter of March 25, 1892
Read and answer the writing prompt below.

Narrative Prompt: The wagon train stopped in Dothan in order to buy supplies for their trip. Think of a time when your mom sent you to the grocery store with a list of ingredients she needed in order to bake a special cake. While shopping in the store, an unexpected adventure happened. If your mom has never sent you to the store to shop for her, imagine what your adventure could have been, and make it up. Be sure to include what happened to you, how you felt about it, and don't forget to add details in your story that will help the reader make a "mind movie" of that unexpected event.

_____

_____

_____

_____

_____

_____

_____

_____

_____

_____

_____

_____

_____

_____

_____

_____

_____

_____

March 26, 1892

Dear Martha,

I loved your letter! I read it three times. I am so happy to hear from you.

I'm sorry about Bernice. Did you bury her in the same little graveyard where we buried your other kitty? I know she was old, but I can't remember if she was 12 or 13. Didn't you tell me your parents already had her when you were born? She was the sweetest little thing. I remember when we would put Bernice in the baby carriage and bring her to our tea parties.

Last night, we all slept outside. It was a bright, starry night with no rain. We couldn't sleep in the wagon because it was piled high with all the purchases we bought yesterday. Mama strung quilts on a line to make a curtain, so we would have some privacy. I had my own pallet next to Mama, Pap, and Dylan. I lay on my back and stared up at the dark sky and the bright stars. It took my breath away.

Pap said, "Teddy, can you show me the Big Dipper?"

I pointed right to it. Then, he said, "What about the North Star?" I had to search for that one. I know it's bright, but it's not the brightest object in the sky. It's easy to mistake for other stars. I pointed to the one I hoped was the North Star.

"That's right," Pap said. "It's the tail of the Little Dipper. Did you know you can navigate by the North Star? The North Star stays fixed in the sky. When you are facing the North Star, east is to your right, south is to your back, west is to your left, and north is straight ahead." I tried to memorize Pap's words by saying them over and over in my mind.

Mama said, "Do you remember how I taught you to find your direction by day?"

I said, "The sun rises in the east and sets in the west."

Mama said, "That girl is a sponge. What did I tell you?"

Today was another busy day, full of chaos.

Mama and I went to church in Dothan. We brought Miss Emily's baby with us to give Miss Emily a chance to make some purchases with her husband, Martin. That meant Mama and I both had a baby to hold during the service. There was a lot of wiggling going on, let me tell you.

Pap couldn't go to church with us. He and Mr. Carter had to take everything out of our wagons, so they could reload them with all of our new purchases. One man can't lift all those loads alone, so they helped each other. Pap arranged the boxes and barrels in the wagon and made a nice bed for Mama, me, and Dylan up on top of the boxes, so we're no longer on the floor. It's a thousand times better! He fit things in every nook and cranny, so things are out of the way but easy to get to if we need them. He also made a baby seat for Dylan and bolted it to the driver's seat, next to where Mama and I sit when we drive the wagon. Now, Dylan can sit up front and not be in danger.

When Mama and I got back from church, we were shocked to see that Jester and Jingo were gone! In their place were two giant oxen. I said, "Pap! I didn't get to say goodbye to Jester and Jingo." I felt terribly sad at the thought of it.

Pap said, "They'll have a good home, Teddy. The dentist that pulled Mama's tooth yesterday bought them to plow his field. He has another mule and two horses. They'll be in good company."

Still, it made my heart hurt something awful. I don't know why, but all of a sudden I started bawling.

Mama said, "Sometimes, we just have to let go of things we love."

Love,
Teddy

Name_____ Date_____

Reading Short Response Questions for the Letter of March 26, 1892
Answer the questions below, and be sure to use complete sentences.

1. How did Pap navigate by the North Star?

_____

_____

_____

_____

_____

2. Why did Mama say, **"That girl is a sponge"**?

_____

_____

_____

_____

3. Why didn't Pap go to church with Mama, Teddy, and Dylan?

_____

_____

_____

_____

4. What happened to Jester and Jingo?

_____

_____

_____

_____

March 27, 1892

Dear Martha,

We are finally under way. It took some "doings" to get us off, but soon, Alabama will be behind us. Tomorrow, we will be camping in Florida, if all goes well. Everyone is talking about it. Florida!

At first light, Pap hitched up our new team of oxen. Their names are Jeb and January, and they are bigger than big. They wear a wooden yoke around their necks to keep them together as they pull the wagon. Pap says they're gentle but as strong as ten giants. Now that we are loaded with supplies, I know that the weight would be too much for mules to pull. Pap is driving the wagon today. He wants to drive for a few days to make sure Jeb and January are settled in.

Since Pap is driving, he let Dylan ride "shotgun" in his new little seat. He loves it! And he's safe because he can't fall out. That left me and Mama free to set up our laundry. Before we left this morning, she helped me gather water from the spring in all six of our big buckets. That was a lot of hauling! She and I divided our dirty clothes into piles: dresses, underclothes, diapers, Pap's shirts, and Pap's overalls. We put the dirty clothes in the buckets and pushed them down under the water. Mama added soap shavings and hung each of the buckets from pegs on the outside of the wagon, three down one side, three down the other.

Then, she said, "Teddy, run back to the spring and gather an apron full of smooth rocks about the size of a hen's egg." When I came back she said, "Now, put five or six rocks in each bucket and all the rest in with your Pap's overalls."

I said, "What on earth for?" It seemed like so much craziness to me.

But Mama said, "See what happens when this wagon rocks back and forth and sloshes these buckets around all day. The sun will heat the water, the rocks will beat the clothes, and all we'll have to do is rinse."

Mama is a genius!

I read your second letter today. Yes, I would love for you to come visit me on our new land. Pap says he heard that the tracks will soon be finished for several trains to run down into Florida to some of the cities. We will be down below Lake Okeechobee, but maybe there will be a way to come fetch you.

We had school again today. Of course, all we could talk about was Florida. What kinds of animals will we see? Will the birds look different from birds in Mississippi and Alabama? Where is the ocean? How will we get fresh water? Do you think we might get eaten by alligators?

Miss Melman said, "The best way to get to know a new place is to study your surroundings and record your observations." She brought out a parcel wrapped in brown paper and string. I had seen her carrying it in Dothan. "I have a gift for each of you." Our eyes widened, and we looked at each other.

She untied the string and opened the wrapping. There was a stack of art sketchbooks and boxes of colored pencils. Great buckets of butterbeans! I'd heard about colored pencils, but I'd never seen any.

Miss Melman smiled. "Open your eyes. Look around you. Make discoveries. Study the sky and the trees. Scrutinize the land. Search out things that are new and intriguing. Record what you see, and the next time we meet, we'll share your drawings and discuss them."

We held our new sketchbooks. The covers are deep red, and Miss Melman has written our names in script. The paper is creamy white and much nicer than notebook paper. But the colored pencils are the best of all, the kind used by artists. Each box holds eight colors: red, yellow, blue, green, purple, orange, brown, and black. They are just too wonderful.

Miss Melman had a huge smile. "Welcome to Florida," she said.

Wonder of wonders and Ethelbert Nevin!

Love,
Teddy

Expository Writing Prompt for the Letter of March 27, 1892
Read and answer the following writing prompt.

Expository Prompt: In today's letter, Miss Melman said, **"The best way to get to know a new place is to study your surroundings and record your observations."** Now take a moment and look around your classroom. Observe your surroundings as if you were a scientist doing research and writing down important notations in a field notebook. Now write an expository piece, and explain what your classroom is like. Make sure to include many specific details so that your reader can "picture it" in her mind. Be sure your piece has a beginning, a middle, and an ending.

_____

_____

_____

_____

_____

_____

_____

_____

_____

_____

_____

_____

_____

_____

_____

_____

_____

_____

_____

_____

_____

March 28, 1892

Dear Martha,

WE ARE IN FLORIDA!

When we stopped to set up camp, Captain Walsh called everyone together for a meeting. He said, "You are now standing on Florida soil." He had to wait for us to stop cheering. "The caravan will stay together as planned, all the way to St. Augustine, Florida. Some folks will leave us there. Then, the rest of us will continue on down below Lake Okeechobee. I expect we'll arrive sometime this summer."

All of the Carters came over for supper last night, and Miss Melman joined us. She and Mama fixed chicken and dumplings. Mama took pity on her and said, "Cassie, you don't have to kill the chicken this time, but watch what I do, so you'll know how to do it next time." Mama gave her an old apron to wear to cover up her pretty white skirt while she boiled the chicken and dropped in the dumplings.

The chicken and dumplings were delicious, by the way. While we were all eating around the fire, Miss Emily said, "Cassie, I have some lovely printed calico. Would you like me to make you a work dress or two, so you won't ruin your pretty things?"

Miss Melman looked from Miss Emily to her mother, Mrs. Carter, and then to Mama, all the while noticing their skirts or dresses. They were all worn and faded. She said, "How foolish I am. Here I've come on a rugged journey, and I'm still dressing like I'm back in Jackson, teaching school. Yes, I would love some calico dresses."

Miss Emily said, "I think we're about the same size. I'll give you one of mine to try on, and if it fits, I already have the patterns."

Today, I started looking at our surroundings like Miss Melman asked us to. I saw hawks and eagles and even tiny hummingbirds. I made a sketch of some kind of white bird that has a big body, enormous wings, long twig-like legs, and a long, thin, curving neck. Its beak is yellow and comes to a sharp point. Pap doesn't know what kind of bird it is, but he said, "It's a beauty, though."

We've passed a number of scruffy short trees that look like pointy bushes. The gigantic leaves look like fans. The bottom of the tree has wooden pieces jutting out this way and that. I sketched a few in my book, using the colored pencils. It's so strange to see color come out when I draw across the page. It's absolutely beautiful! Who would have ever thought we would have colored pencils? Miss Melman said we could blend the colors by rubbing them gently with the side of our finger. I tried rubbing them, and the colors smooth together and look very natural. I'm going to draw all the things I see on our journey. Maybe I'll send you one in a letter.

I read your third letter today while Dylan was taking a nap in the wagon. I'm happy you have a special part in the spring play at school. I must confess that I am a LITTLE jealous about it! If I had stayed in Mississippi, I would probably be in it with you. Is the play one the older kids have done before, or is it a new play? Will there be singing and reciting? Sometimes, I miss going to our recitation class together. I still remember doing "Fireflies on Parade" and "Red, White, and Blue" together.

I can't write anymore tonight. I'm falling asleep.

Love,
Teddy

Name_____ Date_____

Reading Extended Response Questions for the Letter of March 28, 1892

Answer the questions below. Be sure to use complete sentences, reasons, and details.

1. Why did Miss Emily offer to make Miss Melman a work dress? How did Miss Melman feel about this?

_____

_____

_____

_____

_____

_____

_____

_____

_____

_____

2. Describe the drawings Teddy has been sketching in her book. What did she do to make her drawings look natural?

_____

_____

_____

_____

_____

_____

_____

_____

_____

_____

March 29, 1892

Dear Martha,

Today, Pap had me and Mama each take a turn driving, so he could see how we handle Jeb and January. It's really not any harder than driving Jester and Jingo.

When I want the team to start, I say, "Git!" or "Git-up-there you, Jeb" or "Git-up-there you, January." When I want them to stop, I pull the reins and say, "Whoa!" If we need to go left, I say, "Haw!" and if we need to turn right, I say, "Gee!"

We had school again today. I was hoping we'd share our drawings, but some of the kids weren't ready yet, so we'll have to show them next time. Vexation!

Miss Melman said, "Students, I think it is important that we learn some facts about the state that will become our new home." She showed us a map of Florida and let us study it for a while.

Florida is a big state. It's curious because it's part of the United States, but it juts down, all by itself, at the lower right-hand corner. That makes it look like the rest of the United States is a cartoon bubble, and Florida is the part that points to the character's mouth to let you know he's talking, like in a comic strip in the newspaper.

Miss Melman said, "You can see that Florida is a peninsula. Can anyone tell us what a peninsula is?"

Jasper Lowe, Travis's best friend, said, "It's a long piece of land, attached to the mainland but jutting out into the sea."

I knew that, but he got his hand up first.

Miss Melman said, "That's right. Now, who can tell us when Florida became a state?"

Minnie said, "I know. March 3, 1845."

I didn't know that one.

Miss Melman said, "Who can tell us how many years Florida has been a state?"

Travis was the first to raise his hand. "47 years."

I was beginning to feel self-conscious because I hadn't answered a single question yet.

Miss Melman said, "Ah—and who knows the name of the oldest settlement in the United States of America?"

I wasn't going to let anyone out-do me. I blurted out, "St. Augustine," before any other kid could steal the answer. Miss Melman didn't scold me for not raising my hand, but she gave me a look.

"So you all do know something about your new home state," she said. "Good. Here's one more interesting tidbit to add to your knowledge: Florida is the only state that has two rivers with exactly the same name. Does anyone know the name of these rivers?"

No one answered, not even Minnie. Miss Melman said, "There is a Withlacoochee River in north central Florida and a Withlacoochee River in central Florida."

I am learning about this strange wilderness we are traveling through. We've heard that some parts of Florida have cities, but most of the state is still undeveloped. I know one thing: it sure is big.

We have passed a number of swampy areas. Pap says alligators live in some of those swamps, and sometimes they come out on the bank to sleep in the sun. I believe him, but I haven't seen one yet. I've got my sketchbook ready, though. I want to be the first kid to draw an alligator.

Love,
Teddy

Grammar Questions for the Letter of March 29, 1892
Circle the letter of the correct answer.

1. In the following sentence, where does the apostrophe belong?
   A. I've got my sketchbook ready, though.
   B. Ive' got my sketchbook ready, though.
   C. Iv'e got my sketchbook ready, though.
   D. Ive got my sketchbook ready, though.

2. Where do the quotation marks go in the following dialogue?
   A. Miss Melman said, "Who can tell us how many years Florida has been a state?
   B. "Miss Melman said, Who can tell us how many years Florida has been a state?"
   C. Miss Melman said, "Who can tell us how many years Florida has been a state?"
   D. Miss Melman said, Who can tell us how many years Florida has been a state?"

3. In the following sentence, which word is the verb?
   Florida is a big state.
   A. state
   B. big
   C. Florida
   D. is

4. Which of the following words is spelled incorrectly?
   A. peninsula
   B. alligater
   C. character
   D. sketchbook

5. How would you BEST end the following sentence?
   A. It was incredible?
   B. It was incredible,
   C. It was incredible!
   D. It was incredible.

6. What is missing in this dialogue?
   Miss Melman said, You can see that Florida is a peninsula.
   A. quotation marks
   B. a period at the end
   C. a capital letter
   D. good spelling

7. Which is the correct spelling?
   A. florida
   B. Florda
   C. Florida
   D. Florider

March 30, 1892

Dear Martha,

We had a real scare today. Miss Emily Carter was gathering firewood and got bit by a coral snake! At least we thought it was a coral snake. It bit her on the hand when she reached into a pile of wood and dead leaves. She ran back to the wagons screaming, "Martin! Martin! I've been bit by a coral snake!"

Folks came running.

Emily's mother, Mrs. Carter, immediately called out, "Fetch my tincture of purple coneflower, and be quick about it." When she examined the puncture wounds on Emily's hand, she asked, "Are you sure it was a coral snake?"

Emily said, "It was a small snake, black and red and yellow. Right over there in that pile of wood and leaves."

While Mrs. Carter was applying the tincture of purple coneflower, Mr. Carter grabbed a shovel and started digging through the pile of leaves. He found the snake and scooped it up on the blade of the shovel.

"Is this the snake, Emily?"

Emily cried, "Yes!" I felt sorry for her, hearing her sobs.

Mrs. Carter took a good look. "You've been bit, alright, but not by a coral snake. Look carefully. This here is a scarlet king snake. See? The red and black stripes are right next to each other."

Martin's voice was shaky. "What are you talking about?"

Emily said, "Mama, am I going to die?"

Mrs. Carter said, "Not today, daughter!"

Martin asked, "She'll be alright?"

By now, there was a whole group of us standing around watching. Mr. Carter said, "All is well, folks. Emily got bit by a snake, but it was a scarlet king snake. Painful, that's all. Wasn't a coral snake. A coral snake's colored rings are red, yellow, and black. A scarlet king snake's rings are red, black, and yellow. There's a little poem every man, woman, and child should learn when it comes to coral snakes: Red on yellow, kill a fellow. Red on black, won't harm Jack."

Mrs. Carter poured more of the tincture of purple coneflower into the wound. "This will help with infection. You'll be fine in a day or so."

We kids asked Mr. Carter to show us the scarlet king snake up close. He held out the shovel. It was true! The red stripes were next to the black stripes.

I was itching to get to my sketchbook. I tried to memorize what a scarlet king snake looked like, so I could draw it later. Red, black, yellow, black. Small head, body about three feet long.

Travis Lark asked, "Are you going to kill it?"

Mr. Carter said, "Naw! He won't hurt nothing. He mostly eats skinks."

Travis said, "What is a skink?"

Mr. Carter said, "Son, that's another lesson for another day."

So you can see, Martha, if we have many other days like today, our trip through Florida won't be boring.

Great buckets of butterbeans. A snakebite!

Love,
Teddy

Writing Questions for the Letter of March 30, 1892
Circle the letter of the correct answer.

1. Read the following phrases from Teddy's letter today:
    Red, black, yellow, black. Small head, body about three feet long.
    These phrases are examples of which important writing skill?
    A. strong verbs
    B. transitional phrase
    C. onomatopoeia
    D. descriptive writing

2. Read the following sentences from Teddy's letter:
    "There's a little poem every man, woman, and child should learn when it comes to coral snakes: Red on yellow, kill a fellow. Red on black, won't harm Jack."
    What important writing skill is this an example of?
    A. using an idiom as a specific example
    B. strong verb
    C. metaphor
    D. grabber

3. Read the following sentence from Teddy's letter today:
    We had a real scare today.
    This an example of which important writing skill?
    A. strong verb
    B. onomatopoeia
    C. grabber
    D. details you can picture

4. Read the following sentence from Teddy's letter today:
    I was itching to get to my sketchbook.
    The word *itching* is an example of what type of writing skill that we should use in our own writing?
    A. onomatopoeia
    B. strong verb
    C. grabber
    D. juicy color word

5. Read the following sentence from Teddy's letter today:
    So you can see, Martha, if we have many other days like today, our trip through Florida won't be boring.
    The phrase *So you can see* is an example of what type of good writing skill that should occur many times in our writing?
    A. beginning
    B. grabber
    C. transitional phrase
    D. metaphor

March 31, 1892

Dear Martha,

I am getting better with my slingshot. I've been practicing with Travis and Minnie every chance I get. If we have time in the morning before roll-out, Travis sets up targets for us to shoot at. We see who can knock over the can or who can "hit the troll."

Travis filled a burlap sack with some of the gray moss that grows in the trees here, and he painted a troll's head on it. He props it up or hangs it from a tree branch. We take turns shooting, and before we shoot, we call, "Ear!" or "Chin!" or "Nose!" Then, we see who hits the target they said they were aiming for.

Pap was greasing our axles with axle grease, and I guess he was kind of watching us because later he said, "Teddy Girl, you're getting pretty good with that slingshot."

I said, "I want to help you put food on the table, Pap."

Pap said, "You do?" He looked surprised.

I said, "Yes, sir."

Pap said, "Teddy, are you prepared to shoot an animal? Watch him die?"

I hadn't really thought about that part much.

I said, "Maybe."

Pap nodded. "Well, we have to put meat on the table, that's for sure. And I would welcome your company. But we don't hunt for the fun of it. We hunt because we need to eat. That means something has to die."

I said, "I know."

But I didn't know. I love animals. I didn't know if I could kill one. I know we cook the squirrels and rabbits and deer Pap shoots. But now that I had shot my mouth off about putting food on the table, I didn't know if I wanted to. That got me to thinking. I hope none of the boys shoot at animals just to wound or kill them for the fun of it. I hope they don't shoot at songbirds. If they shoot a cardinal, it will break Mama's heart. When she hears one sing, she closes her eyes and smiles.

Then, she says, "I hear a redbird. Teddy, it's a cardinal. See how red he is? Look for his mate. She won't be far behind."

Pap said, "Why don't you let me do the hunting for now, and you stick to the live animals."

That's one of the things I love about Pap. He's always thinking of things like that. I'm glad he's my pap because he's easy to talk to, and he teaches me things about animals and about hunting.

That reminded me. I said, "What about a dog?"

Pap said, "What about a dog?"

I said, "I want one."

Pap said, "I know."

I said, "Do you think one will find me?"

Pap said, "I bet there's one looking for a ten-year-old girl right this very minute."

The thought of a dog filled me with happiness. Jumping jubilation! I hope Pap's right.

Love,
Teddy

Persuasive Writing Prompt for the Letter of March 31, 1892
Read and answer the following prompt.

Persuasive Prompt: Teddy has been practicing with her slingshot every chance she gets. Think of something you enjoy doing, or would enjoy doing, that takes practice. It could be playing the piano, reciting spelling words, playing soccer, doing cartwheels, rapping songs, etc. Persuade your reader that practicing is necessary for this skill. Give examples of how to practice. Use convincing arguments and specific examples to convince your reader how the practice would pay off. Read your paper to see if more details are needed. Share your paper with someone else to make sure that what you wrote is persuasive.

_____

_____

_____

_____

_____

_____

_____

_____

_____

_____

_____

_____

_____

_____

_____

_____

_____

_____

_____

April 1, 1892

Dear Martha,

Today, we had school again, and we finally shared our sketchbooks. It was so much fun looking at everyone's drawings. Kids had drawn all sorts of things: Captain Walsh with his big hat, palm trees, new flowers we hadn't seen before, and every kind of animal you can imagine. Everyone liked my picture of the scarlet king snake.

Jasper Lowe said, "You sure are a good artist. That snake gives me the willies." We had to laugh.

That led to a discussion of snakes. Of course, we were all thinking of the snake that bit Miss Emily Carter two days before. The thought of it still gives me the creeps.

Miss Melman said, "I have some rattlesnake fangs. Would you like to see them?" Of course we all did, so she showed us an envelope that looked like it had something bumpy inside. She asked, "Who would like to be the one to open the envelope and show us what's inside?"

We all raised our hands and said, "Me! Me!" but Jasper pushed right up to the front of all of us.

Miss Melman said, "Alright, Jasper. You may be the one." She handed him the envelope. "But be very careful. Rattlesnake fangs can be dangerous."

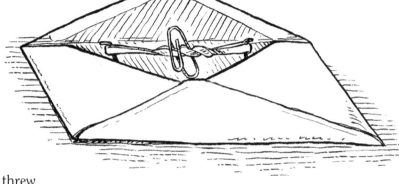

We crowded in real close so we could see. Jasper lifted the flap and opened the envelope, which was not glued shut.

The envelope let out a loud, "Z-z-z-z-z-z-z-z-z!!!"

Jasper screamed at the top of his lungs and threw the envelope up in the air. We ALL screamed and jumped back. We were looking around at each other when we noticed Miss Melman had her hand over her mouth and was laughing so hard tears were coming down her cheeks.

"April fools!" she finally shouted. We stood there with our mouths open.

We had forgotten that today is April 1. Miss Melman got us good! We all started laughing. Jasper asked, "How did you do that? What made that noise?"

Miss Melman said, "Jasper, I'm glad you're such a good sport. My daddy used to play this trick on us when we were children. Here, let me show you how it works." She showed us how she had used a paperclip and hooked it to a rubber band. Then, she had twisted the paperclip over and over until the rubber band was tight.

"The trick is to hold the paperclip, so it doesn't untwist. Slip it down into a paper envelope. Then, hand the envelope to your unsuspecting victim—" We all turned to look at Jasper. He grinned.

"And the rest—is history," she said. The best part is that she gave us each a paperclip, a rubber band, and an envelope, so we could play the same trick on our folks. I played it on Pap, and he laughed, but I know better than to try something like that with Mama. You do not want to get into playing practical jokes with my mama. One time, she swapped the sugar in the sugar bowl with salt. Yikes! And once, she sewed up the bottoms of all my bloomers. And last fall, she put on scarecrow clothes and scared the daylights out of Pap out in the field.

Mama always says, "He who laughs last, laughs best." If I played the rattlesnake fangs joke on her, I might slip into bed some night and find a live frog!

Love,
Teddy

Name_____ Date_____

Reading Multiple Choice Questions for the Letter of April 1, 1892
Circle the letter of the correct answer.

1. What is April Fools' Day?
   A. a day when people dress up in costumes and scare each other
   B. a day when people give each other kind cards and letters
   C. a day when people play tricks on each other
   D. a day when everyone wears green

2. Which items would you need in order to play Miss Melman's "rattlesnake trick" on someone?
   A. rattlesnake fangs, envelope, and rubber band
   B. rubber band, paperclip, and envelope
   C. envelope, tape, and paperclip
   D. paperclip, rubber band, and a paper bag

3. Which one of the students did Miss Melman choose to play the trick on?
   A. Teddy
   B. Travis
   C. Minnie
   D. Jasper

4. Which one of the following examples is NOT a trick that Teddy told us her mama had once played?
   A. She hid Veronica so that Teddy could not find her for a whole day.
   B. She swapped the sugar bowl with salt.
   C. She sewed up the bottoms of Teddy's bloomers.
   D. She put on scarecrow clothes and scared the daylights out of Pap in the field.

5. Teddy said that everyone liked her picture of the snake she drew.
   What kind of snake did Teddy draw?
   A. a rattlesnake
   B. a scarlet king snake
   C. a coral snake
   D. a black racer

6. Which one of the following does Teddy not mention that kids had drawn in their sketchbooks?
   A. palm trees
   B. flowers
   C. animals
   D. wagons

7. What did Jasper say Teddy's drawing of the snake gave him?
   A. the willies
   B. cooties
   C. a headache
   D. the creeps

April 2, 1892

Dear Martha,

Today, we left at the crack of dawn. It was my first day to drive Jeb and January all by myself. Pap sat with me for a while, just to be sure I'd be alright, but I did fine. He said, "Some folks are having trouble with their wagons with all the extra weight and supplies." After he was sure I could handle the team, he rode off on Gabriel to keep an eye on the wagons and help folks shift their supplies if they needed it.

When I drive the wagon by myself, I feel proud that I know how to handle Jeb and January and follow the wagon ahead. I have to watch for ruts in the road or big rocks that might cause our oxen to stumble and fall.

This morning, Miss Emily invited Dylan over to play with Lucy, so Mama went to practice the piano. Miss Melman said Mama has real talent and encouraged her to practice whenever she can. I asked Mama if I could go back there and hear her play, but she said, "Not yet." I begged her, but she said, "Don't meddle."

At first, I was kind of hurt because she wouldn't let me come hear her play, but something exciting happened in the meantime, and I would have been sorry if I hadn't been driving the wagon. Around noon, we met up with another wagon train.

I heard folks up ahead hollering, but I couldn't make out what they were saying. I saw Pap and the rest of the pushers riding hard, up toward the front of the train, where Captain Walsh usually rides. Travis came flying back this way toward the wagons, shouting the news, "Wagon train! Captain says we'll be stopping!"

I pulled gently on the reins and called out, "Whoa, there, Jeb. Whoa, there, January."

Another wagon train! We've passed folks in wagons, on horses, and on foot but never another whole caravan. We stopped for a while, so Captain Walsh could talk to their captain. They talked a long time. Then, Pap came galloping back on Gabriel, telling folks, "Move ahead slowly, follow to circle."

By this time, Mama had come back from the piano wagon, but she was up ahead at Miss Emily's wagon getting Dylan. As the other train passed us, folks waved, and we waved back. And there I was, Teddy Bodain, ten-year-old adventure girl, sitting on our high seat, driving a team of oxen to beat the band!

We made a big half-circle with our wagons, and the other train made a big half-circle with their wagons, so when we were finally stopped, there was a huge circle of wagons. Folks got down from their wagons and off their horses to stretch their legs.

Captain Walsh rode back to speak to us.

"Folks, I know their captain, Marcus Yoner. Good man. They'd like to camp near us for tonight and tomorrow. If you folks are of a mind, we'll have a whoop-de-doo tonight and a preaching service tomorrow. I was planning to stop for a day, anyway, so our teams can rest. We'll leave Monday morning, sharp."

Our mamas immediately began to discuss what dishes to make and what ingredients they would need. Mama and Mrs. Carter and Miss Melman and Miss Emily were talking up a storm.

Mrs. Carter said, "Grace, it won't be a party if you don't make your macaroni and cheese."

Mama said, "Well, Cassie will have to help me. Emily, I hope you bring out a jar of your pickles."

A whoop-de-doo! Goodness gracious and Ethelbert Nevin. We NEED a party!

Love,
Teddy

Narrative Writing Prompt for the Letter of April 2, 1892
Read and answer the writing prompt below.

Narrative Prompt: Teddy drove Jeb and January for the first time all by herself. Think of something you have done for the very first time, all by yourself. Now write a narrative piece, and tell what you did, being sure to include how you felt when you accomplished this task all by yourself. If you can't think of something that is true, make up a story that would be fun for us to read. Add as many good writing skills as you have learned.

_____

_____

_____

_____

_____

_____

_____

_____

_____

_____

_____

_____

_____

_____

_____

_____

_____

_____

_____

April 3, 1892

Dear Martha,

If you ever have a chance to go to a whoop-de-doo, don't miss it. It was so much fun!

Yesterday, as soon as we found out we were going to have a whoop-de-doo with the other train, folks went around to the other wagons to meet each other and find out where they were headed. This train came from Kentucky, and they're headed to a place just 100 miles from here. Their journey is almost over. They had a drought in Kentucky, and the crops failed, so most of them want to try their hand at farming in the Florida wilderness.

Pap and the rest of the pushers from both trains called games for the children. We had sack races, a three-legged race (Minnie and I were together), a wheelbarrow race, drop the handkerchief, and a spelling bee, which was won by a Kentucky girl. Her word was CONSTERNATION. I had just gotten out with the word JOSTLING. Vexation! The Kentucky girl won a silver dollar.

The men played horseshoes, and the competition was fierce. The onlookers clapped and shouted with every toss. It was finally between Martin Carter and a man from the other train. Martin won!

The women cooked supper while the men fashioned tables out of whatever they could find in the wagons: sawhorses, lumber, doors, and a big store sign that said, "Farrier." We piled the pots of food on the tables, and every family brought their own plates and spoons from their wagons.

Guess what? We met another family of Bodains! Pap and the other Mr. Bodain talked about their kin and tried to see if we are related by blood. Pap asked about his cousin, Daniel Bodain, who lives down near Micanopy, Florida, but they did not know of him. We decided that we must be related somehow, way far back in the Bodain family line. It was fun because the rest of the time we called each other "Cousin."

After supper, folks hung their lanterns all around. The place was lit up as bright as day. The men cleared the tables, and Captain Walsh called for a fiddler. We ended up with three fiddlers, three mandolin players, two guitar players, two harmonica players, and two banjo players! There were even more musicians, but the women complained that there wouldn't be anybody left to dance with. Everybody danced: children, women, men, and even the old folks. You didn't even need a partner. You just got out in the circle and danced and danced. Pap and Mama danced with their cheeks together and their eyes closed. Miss Melman danced with Captain Walsh.

When the night was over, folks took the lanterns down and headed off for their wagons.

Today, we gathered again for a preaching service. Captain Walsh had one of the hired drivers drive the piano wagon out toward the middle of the circle. Folks from both trains gathered around the end of it and brought chairs, kegs, barrels, boxes, or whatever they had to sit on. They opened the canvas so the sound could come out, and Miss Melman played hymns. Mr. Carter led the singing. One of the men from the other train did the preaching. He preached the shortest sermon I've ever heard. I said, "Thank goodness!" a little too loud, and Mama pinched me, but I didn't care. I bet she was glad it was short, too.

For the rest of the day, folks visited and helped each other. Kids played everywhere. Women spread quilts out for all the babies. The farrier from the other train looked at our horses and checked to see if they needed shoes. A barber cut folks' hair. Mrs. Carter gave out her liniments and tinctures. Miss Melman wrote letters for folks. Pap and some other farmers talked about which crops would grow in Florida and which crops wouldn't. Mama swapped recipes and looked at pattern books.

I showed some girls from the other train how to make a cat's cradle. They showed me how to make a "button on a string" so that it spins. Travis and the boys played marbles and capture the flag.

We were all going twelve-ways-to-Sunday. What a day!

Love,
Teddy

Name_____ Date_____

Reading Short Response Questions for the Letter of April 3, 1892
Answer the questions below, and be sure to use complete sentences.

1. How did the men make the tables that would be used for supper?

_____

_____

_____

_____

2. Why did they open the canvas on the piano wagon?

_____

_____

_____

_____

3. Why did Mama pinch Teddy after the sermon?

_____

_____

_____

_____

4. Explain the job of a farrier.

_____

_____

_____

_____

April 4, 1892

Dear Martha,

Today, we are all tired. We had such a good time with the folks from the other wagon train. None of us got enough sleep last night. I couldn't stop thinking about the dance, the feast, and the Kentucky kids we played with. I wish we could all travel together, but they are headed in a different direction.

Pap drove the wagon, and Dylan played with Lucy in Miss Emily's wagon.

Mama said, "Let's do something special. I know just the thing."

You'll never guess what it was. She taught me how to make jerky! I've eaten jerky before, but I had no idea how to make it.

First, she scraped off every bit of fat from a big chunk of venison Pap brought home. "Fat goes rancid quickly," she said. "If you make it right, jerky will last for months."

When the meat was scraped clean, which didn't take long since deer meat doesn't have much fat, we sliced it into long, thin strips. Then, we rubbed salt and pepper all over the strips. I covered the meat on both sides.

"Don't skimp," Mama said. "Salt adds lots of flavor."

Now, it might sound strange, but next, we threaded a length of cotton thread in the end of each strip of meat, using a needle. We tied the two ends of the thread to make a loop. After every strip of meat had a loop, Mama stretched a cord on the outside of the wagon from the back to the front. We hung all of the little loops on it and let the venison strips hang free. When we finished, there they were, all in neat rows on either side of the wagon.

"Don't we have to hang the strips over a smoky fire?" I asked.

"We're not staying in one place long enough. We're going to make this Florida sunshine work for us," Mama said. "The heat from the sun will pull out all the moisture. In two days time, we'll have jerky."

I said, "Won't it draw flies?"

Mama said, "Not with all the rocking this wagon does. Flies will want to land, but with all the bouncing around, they won't be able to."

We didn't know Pap was listening. He called, "So if the wagon jerks it around, should we call it 'jerking jerky'?"

We laughed. Mama said, "We should call it jumping, jerking jerky."

I remembered the spelling bee. I said, "We should call it jumping, jostling, jerking jerky."

That tickled Pap. He said, "You win."

Mama showed me a fold of white cloth. She said, "At night, we'll cover the strips with cheesecloth to keep the bugs off. It will also keep off the morning dew. Tomorrow, we'll salt the strips one more time."

Mama is so smart. I hope I turn out like her.

So there we were, rolling along on our way to our new homestead, making the sun work for us to dry out our venison jerky.

It was a good day.

Love,
Teddy

Name_____ Date_____

Expository Writing Prompt for the Letter of April 4, 1892
Read and answer the following writing prompt.

Expository Prompt: In today's letter, Teddy learned how to make venison jerky. People in 1892 didn't just go to the supermarket to get their food items. They had to make many of them. Think of the differences in how people got their food in the 1890s and how we get our food today. Write an expository piece explaining the differences in how people obtained their food in 1892 and today. Be sure to include specific examples from Teddy's story and examples from your family's experiences today. Give specific reasons and great descriptions.

_____

_____

_____

_____

_____

_____

_____

_____

_____

_____

_____

_____

_____

_____

_____

_____

_____

_____

_____

_____

_____

April 5, 1892

Dear Martha,

We had school again today. Leave it to Miss Melman to come up with something fun.

She said, "This wagon train feels like one big family, doesn't it?" We all agreed.

"I've been thinking," she said. "We're like a traveling town. We don't have banks or libraries or stores or even a doctor. But we've got each other. Many people on this train have useful talents and abilities. I've written some names on slips of paper. I'd like each of you to draw a name." She put the slips of paper in her straw hat and passed it around.

I drew Mrs. Carter's name. Miss Melman said, "I'm going to ask you to interview the person whose name you drew. Find out their special gifts. Learn from them. When we meet together another time, we'll teach each other what we've learned."

I was so excited. I love stuff like that. Miss Melman said, "Take your sketchbooks with you. Record what you can. Make drawings. You can use your pictures when we share."

I'm going to interview Mrs. Carter tomorrow. I've never interviewed anyone before, but I'm always asking questions, so I think it will be fun. Besides, Mrs. Carter is nice and is always helping folks.

Miss Melman read more of Tom Sawyer. He reminds me of Travis Lark, always funning around and into foolishment. He is an orphan, but he lives with his Aunt Polly, not in an orphanage, which is good because I've heard you would not want to have to live in an orphanage. Sometimes, the people who run the orphanage are mean and cruel. Remember the orphanage in Oliver Twist, when Miss Pedigrew read it to us?

Anyway, Tom's cousin, Sid, is younger, and he is spoiled and mean. He tattles on Tom and always runs to tell Aunt Polly when Tom sneaks out of their bedroom window or skips school. Then, Tom gets in trouble with Aunt Polly, even though she loves him and wants him to turn out good.

I am waiting for Tom to play some sort of trick on Sid so that Sid gets into trouble, not Tom. Tom is smart, and I bet he's going to think of something clever to play on Sid.

Today, while Miss Melman read aloud, she had a special treat, a peppermint stick, for each of us. I love peppermint sticks! We sucked on them and twisted them back and forth in our mouths so that after a while they had a sharp point. I saw Travis stick Jasper in the back of the neck with his point! See? I told you he is a lot like Tom Sawyer.

Jasper stuck Travis back, and soon we were all sticking each other with our candy points while Miss Melman kept reading away.

We thought she didn't see us, but she said, "That's all for today. Tomorrow's chapter is called, 'Tom and Huck stick each other with peppermint candy points.'"

We looked embarrassed. Miss Melman said, "I know you're not paying attention to the story if you are busy poking each other with candy points."

We felt bad. Miss Melman had bought the candy for us as a special treat. We had repaid her by cutting up while she was reading.

I have to stop writing now. Mama made a little pot of salty water. She wants me to brush it on each of the jerky strips while they are still hanging up. If she's not looking, I might eat one.

Love,
Teddy

Reading Extended Response Questions for the Letter of April 5, 1892
Answer the questions below. Be sure to use complete sentences, reasons, and details.

1. Miss Melman made the statement, **"This wagon train feels like one big family,"** and all the children agreed. In what ways does the wagon train feel like a family?

_____

_____

_____

_____

_____

_____

_____

_____

_____

2. As Miss Melman reads to her students, they start to "cut up" after she gave them peppermint sticks. Describe what they did. How did they feel when they realized Miss Melman saw them?

_____

_____

_____

_____

_____

_____

_____

_____

_____

April 6, 1892

Dear Martha,

Today, the wagons ahead of us slowed and stopped, but we had no idea why. Travis Lark came galloping by, telling us that there was a peddler who wanted to show his wares. Captain Walsh said we could stop for a few minutes in case anyone wanted to make a purchase.

The man was dressed in fancy clothes, including a vest and top hat. His wagon was bright red and yellow, and it opened up on the side, like a little stage. We wondered, what in the world is this?

He said, "Folks, Dr. Xavier Zoren at your service. It is my pleasure to present to you an amazement, a wonder, a staggering demonstration that has confounded commoners and gentry alike."

We gathered around.

Dr. Zoren continued. "My assistant, the lovely Flavia, will help me."

A woman wearing a strange costume came from the side, pushing a large cage to the center of the tiny stage. The cage was covered with a green velvet cloth. She flipped the cloth back for us to see what was inside. A pitiful looking dog sat looking at us. He was so thin his ribs showed.

Dr. Zoren said in a loud voice, "Notice this unhealthy mongrel. Not one of you would want him in this condition." He paused. "Fortunately, I have a regenerative syrup, a life-giving liquid, a restorative recipe, which will dramatically improve this animal's condition, right before your very eyes."

He held up a glass bottle containing a red liquid.

"Dr. Zoren's Elixir of Life. This highly sought-out formula comes from the Rendini People of eastern Rambonia. Its medicinal powers are astounding."

He poured some syrup in a big spoon and stuck it through the bars of the cage. The dog lapped it up hungrily. "See?" Dr. Zoren said. "This dog is eager to get well. He is weak, let me tell you. Even the sun hurts his sore eyes."

His assistant, Flavia, flipped the green cloth back over the front of the cage, so the dog was hidden.

Dr. Zoren said, "My miracle cure, Elixir of Life, only takes a short while to work on small animals. It takes a few days on humans, but it will have the same healing effect on any one of you. It's been known to cure rheumatism, arthritis, ringworm, sleeplessness, gout, headache, teething babies, and general malaise. It works on colic, dyspepsia, fungus, and—the swooning vapors."

He snapped his fingers.

Flavia whipped the cover back, so we could see. The dog was fat and healthy! He held his head high, and his eyes were bright! We crowded forward. The dog was a beauty. He barked and wagged his tail.

Everyone gasped, including me. Folks started digging into their pockets to buy bottles of the syrup.

Dr. Zoren said, "They're going like hotcakes, ladies and gents. Get yours while the getting's good." While he sold his elixir, Flavia pushed the cage off the stage, back into the wagon.

I took one last look at the beautiful dog, wishing he was mine.

A few minutes later, Dr. Zoren and his assistant were gone.

On our way back to the wagon, I said, "Pap, have you ever seen anything like that?"

He said, "I've seen a trickster in a monkey suit before."

That made me mad. I said, "Didn't you see how he healed the sick dog? Made him like new?"

Pap said, "Theodosia, some people will try any trick in the book to cheat you out of your money."

Why does Pap have to be such a fuddy-duddy? Seeing is believing. Why can't he believe?

Love,
Teddy

Grammar Questions for the Letter of April 6, 1892
Circle the letter of the correct answer.

1. Which example has the correct use of capitalization?
   A. Dr. zoren's Elixir of Life
   B. Dr. Zoren's elixir of life
   C. dr. Zoren's Elixir of Life
   D. Dr. Zoren's Elixir of Life

2. Which sentence has the correct use of commas?
   A. His assistant Flavia, flipped the green cloth back over the front of the cage.
   B. His assistant, Flavia, flipped the green cloth back over the front of the cage.
   C. His assistant, Flavia flipped the green cloth back over the front of the cage.
   D. His, assistant Flavia, flipped the green cloth back over the front of the cage.

3. Which of the following words is spelled correctly?
   A. dementrasion
   B. amazment
   C. staggering
   D. pitifool

4. Which example has the correct use of punctuation?
   A. Why does Pap have to be such a fuddy-duddy?
   B. Why does Pap have to be such a fuddy-duddy.
   C. Why does Pap have to be such a fuddy-duddy!
   D. (Why does Pap have to be such a fuddy-duddy)

5. In the following sentence, which word is incorrect?
   He held his head high, and his eyes was bright.
   A. held
   B. and
   C. his
   D. was

6. Why do we capitalize the words Elixir of Life in the following sentence?
   Dr. Zoren said, "My miracle cure, Elixir of Life, only takes a short while to work on small animals.
   A. it is the name of a specific person, place, or thing, called a proper noun
   B. sizzling verb
   C. because Dr. Zoren is special
   D. it is fake medicine

7. Dr. Zoren says, **"Notice this unhealthy mongrel."** What part of speech is the word *unhealthy*?
   A. a noun
   B. a verb
   C. an adjective
   D. a pronoun

April 7, 1892

Dear Martha,

Two good things happened today.

First of all, Travis challenged me to a slingshot contest. I said, "What are we playing for?" He said if he won, I'd have to give him some of our venison jerky. I said, "How many pieces?" and he said three. I said, "What if I win?"

He said, "There's no way you'll win."

I said, "What if I do?"

He looked at Jasper Lowe with a you-and-I-both-know-I-can-beat-Teddy-Bodain look.

He said, "You won't. But if you do, I'll give you all your marbles back."

I said, "And your cat's eye shooter?"

He said, "And my cat's eye shooter."

I trounced him good! Jasper Lowe was our officiator. He said I won fair and square. Travis gave me back all of my marbles, including his cat's eye shooter, in a marble sack. He said, "If I hadn't taught you so much about shooting a slingshot, you wouldn't have won." But he was a good sport about it, all in all.

Jasper said, "Travis, maybe you need a spoonful of Dr. Zoren's Elixir of Life."

The second good thing that happened was my interview with Mrs. Carter. She is such a nice person. I asked her about her tinctures and liniments. I wanted to know how she had learned to use them to heal folks.

She said, "I'm not a doctor or anything like that. My mama just taught me which plants are good for different ailments. That's the way we did in the old days when we couldn't get to a doctor.

"Mama taught me to rub a rhubarb leaf or a slice of lemon on a hornet sting. That will take the pain away every time. She taught me that evening primrose is good for arthritis. Feverfew can cure a headache. Ginger aids in poor digestion." As she talked, she showed me each plant or herb. Some were dry, some were growing in pots, and some she had crushed to a powder.

She said, "Garlic is good for fatigue. You can eat it whole, fresh, or roasted over a fire. Mama taught me how to gather golden seal, bayberry, butternut bark, chamomile, and mayapple. Things like that. They're all found in nature. I make tonics and tinctures to take by mouth and liniments to rub on the body."

I said, "Like Dr. Zoren's Elixir of Life."

She gave me a look. "You didn't buy a bottle of that, did you?"

I shook my head. "No. Pap thinks it was hogwash."

Mrs. Carter said, "Then your pap has got a good head on his shoulders. Maybelle Terwilleger showed me her bottle, and I gave it a taste. It wasn't anything but cheap corn whiskey and red sugar syrup. That man isn't a doctor, let me tell you. He just swindled folks out of their money."

I said, "But what about the dog? Didn't you see how thin he was? After he drank one spoonful of that elixir, he was well."

Mrs. Carter said, "Honey, I don't know exactly how he did it, but that hornswoggler pulled a fast one. His assistant was in on it, somehow."

I said, "But I was standing right next to the cage, Mrs. Carter. I saw it with my own eyes."

Mrs. Carter said, "Like Mr. P.T. Barnum says, 'There's a sucker born every minute.'"

That got me wondering. If it was true what Pap and Mrs. Carter were saying, we'd all been had.

Love,
Teddy

Name_____ Date_____

Writing Questions for the Letter of April 7, 1892
Circle the letter of the correct answer.

1. Read the following sentence from Teddy's letter today:
   I trounced him good!
   The word *trounced* is an example of what kind of good writing skill?
   A. metaphor
   B. simile
   C. strong verb
   D. weak verb

2. Read the following sentences from Teddy's letter today:
   "No. Pap thinks it was hogwash."
   These sentences are examples of what kind of good writing skills?
   A. onomatopoeia
   B. strong verbs
   C. dialogue
   D. simile

3. Read the following phrase from Teddy's letter today:
   Some were dry, some were growing in pots, and some she had crushed to a powder.
   These phrases are examples of what kind of good writing skills?
   A. metaphors
   B. descriptive details
   C. similes
   D. mini story

4. Read the following sentence from Teddy's letter today:
   He looked at Jasper Lowe with a you-and-I-both-know-I-can-beat-Teddy-Bodain look.
   This sentence is an example of what kind of good writing skill?
   A. descriptive writing
   B. voice
   C. simile
   D. onomatopoeia

5. Read the following sentence from Teddy's letter today:
   The second good thing that happened was my interview with Mrs. Carter.
   The phrase *The second good thing that happened* is an example of what type of good writing skill?
   A. descriptive writing
   B. transitional phrase
   C. conclusion
   D. specific emotion word

April 8, 1892

Dear Martha,

Our jerky is ready. I should say our DELICIOUS jerky is ready. I should say our SCRUMPTIOUS jerky is ready. I wish you could taste some right now.

The sun has been shining hot for two days straight, and the strips of meat have turned very dark. That means they've dried out properly. I helped Mama take them down and store them between layers of cheesecloth. Mmmm! I could eat every one.

I said, "May I have three pieces for Travis Lark?"

Mama said, "Travis Lark? What on earth for?"

I told her about the slingshot contest and winning my marbles back and his cat's eye shooter.

Mama said, "Are you sweet on him?"

I practically screamed, "MAMA! Of course not. He's just my friend."

Mama said, "Well, alright then. You're just being neighborly."

We had school again today. Miss Melman said, "I hope your interviews are going well. I'm going to give you a few more days to work on them. Don't forget to include some pictures in your sketchbooks." I'm glad she gave us more time. I haven't had much time to do my drawings. Life is so busy on a wagon train. Where does all the time go?

We settled in for Miss Melman to read several more chapters of Tom Sawyer. This time we were quiet and listened to every word. Tom Sawyer is such a good book. Miss Melman was just getting to the part about Tom and Becky Thatcher being sweet on each other. She liked him, but she pushed him off a bridge into the water.

I thought about Travis Lark. He's a boy, and he's my friend, but he's not my boyfriend. I don't know why Mama had to say that. I only wanted to give him the jerky because he was such a good sport about losing his marbles and his shooter. He would love our jerky.

I looked around for Travis, but to my surprise, he wasn't there. I was wondering where in the world he could be when he rode up on Dixie, all huffy and out of breath.

He said, "Sorry I'm late, Miss Melman. A constable rode up a few minutes ago with his deputy and asked Captain Walsh if we had seen a Dr. Xavier Zoren, selling his Elixir of Life. He said Dr. Zoren swindled his townspeople out of their money. He had sold them bogus medicine. The constable's wife gave the stuff to her pet kitty—and the cat got drunk."

We burst out laughing. Miss Melman said, "Oh dear! I had my suspicions about Dr. Zoren. I studied my maps and the globe, and I'm afraid the country of Rambonia simply doesn't exist."

I said, "It doesn't?"

Miss Melman said, "No, and I've never heard of the Rendini people, either. I think Dr. Zoren is a swindler, and I don't think we're the first group of people to fall for his scheme."

Hallie said, "But why would he lie to us?"

Miss Melman looked thoughtful. "It's sad to think about it, but there are dishonest people in this world. Instead of doing an honest day's work, they would rather trick people out of their hard-earned money. In my book, that's just not right."

I remembered folks handing their dollars over, dollars that had been earned with hard work.

I felt sick with shame. I'd been so wrong about Pap.

Love,
Teddy

Name_____ Date_____

Persuasive Writing Prompt for the Letter of April 8, 1892
Read and answer the following prompt.

Persuasive Prompt: In talking about her suspicions about Dr. Zoren, Miss Melman said, **"It's sad to think about it, but there are dishonest people in this world. Instead of doing an honest day's work, they would rather trick people out of their hard-earned money."** We know it is better to earn your money by working hard. Pretend you have met a trickster who is cheating people out of their money. Use convincing arguments to persuade him to get a job and earn his money the honest way. Give examples of how his cheating can be hurtful. Tell him what the consequences could be for dishonesty, and give ways in which he could possibly earn his money in an honest manner. Read over your paper carefully. Does your paper have plenty of "weight" and logical reasons?

_____

_____

_____

_____

_____

_____

_____

_____

_____

_____

_____

_____

_____

_____

_____

_____

_____

_____

April 9, 1892

Dear Martha,

Today, our caravan stopped by a swamp. We weren't expecting anything special, but one by one all the wagons ahead of us stopped, so we did, too. Captain Walsh came riding by on his horse, Highlander. We were a little surprised because he usually sends Travis with all of the messages.

Captain Walsh called out, "I'm inviting all children who are old enough to behave to join me out here. I want to show you a real Florida swamp. You must have on shoes or boots. Some of you adults may want to join us. That is, if you can behave."

That tickled Mama. She said, "Go do it!" I grabbed my sketchbook and took off flying.

Captain Walsh led us to the edge of a low, muddy river. Strange wooden points jutted up out of the water. I sketched them quickly, so I could ask about them later. Some of the trees that lined the shore were full and leafy, and moss hung from their branches. Other trees looked like dead skeletons. There were birds in the sky, birds floating on the water, and birds sitting in the branches of dead trees. Fish jumped right out of the water and splashed back in again.

Captain Walsh said, "I've led wagon trains down this way since just after The War Between the States. I've learned a thing or two from Indians, naturalists, settlers, and original pioneers, known as 'Florida Crackers,' who have grown up on the land. I'd like to teach you a few things about the swamps you'll be seeing all along our journey."

Right away he cautioned us. "Always stay back from the edge of the water, children. See who's taking a nap in the morning sun?" I looked, but I couldn't make out what he was talking about. Captain Walsh said, "Right there. See those long, scaly animals?" He waited for us to focus. "Those are reptiles. American alligators."

Alligators! I'd heard about them. I'd had nightmares about them. Now, I was seeing them with my own eyes. They were absolutely still. They didn't move a muscle or even blink their eyes. I thought they might be dead. Captain Walsh said, "These are the little fellows. Their big brothers are about five times this big." I was astonished! The "little fellows" were about as long as I am tall. Can you imagine how big their big brothers must be? I sketched as fast as I could while Captain Walsh answered questions.

Miss Essie Mae Pitts asked, "Are they always this still?"

Captain Walsh said, "When they're sunning themselves, they remain perfectly still. But don't let that fool you. Alligators can run faster than a full-grown man. In short bursts, they can run as fast as a horse."

Immediately, everyone backed up. We snickered, embarrassed.

"Florida swamps are interesting, to be sure, but danger is always lurking. Look there, in the fork of this tree." He pointed nearby. Once again, I had to search for what he wanted us to see. Then, I saw it! A snake was coiled right where several branches joined the trunk of the tree. I shivered. I hadn't seen it because the snake's skin was the exact same color of the tree bark.

Captain Walsh pointed to a high tree across the water. "See that big bird over yonder?"

Minnie Good asked, "Is that an eagle?"

Captain Walsh said, "Looks like it, but it's an osprey. Ospreys always make their nests near water because they're fish eaters. Many's the time I've seen an osprey swoop down from high above, dip deep into the water with his talons, and come up with a fish."

Florida is amazing! There is nature everywhere. But there is danger, too.

Love,
Teddy

Name_____ Date_____

Reading Multiple Choice Questions for the Letter of April 9, 1892
Circle the letter of the correct answer.

1. What was the name of Captain Walsh's horse?
    A. Silver
    B. Midnight
    C. Bessie
    D. Highlander

2. Captain Walsh told the kids that original pioneers of Florida who have grown up on the land are called what?
    A. Pilgrims
    B. Florida Crackers
    C. Colony People
    D. Florida Natives

3. What kind of animal is an American alligator?
    A. a mammal
    B. an amphibian
    C. a reptile
    D. a marsupial

4. What did Captain Walsh say that ospreys eat?
    A. fish
    B. bugs
    C. swamp grass
    D. alligators

5. What kind of bird did Minnie Good think the osprey was?
    A. a heron
    B. a cardinal
    C. an eagle
    D. a pelican

6. Why did Teddy have trouble seeing the snake that was coiled up in the tree?
    A. The snake was too small for her to see it well.
    B. The snake was hiding in a bunch of tree moss.
    C. The snake slithered into a hole in the tree before she could get a good look at it.
    D. The snake was the same color as the tree.

7. Why did Captain Walsh say that ospreys make their nests near water?
    A. They love to bathe themselves every morning.
    B. They eat fish.
    C. They need water to drink.
    D. The evaporating water keeps them cool.

April 10, 1892

Dear Martha,

I'm supposed to be drawing pictures of Mrs. Carter for my interview report, but I can't help myself. I'm drawing the plants and animals we saw in the swamp yesterday. It's not that I don't think Mrs. Carter is interesting. It's just that I saw so many fascinating new animals, I want to sketch them before I forget a single detail. I could draw forever.

Yesterday, while Captain Walsh was telling us about ospreys, eagles, and other birds of prey, which means they are hunters, all of a sudden he stopped, right in the middle of his sentence, and pointed.

He said, "Well, would you look at that! We've got company."

Two darling little brown animals were swimming and doing tricks. They had big brown eyes, whiskers, and long sleek bodies. I was just going to ask what they were when Captain Walsh said, "Otters are usually found in rivers, but this swamp is fed by a river, so they're using it as a playground. They're funny little creatures and about as cute an animal as you'll ever see. But don't let that fool you. They bite, so keep your distance."

He pointed to the woody "knees" that jutted out of the water. "Anyone know what these are?" We studied them.

"These are cypress knees. They come from the roots of the cypress trees you see all around here."

Cypress knees. What a strange term.

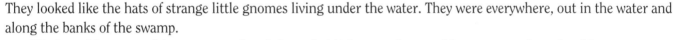

They looked like the hats of strange little gnomes living under the water. They were everywhere, out in the water and along the banks of the swamp.

All of a sudden, something stung my leg. I slapped at it, but another one bit my arm and another bit me under my chin.

I was not alone. Folks started slapping themselves all around. It's funny, thinking back on it.

Captain Walsh said, "Mosquitoes! It's a swarm! They love the swamps. We'll have to go back. They're all around us." Was he ever right! We were surrounded by clouds of mosquitoes, buzzing and biting like crazy. We were slapping and scratching like maniacs as we ran back to the wagons.

I told Mama all about our trip to the swamp because she had to stay home, so Dylan could nap in the wagon. I told her about the otters and the ospreys and the alligators and the cypress knees. Mama made me promise to draw them all for her in my sketchbook, so she can see what they looked like.

Now tonight, I can't stop scratching. I draw a little, and then stop to scratch. I have lumpy bug bites all over my body. I hope I never see a mosquito again, as long as I live!

I've drawn the otters, the osprey, the alligator, and the sleeping snake that scared me. I want to draw the cloud of mosquitoes that surrounded us so suddenly. But I've got to stop drawing swamp critters and start my sketches of Mrs. Carter and her herbs. Vexation.

I wonder if she has a cure for itchy mosquito bites.

Love,
Teddy

Name_____   Date _____

Narrative Writing Prompt for the Letter of April 10, 1892
Read and answer the reading prompt below.

Narrative Prompt: Otters are very playful creatures whose hilarious antics are fun to watch. Pretend you are walking along a beautiful, shade-covered riverbank when you meet two otters. Now write a narrative piece and tell a story about meeting these two otters. Be sure to give many juicy details about this meeting. Where exactly did you meet them on the riverbank, what did their home look like, what did they do when they played among the rocks and leafy ferns on the riverbank? Make sure to include many specific details so that your reader can "picture it" in his mind.

_____

_____

_____

_____

_____

_____

_____

_____

_____

_____

_____

_____

_____

_____

_____

_____

_____

_____

April 11, 1892

Dear Martha,

This morning, it was my turn to drive. Our train moves so slowly that I could work on some of my sketches. I drew Mrs. Carter as a girl, gathering herbs and plants in the forest with her mother. I sketched some of the plants and berries she had shown me. I drew the bundles of herbs hanging upside down from the rafters in the barn while they dried. I drew Mrs. Carter crushing some of the herbs in a mortar and pestle to grind them into a fine powder. My favorite drawing was of the cute little glass bottles she uses for storing her liniments, tonics, and tinctures.

After her piano lesson, Mama slid up on the seat beside me. "What are you drawing?"

I showed her my sketchbook.

She said, "You never told me you could draw so well, Teddy."

She flipped the pages, looking this way and that. I felt a little shy about her seeing my sketches.

I said, "How are your piano lessons coming?"

She smiled from ear to ear. "I love learning to play."

"Miss Melman said I've taken to it like a duck to water. Teddy, I'm learning a beautiful new piece. It's difficult, but I'm taking it slow. It's called 'Narcissus.'"

I said, "By Ethelbert Nevin."

She said, "How did you know? Girl, you are a sponge!"

I said, "Will you play it for me?"

Mama acted shy. "Maybe—when I get a little better."

Mama took over the driving, so I could fix our noon meal.

At breakfast, I had made oatmeal while Mama milked Girlie. While the oatmeal was cooking, I made some corn cakes and fried them in a skillet over the fire. I wrapped the corn cakes in brown paper, so we could have them later and not have to stop and build a fire. Mama had given Dylan a cup of milk and put the rest in her "ice box." Leave it to Mama to think of something good. She had bought an enormous chunk of ice from the supply wagon two days ago. She lined our wood box with sawdust and buried the slab of ice down in the shavings. When she wants to keep something cold, like Girlie's milk, she exposes part of the ice and sets the milk pitcher on top of it. Then, she covers it with a woolen quilt, folded thick.

"That quilt's too hot to use as cover, but it will make ice last almost a week," she said.

For our noon meal, I buttered two corn cakes for each of us and stuck them together with syrup. I put Mama's cakes on a tin plate with two strips of jerky. I put Pap's meal in the tin box Mama and I carry to him each day. I cut an apple for Gabriel and one for Girlie and poured a cup of milk for Mama and Dylan. I poured Pap's milk into a canteen and another canteen for me. I wrapped my lunch in brown paper.

When I took Pap his lunch, he said, "What's that you've got with you?" I told him it was my lunch. He said, "Get on up here with me. I've got an idea." He took our lunches and hauled me up behind him.

Pap told Captain Walsh that he would go ahead and scout awhile.

Captain Walsh said, "I see you've got company."

Pap and I rode ahead until our wagon train was out of sight. We stopped for a picnic.

"See that line of willow trees?" Pap said, pointing. "They're telling us where the river is. Willows like water. Captain Walsh says to watch for willows if you want to find water."

When we finished our lunch, we rode ahead, and sure enough, there was a river. There were people, too. Several men worked a flat, wooden ferry that was surrounded by ropes and pulleys. Pap pulled a folded map from his pocket and studied it.

He said, "Yep. This is the Apalachicola. This is where we'll cross with the wagons."

I wonder what it will be like to cross a river.

Love,
Teddy

Name_____ Date_____

Reading Short Response Questions for the Letter of April 11, 1892
Answer the questions below, and be sure to use complete sentences.

1. What does Mrs. Carter do with the herbs and plants she gathers?

_____

_____

_____

_____

2. Why does Mama act shy when Teddy asks her to play "Narcissus" for her?

_____

_____

_____

_____

3. How does Mama keep the ice from melting too quickly?

_____

_____

_____

_____

4. What did the line of willow trees mean to Teddy?

_____

_____

_____

_____

_____

April 12, 1892

Dear Martha,

　　We are camped on the banks of the Apalachicola River. Today is a day of rest. Folks are visiting, cooking together, and tending to the stock. There's going to be a singing after a while.

　　Tomorrow, we will wait for our turn for the ferry. It will take two days, maybe, for all 24 wagons to cross the river, if all goes well. Crossing the river can be dangerous. Captain Walsh met with us today and explained how the crossing will take place. The ferry can take just one wagon at a time since the wagons are so big and heavy. Pap and the other pushers will help each family roll their wagon onto the ferry without any oxen. The ferry will float the wagon to the other side of the river. The men will swim the oxen across the river, one team at a time.

　　Crossing is expensive. We have to pay the ferrymen to take our wagon across. We have to pay the stockman to corral our team on the other side of the river. We even have to pay to camp here, and we've never had to pay for camping before.

　　Late last night, while Mama rocked Dylan, Pap and I opened the secret compartment under the wagon to take out money for the crossing. Pap held the lantern while I opened the hidden drawer. Something sparkled in the light.

　　"What's that?" I asked.

　　"That's my pap's pocket watch," Pap said.

　　I saw a thick paper, folded. "What's that?"

　　Pap said, "That's the deed to our land, Teddy. That paper is going to make a new life for our family."

　　I said, "Tell me again how we got it." Pap counted out some money and put it in his pocket. Then, he carefully shut the drawer. Now, the drawer was invisible again.

　　"Come sit a spell," Pap said. We sat by our fire, which had burned down to just the coals.

　　"Times were hard in Mississippi. I'd been working on Mr. Albritton's land since before you were born. I always wanted to buy land of my own, but there never seemed to be enough money after we paid all of our bills. You remember when the corn crop failed two years ago?"

　　I nodded. That had been a hard year. The year Dylan was born. The year we hardly had enough food. The year Mama made our clothes from feed sacks.

　　Pap said, "Mr. Albritton lost big when the crop failed. He called me in and said, 'Bodain, here's the truth of it. I have little money to pay you. However, I can offer you a land deed for 40 acres down in Florida. If you work for me one more year, I'll deed that land over to you.' It was a shock that he couldn't pay me in cash for my work. But land! I told Mr. Albritton, if he would throw in Jester and Jingo, he had a deal."

　　My heart was sad again when I heard the names Jester and Jingo.

　　Pap said, "We barely made it through, but Mr. Albritton was a man of his word. He presented me with the deed, signed over to Mr. Dalton Bodain."

　　I said, "Where did you get the money for our wagon and all the supplies?"

　　Pap said, "Captain Walsh took me on as one of the pushers for this caravan. He advanced me the money for the wagon and for our supplies in Dothan. That's why I work every day to pay him back."

　　Pap's story made me think about our life in Mississippi. There are things I miss there. I loved living near you, Martha. You will always be my best friend. But I am happy that Mama and Pap will have a chance to own their own land.

　　Love,
　　Teddy

Expository Writing Prompt for the Letter of April 12, 1892
Read and answer the following writing prompt.

Expository Prompt: Teddy saw Pap's precious pocket watch in the secret compartment under the wagon. Think of something that you own that is very precious to you. Now write an expository piece and explain the item that is special to you. Be sure to include what the object is, its detailed description, where you got it, how you keep it or store it, and any other details that would help the reader understand about your special object.

_____

_____

_____

_____

_____

_____

_____

_____

_____

_____

_____

_____

_____

_____

_____

_____

_____

_____

April 13, 1892

Dear Martha,

Pap startled me awake today with the words, "Teddy, you got to get up, girl, 'cause we're crossing the river today." I was so deep asleep that, at first, I was confused. My mind was hazy and full of cobwebs, but then I remembered one word—ferryboat. I jumped up, so I wouldn't miss any of the excitement.

Fortunately, we were camped near the river. But we first had to secure everything in the wagon or, as Pap said, "batten down the hatches." Mama always chuckles when he says that. Pap said it's something sailors say.

The pushers and the rest of the men struggled to line up the wagons in front of the ferryboat. They unhitched a team of oxen and moved them out of the way. Then, they pushed one wagon at a time on board the flat deck of the ferry. The ferrymen lashed down the wagon wheels to large planks nailed to the ferry deck, so the wheels were locked in place. The wagons were floated and pulled across the river by ropes and pulleys. A team of mules on the other side were driven away from the river, pulling the ferry across. Great buckets of butterbeans, was that ferry sitting low in the water! The men in front got splashed as the river churned up and gushed over the bow.

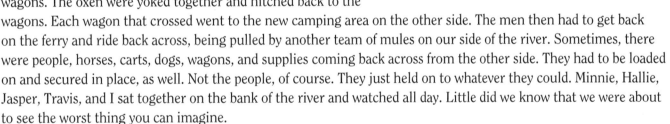

One of the pushers led the oxen to the river in pairs, unyoked them from each other, and a man on horseback swam them across. When he got them to the other side, they were herded into a corral. I couldn't imagine how those huge oxen could swim, but they were as graceful as horses.

Once on the other side, the men had to unlash the wagons, unlock the wheels, and push the wagons off of the boat. Sometimes, it took as many as ten men to push those heavy wagons. The oxen were yoked together and hitched back to the wagons. Each wagon that crossed went to the new camping area on the other side. The men then had to get back on the ferry and ride back across, being pulled by another team of mules on our side of the river. Sometimes, there were people, horses, carts, dogs, wagons, and supplies coming back across from the other side. They had to be loaded on and secured in place, as well. Not the people, of course. They just held on to whatever they could. Minnie, Hallie, Jasper, Travis, and I sat together on the bank of the river and watched all day. Little did we know that we were about to see the worst thing you can imagine.

The animals could get pretty skittish on the ferry. Late that afternoon, a mule got scared and started kicking. A man who was not from our caravan was standing nearby. The mule kicked him in the chest, and he went flying right into the river. They threw him a lifeline, but he was too badly hurt to hold on. Martin, Miss Emily's husband, dived into the river and swam after him. The man was unconscious and coughing up blood by the time Martin got him to shore.

There was no doctor, so Mrs. Carter examined the man. She said, "It might be too late, but this man needs a doctor." The way she said it, we all knew he might die. The farmer who owned the mule offered to take him to a doctor.

Of course, all the excitement completely stopped the river crossing for the day. It was about dark, anyway. This wagon crossing takes a long time. Ten wagons did cross today, but ours wasn't one of them.

Tomorrow, the remaining wagons will cross, and we will become a train again.

Love,
Teddy

Reading Extended Response Questions for the Letter of April 13, 1892
Answer the questions below. Be sure to use complete sentences, reasons, and details.

1. Describe how the wagon pushers get the wagons across the river.

_____

_____

_____

_____

_____

_____

_____

_____

_____

2. Explain why Mrs. Carter said, **"This man needs a doctor."** What did Teddy know from her tone?

_____

_____

_____

_____

_____

_____

_____

_____

_____

April 14, 1892

Dear Martha,

We crossed the river today. I sat on the bank again with Minnie, Hallie, Jasper, and Travis, only today, I had Dylan with me. I had to watch him, so Mama could help make sure all our things on the wagon stayed tied down and weren't damaged. After our wagon was locked in place on the ferry, Pap swam Jeb and January across the river. I was so proud. They swam over as pretty as you please and scrambled up the bank. Mama stayed with the wagon as it crossed on the ferry.

Minnie and Hallie held Veronica for me, so Dylan wouldn't ruin her or get her dirty. I wasn't about to leave her on the wagon. Captain Walsh said that, once in a while, the ferry might tip over if the load wasn't balanced just right, and our belongings would all be swept down river.

While we were sitting on the bank, Travis asked, "Whose doll is that?" and pointed at Veronica.

I said, "Mine."

He asked, "How did her hair get so real looking?"

I told him about how your mother used cuttings of your real hair to make Veronica's hair.

He said, "Oh, Jasper, will you cut my hair, so I can glue it on some dumb doll?"

I said, "Hush up, Travis."

And of course, he said, "Hush up, Travis," in a girl's voice.

He said, "And we can dress her in frilly clothes and have a tea party."

I said, "Just remember that I whipped you in the slingshot competition."

He said, "I taught you everything you know!"

I said, "I'm not sharing any more of my jerky with you!"

Before I could realize what was happening, Travis snatched Veronica from Hallie and ran down to the river. He held her over the water and said, "How would you like it if I dropped your precious doll baby in this river? Then, would you share your jerky? Huh? Huh?"

I screamed, "Stop! No!" I reached for Veronica. Travis tried to hold her up over his head, but she flew out of his hand and sailed into the river.

We both had the most astonished looks on our faces. I was furious! I screamed, "My baby! She's in the river!"

Travis was in a panic. He shouted, "Jasper, help! I dropped her in the river." He dived in and began searching. When he came up for air, he called to Jasper again, "Help me!" I'm sure Travis knew he had done something terrible.

I stood there frozen to the spot. I heard some adults start shouting. Folks came running from all directions. I heard Mama scream. I turned my head just in time to see her jump off the ferry into the water. She swam like her life depended on it. I thought, what on earth is she doing?

Captain Walsh shouted, "You men! Come help here!"

Mama staggered through the shallower water, her arms reaching out. She screamed, "Where is he? Where is he?" I had no idea what she was talking about. She looked more frightened than I had ever seen. She screamed, "Where is my baby? Where is my baby?"

I yelled, "Mama, Dylan's right here with Minnie. Travis threw Veronica in the river!"

Mama's face changed immediately. She found Dylan with her eyes, sitting on Minnie's lap. She glared at me. "What were you screaming about? I thought the baby had drowned!" Mama burst into tears.

I said, "Travis threw Veronica in the river."

Everyone standing there looked over at Travis. He held Veronica in his hands. She was dripping wet and most of her hair had come off.

Today was not a good day.

Love,
Teddy

Grammar Questions for the Letter of April 14, 1892
Circle the letter of the correct answer.

1. Where do the quotation marks go in the following sentence?
   A. I said, "Just remember that I whipped you in the slingshot competition.
   B. I said, Just remember that I whipped you in the slingshot competition."
   C. "I said, Just remember that I whipped you in the slingshot competition."
   D. I said, "Just remember that I whipped you in the slingshot competition."

2. After Travis dropped Veronica in the river, Teddy said they both had the most astonished looks on their faces. What does the word *astonished* mean?
   A. happy
   B. shocked
   C. mad
   D. sad

3. Which word is the subject in the following example?
   He held Veronica in his hands.
   A. Veronica
   B. his
   C. He
   D. hands

4. Which sentence has the correct use of commas?
   A. After our wagon was locked in place on the ferry, Pap swam Jeb and January across the river.
   B. After our wagon was locked in place, on the ferry, Pap swam Jeb and January across the river.
   C. After our wagon was locked in place on the ferry Pap, swam Jeb and January across the river.
   D. After out wagon was locked in place on the ferry, Pap, swam Jeb and January across the river.

5. What did Teddy mean when she said that Mama swam **"like her life depended on it."**
   A. Mama doesn't know how to swim very well.
   B. The water was cold and Mama hates to swim.
   C. Mama swam very fast because she was afraid that Baby Dylan would drown.
   D. Mama was drowning in the river.

6. Teddy wrote, **"Mama's face changed immediately."** What part of speech is the word *immediately*?
   A. an adverb
   B. a verb
   C. an adjective
   D. a prepositional phrase

7. Why did Teddy capitalize the words *Captain Walsh*?
   A. He's her pap's boss.
   B. Captain Walsh is the subject.
   C. Captain Walsh is a proper noun.
   D. The words Captain Walsh started the sentence.

April 15, 1892

Dear Martha,

Travis and I are both in big trouble.

Mama is still pretty mad. Last night she had to stay in her wet clothes until we could get the wagon hooked back up to Jeb and January and make our way to the new campsite. She wouldn't talk to me and didn't want to hear a word I had to say.

Pap whispered, "Let her stew awhile. She'll come around."

At bedtime, I tried again.

I said, "Mama, I really am sorry."

She said, "Teddy, sometimes you can be a vexation of a girl. You almost scared the life out of me."

I said, "I didn't mean to. I just wasn't thinking."

Mama said, "Well, you had better think next time."

I am confined to the wagon for two days. I can't go anywhere, not even to school, which means I will miss the next installment of Tom Sawyer. Rats! I'm just sick about it, but Mama won't budge.

She said, "A day or two in this wagon is just the schooling you need." She won't let me sketch or read, either. "You just sit there on that wagon seat and think about how to behave properly." .

I was bored out of my mind. I just had to sit there mile after mile, watching the scenery go by. There was nothing to do. Absolutely nothing.

I thought about our life in Mississippi. We had a good life there, but it was a hard life. Pap had to work day and night, and most of his hard work went toward making money for Mr. Albritton. Mr. Albritton was a good man, but Pap and Mama wanted to own their own land.

I remembered the day Pap came home with the news of the land deed. He said, "Grace, you know things have been hard. Since the crops failed, Mr. Albritton has taken a terrible loss. He can't pay me in money, but he gave me something that might mean a new life for our family. It's a deed for some land. Not here in Mississippi. In Florida. But it's 40 acres, and it's ours."

I thought about how it had been to prepare for the new adventure. Leaving Mississippi for Florida meant giving up our friends, our school, our church, our life. I thought and thought, mostly about those things and about leaving you. And about the adventures we've had so far.

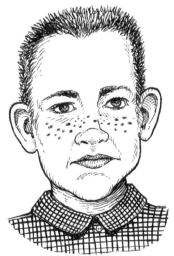

About mid-afternoon, Travis Lark caught up with our wagon. I was shocked to see how short his hair was. His mother must have cut it this very morning. He was going to speak to me, but he saw the look on Mama's face.

"Mrs. Bodain, I've come to apologize, ma'am. I am truly sorry for the terrible trouble I caused you and your family yesterday."

Mama said, "You children put a terrible scare in us. But I accept your apology. I appreciate the fact that you came over."

Travis said, "May I speak to Teddy, please?"

Mama said, "No, you may not. Teddy is being punished."

Travis said, "I'm being punished, too. My ma only let me come over so I could apologize."

Mama said, "Well, you have apologized. Now, good day, Travis."

I told myself I would not talk to him, ever, ever, ever again. He ruined Veronica, my most prized possession. He was acting like a big old show-off, and now he'll have to pay for it.

But I couldn't help but notice how sad he looked, how ashamed. I almost felt sorry for him. Almost.

Love,
Teddy

Writing Questions for the Letter of April 15, 1892
Circle the letter of the correct answer.

1. Read the following sentence from Teddy's letter today:
    Travis and I are both in big trouble.
    This sentence is an example of what type of good writing skill that we should include in our writing?
    A. strong verb
    B. details that you can picture
    C. grabber
    D. zinger

2. Read the following sentences from Teddy's letter today:
    Rats! I'm just sick about it, but Mama won't budge.
    These sentences are examples of what type of good writing skill?
    A. onomatopoeia
    B. voice
    C. grabber
    D. juicy color words

3. Read the following sentences from Teddy's letter today:
    I was bored out of my mind. I just had to sit there mile after mile, watching the scenery go by.
    These sentences are examples of what kind of good writing skill?
    A. descriptive writing
    B. persuasive writing
    C. juicy color words
    D. transitional phrase

4. Read the following sentences from Teddy's letter today:
    Pap whispered, "Let her stew awhile. She'll come around."
    The word *stew* is an example of what kind of good writing skill?
    A. transitional phrase
    B. strong verb
    C. onomatopoeia
    D. juicy color word

5. Read the following sentence from Teddy's letter today:
    About mid-afternoon, Travis Lark caught up with our wagon.
    The words *About mid-afternoon* are an example of what kind of good writing skill?
    A. takeaway ending
    B. metaphor
    C. specific emotion word
    D. transitional phrase

April 16, 1892

Dear Martha,

Another long day of punishment, only today's punishment was a little better than yesterday's.

Mama gave me every single chore she could think of. I had to reinforce all the buttons on Pap's work shirts. I had to clean the lamp chimney and fill the base with oil. I had to sift the sugar to get the lumps out. I had to brush all the dust off the supply boxes in the wagon with a stiff brush, sweep the floor, and cut the mold off the cheese. I had to pour the salt out on a tray to dry in the sun, put lemon juice on the stains on Mama's apron, and pull the wicks out of the candle stubs.

But no matter what she gave me to do, it was better than just sitting there with NOTHING to do.

Late this afternoon Mama said, "Teddy, I think that's enough. Come on up here and sit with me."

I crawled up on the seat and sat beside her. Dylan was in his little seat leaning back against a blanket, sound asleep. Mama said, "Have you learned your lesson?"

I said, "I have. I'm sorry. Real sorry. I'll think next time."

We rode for a while. Mama said, "You are so much like me."

I liked the sound of that. I was going to ask her what she meant, but Travis caught up with us again. He had a package, wrapped in brown paper and tied with white string. I noticed his short haircut again.

He said, "Mrs. Bodain, please, would you let me talk to Teddy today?"

Mama said, "You may say what you've come to say, Travis."

He probably hoped Mama would go back in the wagon, but she stayed right where she was. He handed me the package and said, "Teddy, I never meant to drop your doll in the river. I'm sorry. My ma had Miss Emily Carter fix her as best as she could." I didn't answer. I sat as quiet as a mouse. Travis finally realized I wasn't going to say anything, so he turned and left.

I stared at the package. It could sit there forever. I didn't want to see Veronica all ruined and dirty. I wanted to fling that package under the wagon wheels.

Mama said, "Well, I see you've chosen not to forgive Travis. I think that's a fine idea. Hold a grudge. Stay mad. Keep all that bitterness bundled up inside. Try to hurt him as much as he hurt you. Isn't that what the Good Book says?"

I felt ashamed. I hung my head. She was right, of course. Travis had apologized.

It was just that I dreaded so much what Veronica would look like now that she was ruined.

Mama said, "You've got to look at her sooner or later."

I untied the string and opened the brown paper. I stared in amazement.

Veronica was more beautiful than ever.

Miss Emily must be a miracle worker! She made a new dress out of some fancy, blue material. She cleaned and polished Veronica's leather shoes, like new. Miss Emily made pantalettes and lace stockings. All the traces of the muddy water had been washed away from Veronica's porcelain head, hands, and feet. Miss Emily fastened them to a new shapely body, fashioned from clean muslin, and stuffed her with kapok. I examined every part of her. I was totally amazed.

But the thing that I couldn't figure out was Veronica has hair! It was glued on just so, all lovely and curled, and the same color as before. I had clearly seen her in the river with most of her hair washed away. Just a few strands had been left. Now, she has a full head of hair.

I said, "Where on earth did Miss Emily get real hair?"

Mama and I sat wondering. Then, it finally dawned on us, both at the same time, and we burst out laughing!

Poor Travis. He's suffered enough.

Love,
Teddy

Name_____ Date _____

Persuasive Writing Prompt for the Letter of April 16, 1892
Read and answer the prompt below.

Persuasive Prompt: Accident or not, Travis came to Teddy to apologize for dropping her doll, Veronica, in the river. Travis then had Teddy's doll restored, so she was **"more beautiful than ever."** Do you think we should fix or replace something we've broken? Pretend someone you know broke your teacher's favorite pen. Persuade that person he should apologize, fix the pen, replace it with a new one, or just pay for it. Use convincing arguments to show how important it is to take responsibility for our actions. Read through your paper carefully. Underline your important, convincing reasons.

_____

_____

_____

_____

_____

_____

_____

_____

_____

_____

_____

_____

_____

_____

_____

_____

_____

_____

April 17, 1892

Dear Martha,

Today was an ordinary day, thank heavens.

We had school again. Miss Melman told me and Travis that she had not read ahead in Tom Sawyer on Tuesday, so we didn't miss any of the story. I am so glad.

First, we listened to each other's interviews. Angel Jones reported about Mr. James Good, Minnie's father. He's a butcher by trade, and Angel told us that he orders special knives made in Solingen, Germany. The steel that the knives are made of keeps its sharp edge longer than other knives. She also showed us a drawing of the different parts of a pig. She said, "Mr. Good said that every part of a pig is useful except his oink." I thought that was funny. Everything except the oink.

Will Cranberry, the lucky duck, interviewed Captain Walsh. We were all a little jealous that he had drawn the captain's name. He said, "Captain Walsh fought in The War Between the States, and he was an officer. That's why we call him Captain." He told us that when Captain Walsh was a young man, he trained as a scout in Montana. Now, he leads travelers down into the state of Florida because he says it's one of the last frontiers. He's free to travel because his wife, Elmira, died many years ago, and his sons are grown.

Several more kids told about their interviews, but I was surprised when Jasper Lowe's turn came.

"I drew Mrs. Grace Bodain's name," he said.

What? Mama hadn't told me. What would Jasper have to say about Mama? I couldn't imagine.

Jasper said, "Mrs. Bodain is a homemaker. Before she was married, she attended the Birmingham Art School for one year."

Mama, a college girl? I couldn't believe my ears. Mama had never said anything about it to me.

Jasper continued, "But what Mrs. Bodain is most noted for are her beautiful quilts. My mama told me that other women envy her designs and consider her quilts to be heirlooms."

I'd never noticed Mama's quilts before. To me, they're just old blankets to keep us warm in the winter. Are they special? I thought every mother made quilts for her family. Jasper went on and on about Mama, if you can believe it.

The rest of us will have to wait to present our interviews another day.

Miss Melman read the next few chapters of Tom Sawyer. It was a scary part, where Becky Thatcher and Tom get lost in a deep, dark cave. Becky was afraid and Tom was doing his best to find their way out. The scary thing was that they were being followed by a man who wanted to kill Tom. Miss Melman left off at the most exciting part. Rats!

On the way back to our wagon, Travis stopped me. He said, "Are you still mad?"

I said, "No, I'm not mad anymore. Veronica looks great, especially her hair."

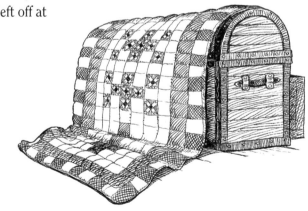

Travis's face turned beet red.

I looked at his hair and raised my eyebrows.

He said, "You going to tell anybody?" He looked desperate. His face turned redder.

I said, "No, I promise."

He said, "I'm really sorry, Teddy. I know Veronica had hair from one of your best friends."

I said, "She still does."

Today was an ordinary day, but ordinary days can be good, too.

Love,
Teddy

Reading Multiple Choice Questions for the Letter of April 17, 1892
Circle the letter of the correct answer.

1. What is Mr. James Good's profession?
   A. a school teacher
   B. a locksmith
   C. a constable
   D. a butcher

2. Mr. Good said that only one part of the pig is not useful. Which part is that?
   A. the tail
   B. the oink
   C. the snout
   D. the feet

3. Teddy said, **"Today was an ordinary day."** What does the word *ordinary* mean?
   A. fast and exciting
   B. slow and boring
   C. regular or average
   D. fun and adventuresome

4. Where did Captain Walsh train as a scout when he was a young man?
   A. Montana
   B. Florida
   C. Mississippi
   D. Alabama

5. What fact was Teddy shocked to learn about her mama from Jasper's interview?
   A. Mama helped her father herd cattle when she was a girl.
   B. Mama was a champion jump roper.
   C. Mama had attended art school for one year before she married Pap.
   D. Mama sang tenor in the church choir before Teddy was born.

6. What did Jasper say that Mrs. Bodain was most noted for?
   A. her fabulous beef jerky
   B. her skills on the piano
   C. her candle making
   D. her beautiful quilts

7. Why did Mr. Good order his knives from Germany?
   A. The steel keeps its sharp edge longer.
   B. He was German and so was his wife.
   C. They were cheaper than other knives.
   D. The German blades were longer.

April 18, 1892

Dear Martha,

Well, you just won't believe what happened today. I still have trouble believing it myself! I hope I have time to write it all. I'm sitting on the ground, almost under the wagon, writing by lamplight.

We left early today. Mama drove, Dylan sat in his little seat, and I sat on the seat with Mama. About midmorning, Travis came riding by on Dixie. He said that the next town, Hampton Springs, was having a fair right outside town. Captain Walsh said we could stop for two hours, so everyone could eat at the fair and play some of the games since we were going to pass right by there. We scurried to get ready!

The fair wasn't too big, but it was full of people. I guess they were from the town of Hampton Springs and other parts around here. Anyway, Pap and Mama and Dylan and I walked around to the different booths. Pap bought us hot dogs. Boy, were they tasty! We bought cups of lemonade. Mama looked at the quilts and the jellies while we stuffed our faces.

Pap put Dylan on his shoulders. The three of us went to look at the livestock and the small animals. Dylan loved the rabbits and the ducks.

But here's the part I've been waiting to tell you. We noticed there was a crowd of people gathered. We went over to see what was going on. It was Dr. Zoren, selling his Elixir of Life! There he was, right in front of his red and yellow wagon, giving the same speech he had given us. The same skinny dog was in the cage and then, after he lapped up the spoonful of Dr. Zoren's Elixir of Life, Flavia covered the cage with the green cloth. And, just like before, after he talked to the crowd for a while, she flipped up the cloth, and the dog looked fat and healthy. The crowd gasped and clapped, just like we had. Folks were trying to give Dr. Zoren their money for his elixir while he was still talking. He had fistfuls of money by the time he was finished.

All of a sudden, a man came into the crowd not three feet away from me and Pap. He yelled out, "You are a thief and a liar!" Everyone turned to look. The man screamed out again, "You ain't no doctor, either. I bought this elixir from you two weeks ago and gave it to my sick bull. Two days later, he was dead."

The crowd looked at Dr. Zoren and then back at the man. He shouted, "I've been trying to catch up with you for three days. Everywhere I go, people tell the same story: they've been swindled!"

The crowd pressed forward and began to snatch their money out of Dr. Zoren's hand!

The man wasn't through. He pushed his way up front and opened the door of the cage. The dog jumped out, but the man didn't seem interested in him. He was searching the cage, as if looking for something.

Dr. Zoren tried to stop him. He shouted, "Wait just a minute, sir. You are interfering with my—"

But before he could finish, the man yanked on the back of the cage.

Dr. Zoren yelled, "Stop! Sir, you are disturbing my business! This is outrageous! Get away from there!"

The angry man yanked harder. The back of the cage fell forward. Great buckets of butterbeans! There stood the thin dog! The crowd gasped!

Vexation! Pap just said, "Teddy, put that light out, and get to sleep. We've had enough excitement for one day." I'll have to tell you all about it tomorrow. Rats!

Love,
Teddy

Name_____ Date_____

Narrative Writing Prompt for the Letter of April 18, 1892
Read and answer the prompt below.

Narrative Prompt: Fairs are exciting. There's scrumptious food, dizzying rides, daring games, plenty of livestock, and crowds of people. Think about a time you went to a fair, or make up a time. Did you eat cotton candy, win a stuffed panda bear at the baseball throw, pet the animals, or throw up on the ferris wheel? Now write a narrative piece and, using as many specific details as you can, tell about your day at the fair. If you have never been to a fair, imagine what it would be like, and write from your imagination. Be sure to use your senses and lots of describing details, so your reader will be able to feel as if she is right there at the fair with you.

_____

_____

_____

_____

_____

_____

_____

_____

_____

_____

_____

_____

_____

_____

_____

_____

_____

_____

April 19, 1892

Dear Martha,

Let me get right back to my story. I know you are wondering what on earth happened.

The angry man showed everyone in the crowd that the sick dog was still in the cage. He said, "See? That elixir doesn't cure a thing! Elixir of Life, my foot! This man is a scoundrel, a cheat, and a liar!"

Martha, I was absolutely astonished! The pitiful dog was trembling something fierce. The angry man pulled him out and set him on the ground. He yelled, "Someone get the constable!"

Well, that did it. Some of the men took hold of Dr. Zoren. People started yelling, "You tried to cheat us out of our money!" and "This man is a quack!"

In a few moments, the constable arrived. He listened to the angry man's story. Then, he questioned Dr. Zoren. He looked carefully at the cage, moving the false wall up and down.

Finally, he said, "Mister, I could put you in jail for cheating folks out of their money and for pretending to be a doctor. But I don't want to have to deal with the likes of you another minute. Pack your things and get out of town."

Dr. Zoren whistled for his two dogs to return. A family with three children was petting the healthy dog. It wagged its tail.

The pitiful dog was standing all alone, trembling.

The constable said, "And you won't be taking your dogs with you, either. It's obvious you don't know how to treat an animal with kindness."

This made Dr. Zoren stomp his foot and wave his fist. He said, "Sir, this is my livelihood!"

But the constable ignored him. He called, "Gus, you want a good dog?"

The man with the three children nodded. "Sure. We'll take him."

The constable pointed to the skinny dog, "Anyone interested in this dog?"

For a moment, no one said a word. Then, someone actually laughed.

Another man called, "Now, that is a joke. Best thing you could do is put him out of his misery."

Folks turned and walked away.

The skinny dog looked right at me. He wagged his tail, just the slightest wag.

I raised my hand to get the constable's attention. I said, "Sir, I would love to have this dog."

The constable looked at Pap and then at me. He said, "He's known cruelty."

Pap said, "If anyone can love this animal back to health, it's this girl."

I knelt down to look at the dog. I could count his ribs. His head drooped, and his fur was matted and dirty. The thought of how he had been starved made me shudder. How could anyone be so cruel? This dog needed food, medicine, and most of all, love.

I said, "Hey, boy." He cocked his head to one side, looking at me.

I scratched his ears. I said, "You want to be my dog?" He licked my hand.

He barked. Just a little one, mind you, but it was a sign.

Pap said, "Theodosia. I told you a dog was looking for you. It seems like he just found you."

I thought my heart would burst.

Love,
Teddy

Reading Short Response Questions for the Letter of April 19, 1892

Answer the question below, and be sure to use complete sentences.

1. Why did the people call Dr. Zoren a quack?

_____

_____

_____

_____

2. Explain why the constable did not allow Dr. Zoren to keep his dogs.

_____

_____

_____

_____

3. What happened when the crowd was asked, **"Anyone interested in this dog?"**

_____

_____

_____

4. What did the constable mean when he said, **"He's known cruelty"**?

_____

_____

_____

_____

April 20, 1892

Dear Martha,

The whole train knows about my new dog, Ethelbert, even Miss Melman. Even Captain Walsh. That first night, the reason Pap said, "Teddy, put that light out!" is because I slept outside next to him under the wagon, and my lamplight was keeping him awake. Mama said she was happy I had a dog, and she would help me nurse him back to health, but he had to sleep outside. Since it was his first night, I begged if I could sleep outside next to Pap.

Mama said, "You're knocking on my soft spot," but she made me a hammock out of one of her old blankets and hung it under the wagon. Then, she made Ethelbert a pallet, so he wouldn't have to sleep on the damp ground. He slept right next to me. He whined some during the night, but if I put my hand on him, he hushed and lay still.

At breakfast, Mama said, "Try that dog on a little oatmeal." He lapped it up and then drank some fresh water. I was so happy about it, I could have leaped over the moon.

But when roll-out came, there was the problem of what to do with Ethelbert. He was too weak to walk all day beside the wagons. We usually cover ten miles before we stop to camp for the night. Pap said, "Put him in the laundry basket, and let him lay at your feet. He'll be able to walk on his own in a few days."

We passed a spring. Mama said, "You better fill some buckets with water and let them warm in the sun. You've got a dog that needs tending." I filled three buckets and hung them on the side of the wagon that faces west, so they would heat up in the afternoon sun.

I said, "Mama, what can we feed him, so he'll be healthy again?"

Mama said, "I've been studying on that. This dog's been starved half to death. He needs meat."

When we stopped to make camp, Pap went to hunt up our supper. Mama brought out her laundry tub and helped me bathe Ethel with warm water. Dogs don't usually like baths, but he sat as still as you please and let us soap him all over and rinse him twice.

I dried him by our campfire and combed his hair with the currycomb Pap used for Jester and Jingo. Ethel looked about a million times better after he had his bath. He lay on his pallet by the fire and put his head on his paws.

At supper, Mama fried rabbit for us and gave the raw liver and part of the meat to Ethelbert. You have never seen a dog gulp down food so fast!

Mrs. Carter came over after supper and ran her hands over Ethel from head to toe. She said, "No broken bones. No disease. Just feed him well. He might need to eat lots of little meals all during the day. And by all means, give him a spoonful of this iron tonic in the morning and a spoonful at night."

Pap said, "Are you sure that isn't Dr. Zoren's Elixir of Life?"

We had a good laugh at that one. While the men were telling stories, Ethelbert rested his head in my lap, and Mama and Miss Emily rocked their babies to sleep by the fire.

Did you ever have a day when you thought you might just die of happiness?

Well, this was one of those days.

Love,
Teddy

Name_____ Date _____

Expository Writing Prompt for the Letter of April 20, 1892
Read and answer the following writing prompt.

Expository Prompt: Teddy describes for us how she is learning to take care of her new dog, Ethelbert. Think of how you have to take care of a pet of yours. If you don't have a pet, imagine the kind of pet you would like to have and all the many things you would need to do to care for it. Now write an expository piece and explain how you would take care of your pet animal. Support with reasons and descriptive details as you write. Be sure to include a beginning, a middle, and an ending and several writing skills to add beauty and maturity to your writing.

_____

_____

_____

_____

_____

_____

_____

_____

_____

_____

_____

_____

_____

_____

_____

_____

_____

_____

_____

April 21, 1892

Dear Martha,

We had school again today. Ethelbert went with me. He's strong enough to walk, just not strong enough to walk all day.

Miss Melman said, "I see we have a new student." When we laughed, she said, "That's the nice thing about a school like this. We meet in different places, at different times, and all because you just want to learn. We're surrounded by nature on all sides. I see no reason why we can't have a dog in our midst."

When I told Miss Melman his name, she said, "Teddy, you must be the only girl in the world to have a dog named Ethelbert."

I said, "His full name is Ethelbert Nevin Bodain."

Miss Melman said, "I will never play 'Narcissus' again without thinking of this handsome dog."

I wonder why Miss Melman doesn't have a husband. I heard Mama and your mama talking one time, and they said if you are older than 25 and aren't married, you're an old maid.

Miss Melman doesn't seem like an old maid. She's not homely, and she smells good. Besides, she plays the piano. But I can't think of any man on this train that she could marry. They're all married already, except Captain Walsh, and he's old.

This afternoon, Minnie, Travis, Jasper, and I made kites. Jasper's mama gave us some brown paper. Mrs. Good gave us some string. Travis and Jasper cut some branches we could split into the spine and the frame. Miss Emily gave us some calico scraps for the tail. Mama had a little pot of glue she let us use. We didn't have enough string to fly four kites, so we decided to make two kites: a girls' kite and a boys' kite. It would be a competition, a war.

Minnie and I chose two sturdy pieces of the wood to act as the spine and the cross spar. We cut notches in the strips and fitted them together. I held them in place while Minnie stretched the string through the notches and tied them off. We lay the frame over the brown paper, and I drew it off about two inches bigger than the frame.

We were just going to glue it on the string, when Minnie said, "Wait. Let's use our colored pencils to decorate it." I thought that was a brilliant idea. We decided to call it The Florida Belle, so I printed the name and filled in the letters, and Minnie drew some palm trees and a big sun. That's all we had time for. We folded the paper over the string and glued it in place. It was a sunny day, so it didn't take long to dry. It wasn't hard, but we did all this in Minnie's wagon, so we were crowded. We plan to test it out this afternoon when we stop for the day.

Minnie's mother, Mrs. Good, let Ethel sit on the floor of their wagon while we worked. She said he looked much better than he did when he was in Dr. Zoren's cage. I explained about the bath, the good food, and Mrs. Carter's iron tonic. Mrs. Good gave me a ham bone for Ethelbert's supper.

I can't wait to fly our beauty.

We'll show those boys whose kite is boss.

The Florida Belle will be the queen of the sky!

Love,
Teddy

Name_____ Date _____

Reading Extended Response Questions for the Letter of April 21, 1892

Answer the question below. Be sure to use complete sentences, reasons, and details.

1. Describe how Teddy and Minnie went about making The Florida Belle. How did the girls feel about their finished product?

_____

_____

_____

_____

_____

_____

_____

_____

_____

_____

_____

2. Why did Miss Melman allow the "new student" to come to school with Teddy?

_____

_____

_____

_____

_____

_____

_____

_____

_____

_____

_____

April 22, 1892

Dear Martha,

I have to report on the kite-flying contest. Our kite, The Florida Belle, was more beautiful, but Travis and Jasper's kite, The Destroyer, won. After the wagons stopped for camp, we met for a kite war! Their kite was not pretty. It was just plain. Ours was gorgeous with strips of bright colored calico all down the tail. The boys used rags for their tail. The contest was to see whose kite stayed up in the air the longest. I think every kid on the train came to see who would win.

Travis launched their kite, and I launched ours. Jasper and Minnie held the kites while we ran in the opposite direction with the string. Both kites popped up into the air at about the same time. Lots of adults stopped what they were doing and came to watch. It really was very exciting.

Our kites sailed high into the sky. I let out a lot of line. The Florida Belle took to the sky like a bird, dipping and turning in the wind. I heard Miss Melman say, "Oh, isn't the girls' kite darling!"

But then, without warning, Travis crossed my line with his. I thought, what is he doing? I tried to get away, but I couldn't. He and Jasper started laughing an evil laugh because they knew they had a secret weapon.

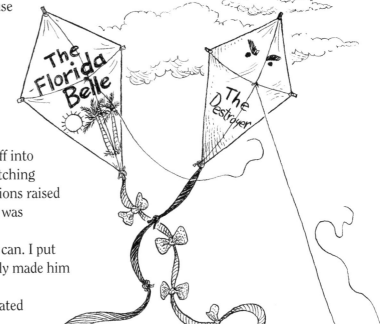

The day before, they had put some marbles in an old sock and beat them with a hammer. They coated six feet of their string nearest their kite with glue and crushed glass! The glass was as sharp as a razor.

When Travis sawed their string against ours, The Florida Belle's line cut through and she flew off into the wind. Minnie and I screamed, but everyone watching laughed and clapped. Of course, those two rapscallions raised their hands and jumped up and down in victory. It was Tom Sawyer and Huckleberry Finn all over again.

There stood Travis Lark, laughing like only he can. I put my hands on my hips and shook my head. That only made him laugh harder.

And to think that, once again, Travis Lark defeated me with a MARBLE. Vexation! The only thing that makes me feel better about it is that it wasn't one of MY marbles that defeated our kite. That would have been too much to bear.

Minnie and I have taken an oath to get them back! We will, too. Just wait and see. Our day will come, and I'll show that Travis a thing or two about flying a kite.

Pap missed the kite war because he was off scouting for Captain Walsh. But later, when I was milking Girlie, he came by to see me. I told the story of how Travis had cut my line. Pap and I had a good laugh. I couldn't help it. The glass dust on the string was a great trick. I wish I had thought of it myself.

Pap said, "I did the same exact thing to someone when I was a boy. I should have taught you my secret kite-flying tricks."

"Yeah," I said. "Whose side are you on?"

So much for The Florida Belle. She was beautiful while she lasted.

I'll never forget how glamorous she was, sailing through the sky, up, up, and out of sight.

Love,
Teddy

Grammar Questions for the Letter of April 22, 1892
Circle the letter of the correct answer.

1. Which example has the correct use of capitalization?
   A. Our kite, the Florida belle, was more beautiful.
   B. Our kite, the Florida Belle, was more beautiful.
   C. Our kite, the florida belle, was more beautiful.
   D. Our kite, The Florida Belle, was more beautiful.

2. In the following sentence, what type of word is *sharp*?
   The glass was sharp.
   A. noun
   B. verb
   C. adjective
   D. adverb

3. In the following sentence, which word is incorrect?
   Minnie and me have taken an oath to get them back!
   A. me
   B. have
   C. an
   D. oath

4. Which word is spelled incorrectly?
   A. glamorous
   B. launched
   C. probabley
   D. exciting

5. In the following sentence, which word is the verb, or action word?
   They coated six feet of their kite's string with glue and crushed glass.
   A. of
   B. coated
   C. with
   D. crushed

6. What does the word *glamorous* mean?
   A. rude and unkind
   B. ugly and wrinkled
   C. beautiful and elegant
   D. sticky and ruined

7. Why does Teddy capitalize the word *Girlie*?
   A. It is a proper noun.
   B. She likes to write an uppercase G.
   C. Girlie is a descriptive word.
   D. It is a place.

April 23, 1892

Dear Martha,

We had trouble today. BIG trouble. It was very upsetting for everyone.

We were rolling along, everything was peaceful, when suddenly we heard someone scream. A wheel had come off the wagon five wagons up from us. One minute they were driving, and the next thing we knew, they were tipping over, sliding down a hill.

I don't know how it happened. Pap said he thinks that when the wheel came off, the load shifted. The wagon began to tip, and then it fell completely over. The Porters (the people who own the wagon) were in the wagon. Mr. Tip Porter was driving, but Mrs. Porter was in the wagon with her two little girls, Mary and Anna. When the wagon tipped over, all of their possessions came crashing down around them. The noise was frightening. As the wagon slid down the hill, the canvas top ripped open. Boxes bounced out and cracked open. Clothes flew through the air. Fruit, potatoes, and 100 pounds of sugar bounced out.

I could hear Mary and Anna screaming and the terrible bellowing of their oxen. I had to put my hands over my ears because it was so awful. I think I might have been screaming, myself.

Folks started running toward them even before the wagon came to a stop at the bottom of the hill. Mama handed Dylan to me and said, "Stay here." I know I was supposed to stay put, but I couldn't help myself. I gathered Dylan in my arms and ran right behind her.

Mr. Porter had been thrown from the seat. He was dirty and scraped up, but he was not hurt in a big way. He had already jumped up by the time folks got down the hill. Mrs. Porter and the girls were inside the broken wagon. When it came to a stop, we could hear them crying.

Mr. Porter shouted, "Ellen! Ellen! Are you hurt bad?"

We could hear Mrs. Porter's muffled voice. "Help us! The girls are under boxes!"

I have never seen people move so quickly. Pap and some of the other men lifted the ripped canvas and began to hoist the boxes and piles of broken goods. It wasn't long till we saw arms and legs. One by one, they lifted out Mary, and then Mrs. Porter, and then little Anna.

They were banged up something awful, and all of them were crying. Mrs. Porter's dress was ripped to ruins. Mama took her shawl off and wrapped it around her shoulders. Mr. Porter's face was as white as a bed sheet.

Mrs. Carter was a little too old to climb down the hill, so the men carried the Porters up the hill. Then, Mrs. Carter asked Mama and Miss Emily to hold up some quilts, so they would form a little examining room.

She said, "Ellen and Mary are awfully bruised. They'll be sore, but they'll be alright in a week or so. Tip wrenched his shoulder. I can bind that and put him in a sling for a few weeks. But I'm worried about Anna. She has a gash on her arm, and I think she may have some broken ribs."

Poor little Anna. Just seven years old! I hope she will be alright.

Captain Walsh said, "Folks, we'll have to make camp here. Men, settle your families, and then let's see what can be done for the Porter's wagon and ox team."

Folks have taken the Porters in, here and there, until their wagon is fixed. Their things are in ruins. Tonight, I was in charge of everything: watching Dylan, making a campfire, milking Girlie, and I thought I was going to have to fix supper, but Mrs. Lark came by and said, "Teddy, we'll be cooking vittles for you and the Carters and the Porters." That was the best news I'd heard all day. Jubilation.

Love,
Teddy

Writing Questions for the Letter of April 23, 1892
Circle the letter of the correct answer.

1. Read the following sentence from Teddy's letter today:
   It was very upsetting for everyone.
   The word *upsetting* is an example of what type of good writing skill that we should include in our writing?
   A. simile
   B. specific emotion word
   C. onomatopoeia
   D. transitional phrase

2. Read the following sentence from Teddy's letter today:
   Boxes bounced out and cracked open. Clothes flew through the air.
   If we join these two sentences with the word *and*, and produce a compound sentence, what writing skill have we demonstrated?
   A. sentence combining
   B. sentence variety
   C. juicy color sentence
   D. run-on sentence

3. Read the following sentences from Teddy's letter today:
   Mr. Porter shouted, "Ellen! Ellen! Are you hurt bad?"
   These sentences are examples of what type of good writing skills?
   A. specific emotion word
   B. dialogue
   C. strong verb
   D. onomatopoeia

4. Read the following sentence from Teddy's letter today:
   Mr. Porter's face was as white as a bed sheet.
   The phrase *was as white as a bed sheet* is an example of what type of good writing skill that we should include in our writing?
   A. transitional phrase
   B. simile
   C. metaphor
   D. dialogue

5. Read the following sentence from Teddy's letter today:
   Pap and some of the other men lifted the ripped canvas and began to hoist the boxes and piles of broken goods.
   This sentence is an example of what type of good writing skill?
   A. transitional sentence
   B. specific examples
   C. metaphor
   D. opinion

April 24, 1892

Dear Martha,

Everyone is still in shock about the accident.

Last night, Pap stayed out very late with the other men, I imagine talking about how to help the Porters get their wagon and their belongings back up the hill. Lots of people had helped save whatever they could, but the wagon was still piled in a broken heap. The oxen, luckily, had escaped serious harm.

I was alone at our wagon, so I fed Dylan and rocked him to sleep. He is the most precious baby in the world. I am so lucky to be a big sister.

Mama still hadn't come home from Mrs. Carter's, so I fixed her plate and covered it with a piece of cheesecloth. I took out one of her lemons and squeezed it in a cup, added fresh water and a big lump of sugar. I stirred it around real good. There was enough lemon juice for another cup, so I made me one, too. I decided I'd wait for Mama, so we could drink our lemonade together.

Jasper Lowe's daddy brought us by two buckets of water. I don't know why he did it, but it sure was handy. I hauled Mama's tub to the far side of the wagon and hung a quilt. Then, I warmed the buckets of water over the campfire until they were steaming and poured them in Mama's tub.

That was a lot of work, let me tell you! I added some of the French soap your mother gave us before we left Mississippi. It smelled heavenly! I lit the lamp and waited. When Mama came home from Mrs. Carter's, she looked like she was about to fall over. I gathered her nightgown, took her hand, and led her out to the far side of the wagon.

When she saw the tub, she smiled. She said, "What would I do without you, Teddy?"

We ate together by the fire, but Mama was almost too tired to eat. I handed her the lemonade, and she said, "How did you know lemonade is just what I was craving?"

Mama told me that Mrs. Carter had to bind Tip Porter's shoulder and fashion a sling. Then, she gave Anna some drops that made her very sleepy. Mama helped Mrs. Carter bind Anna's ribs from her chest down to her waist. They had to make the bindings tight, so her broken ribs would not move. Then, Mrs. Carter gave Anna more sleepy drops, and she fell asleep in Mama's arms. Mrs. Carter cleaned the cut on Anna's arm and sewed it together with clean, white thread she had soaked in antiseptic. Anna did not wake up. The thought of sewing on someone's arm is strange to me.

I asked, "Will she be alright?"

Mama said, "I think she will. She's going to have some painful days, but hopefully she'll mend, poor little bird." She brushed her hair, tugging and smoothing out the knots until her hair was silky.

Mama was in a thoughtful mood. She was tired but relaxed as she sipped her lemonade. She said, "The stars are out tonight. Aren't they beautiful?"

I hadn't even looked at the stars. They were beautiful. They sparkled and shimmered like a sea full of diamonds. We stared at them for the longest time.

Then, Mama said, "Teddy, do you see all those stars?"

I said, "I see a sky FULL of stars."

Mama said, "Well, you mean more to me than all those stars put together."

I thought my heart would fly up to the moon.

Love,
Teddy

Persuasive Writing Prompt for the Letter of April 24, 1892
Read and answer the following prompt.

Persuasive Prompt: Teddy did chores, not just the chores Mama had assigned her, but things she saw that needed doing. Imagine you know someone who is lazy and doesn't want to do anything but the chores he absolutely HAS to do. Persuade him how a family works better if everyone is willing to pitch in and do MORE than his assigned chores. Make a convincing argument about what attitude to have. Give examples of chores and thoughtful deeds kids can do. Give reasons and details of how these actions would be a huge help to someone else. Make sure your arguments and specific examples will persuade this person to move into ACTION.

_____

_____

_____

_____

_____

_____

_____

_____

_____

_____

_____

_____

_____

_____

_____

_____

_____

_____

_____

April 25, 1892

Dear Martha,

This morning when we woke, a cardinal was singing.

I searched the bushes until I found him, sitting on a branch. Mama whispered, "Do you see his mate? She won't be far behind." I looked and looked till I saw the brown-feathered bird perched on a nearby branch. Mama said, "It's a good day when a redbird sings."

The bad news is, we will have to stay here for a few days. The Porter's wagon needs some repairs that have to be made with special parts. One of the pushers will have to ride to the next town to buy the supplies from a wagon maker. I hope it's not Pap.

The good news is that we are camping by a spring! Yesterday, Captain Walsh told us that we were only three miles from Fanning Springs. He thought it would be a better place for us to camp while we wait for the parts for the Porter's wagon.

I'd seen springs before, but not like this. Miss Melman told us all about them today when we had school. We were sitting on some rocks right by a pool of blue, iridescent, shimmery water. It looked like an inviting oasis with shady palms and a gentle breeze.

She said, "A spring is a body of clear, fresh water that is fed by an underground aquifer. An aquifer is like a river that runs underground. The water is filtered through tons of limestone and gravel. Gravity causes the water to be pushed up through holes in the limestone. This creates a series of connected ponds, known as 'springs.' Isn't it enchanting?"

I asked, "What makes it so blue?"

She said, "Pureness and filtering give the water its spectacular blue color. It's nature's beauty."

She brought out her big picture book on Florida. "This says that springs are 72 degrees year round. That will feel rather cold when you jump in, but you'll get used to it after a while. When the water bubbles up through the boil—"

Will Cranberry said, "What's a boil? Wouldn't a boil be hot? If it's a boil, where is the steam?"

Miss Melman said, "You are inquisitive, Will. The boil is the spot that shows the force of the water coming out of the ground. It ripples and moves, like water boiling in a kettle."

For about the millionth time, I thought about what an adventure we are on. Miss Melman said, "I'd like for you to learn as much as you can about the springs, the plants and vegetation, and the fish and the wildlife through observation. Learn all you can, and we'll share information."

Later, Travis told me that Captain Walsh said that springs are not only a great place to go swimming, but you can also fan for treasure. I practically shouted, "Treasure? What kind of treasure? What do you mean by fan for treasure? Where?"

Travis said, "Pipe down. We don't want everyone looking." He lowered his voice. "The captain says we might find pieces of gold or lost jewelry or doubloons. The Spanish were all over this place. So were pirates."

Great buckets of butterbeans. Treasure! I wonder if it was left by the pirates of Penzance!

Love,
Teddy

Reading Multiple Choice Questions for the Letter of April 25, 1892
Circle the letter of the correct answer.

1. What did Miss Melman say an aquifer is like?
   A. a trickling brook
   B. a steady stream of water
   C. a boiling hot spring
   D. a river that runs underground

2. What color is the cardinal, or redbird's, mate?
   A. red
   B. brown
   C. yellow
   D. black

3. What did Miss Melman say makes the spring's water so blue?
   A. chlorine
   B. oxygen
   C. pureness and filtering
   D. the fish and plants that live in it

4. What did Travis mean when he told Teddy to **"pipe down"** when she asked him about the treasure?
   A. He wanted her to be quiet.
   B. He wanted her to sit down.
   C. He wanted her to talk louder.
   D. He wanted her to crouch down on the ground.

5. What does Miss Melman say causes the water to be pushed up through holes in the limestone?
   A. fish
   B. pressure
   C. gravity
   D. moisture

6. Who told Travis about the treasure they could look for in the spring?
   A. Mr. Bodain
   B. Teddy
   C. Miss Melman
   D. Captain Walsh

7. What temperature did Miss Melman say the spring stays year round?
   A. 70 degrees
   B. 72 degrees
   C. 75 degrees
   D. 80 degrees

April 26, 1892

Dear Martha,

When you come to Florida to visit me someday, we must go swimming in a spring. WE MUST!!

This afternoon, when the sun was fierce, we all went swimming at the spring. The pressure of the water squirting up out of the ground erodes the limestone and makes a perfect swimming hole.

None of us had a proper bathing costume, so we all wore old clothes. I wore a pair of cut-off overalls and an old shirt. The spring water is quite cold, just like Miss Melman said, but we warmed up in the sunshine. Soon, it didn't feel cold at all. We jumped and swam and dived like mermaids! Even Mama got in with Dylan and had a great time swimming.

One of my favorite things is the rope swing that hangs down from a tree on the far bluff. We took turns holding the rope, swinging out over the boil, and dropping in with a big splash. It was a blast!

I opened my eyes under the water. It was amazing. I could see each individual grain of sand on the bottom. I saw clumps of green grass and tiny little fish. In Mississippi, the creeks and rivers were muddy. I don't ever remember being able to see the bottom. But Fanning Springs is crystal clear. I had to warn Miss Melman because her swimming dress floated up, and when I was under water, I could see her bloomers.

Travis called me over to the side where he and Jasper were. He said, "Let's fan for treasure."

I said, "How do you do it?"

He said, "I told Miss Melman what we were going to do, and she thought it was a great idea. She gave me this piece of slate to fan with. Captain Walsh said we should find a sunny spot, take a deep breath, dive down, and start fanning the sand away.

Jasper said, "Gold and silver are metals. Metal is heavy, so it sinks to the bottom. We don't actually know that something is there, but it will be fun to look. We might find something! We could get rich!"

So that's what we did. We took turns sitting on the bottom, fanning the sand away, and looking for anything that glinted or gleamed in the sunlight. The spring gets more shallow as you move away from the boil, but still, none of us could stay on the bottom. We kept floating up to the top! Finally, we figured out that we needed a heavy rock to put on our lap when we were down there. I wanted to find something valuable! When it was my turn, I fanned and fanned. The sand rose up in the water, and I fanned it away with the slate. I never found anything, but I kept looking. I thought about the Spanish explorers who were here long ago, and the pirates who crossed the land with stolen treasure.

All of a sudden, I heard an ear-splitting scream, "There's a monster in the water!" You have never seen people get out of a spring so fast. Debbie Goguen pointed. "Over there!" We thought she was just joking, but sure enough, there was a large creature in the water. It had a huge gray body, a round tail, and flippers.

Miss Melman went closer and took a good look. She called out, "Not to worry, everybody. This is not a monster. I can see how it looks like a monster because of its size, but I assure you, it is not. This is a sea cow. I've read about them in books. They are also known as manatees. They are gentle herbivores so not to worry."

No one moved.

"They eat plants and grasses," Miss Melman said. "They're harmless, really." To prove it, she dived back into the spring. The manatee watched her for a moment and then slowly swam away.

Soon, we were all back in the water, diving, swimming, and fanning for treasure.

You've got to love Miss Melman.

Love,
Teddy

Name_____ Date_____

Narrative Writing Prompt for the Letter of April 26, 1892
Read and answer the writing prompt below.

Narrative Prompt: Teddy and Travis are fanning for treasure. What fun! Pretend you and your friend are going fanning for treasure. Think about which friend you will choose to go with you, where you will want to look for your treasure, how you will fan for treasure, and what magnificent treasures you will find. What emotions will you feel when you find the treasure? What will you say? Now write a narrative piece, and include all the fabulous details, so your reader can form a "mind movie." Use your imagination!

_____

_____

_____

_____

_____

_____

_____

_____

_____

_____

_____

_____

_____

_____

_____

_____

_____

_____

_____

April 27, 1892

Dear Martha,

Mr. Tip Porter's best friend, Harold, returned today with two wagon makers. He had ridden his horse to the nearest town and told the wagon maker about the Porters' accident. One of the wagon makers was an old man with dark skin and snow white hair. His name was Obadiah Lincoln, and he used to be a slave. His son, Lucas Lincoln, was also a wagon maker, and he was the biggest, strongest man I have ever seen.

They brought their own wagon. It was not a covered wagon, like ours. It was a long wagon with enormous tools and sawhorses in the back. It also contained about every wagon part you can imagine, including wheels, pulleys, tongues, axles, and I don't know what all. There was even a coop with a bunch of chickens!

Yesterday, while we were swimming, the men had hooked up six teams of oxen and pulled the Porters' wagon upright. They put a wheel jack under the wagon where the wheel had been. Then, they fitted on a spare wheel and somehow got the oxen to pull the broken wagon up the hill. Pap said it was a Herculean task. Now today, they watched together with all of us as the two wagon makers looked at the damage.

Obadiah and Lucas walked around the wagon over and over, prodding and pulling, rubbing their chins. They talked in low tones. Lucas crawled under and studied the brake system. Obadiah climbed up into the wagon and rocked his weight back and forth.

At last, Mr. Obadiah Lincoln said, "Well, I think if we replace the felly rim, and the doubletree, and shore up the sides, you'll be in good shape as far as the body of the wagon goes. My son, Lucas, is also a wheelwright. He'll have to replace the wheel that came off during the accident."

Captain Walsh asked, "How long?"

The two Mr. Lincolns talked for a moment. Then, Lucas said, "Two days, if it doesn't rain."

That means that we have two more days at the spring. Jubilation!

I went back to the swimming hole this afternoon. This time, Minnie and I each took turns fanning the sand. We looked in a different location. We only found a broken bottle. After a while, we joined all the other kids who were jumping into the boil with the rope swing. We swam and splashed each other and played most of the afternoon. Miss Melman taught us a water game called "Marco Polo."

When we came back to the wagons, we were hungrier than bears. I found out the chickens I saw in the Lincolns' wagon earlier were bought by the Porters for the Carters and our family.

Mrs. Porter said, "You've been such a help doctoring us up. We wanted to thank you."

Mama made fried chicken for supper. The skin was crispy and brown and would almost melt in your mouth. Miss Emily made potato salad and a plate of sliced pickles. Mrs. Carter made a pot of beans and peach cobbler. I made skillet biscuits, just the way Mama taught me.

Pap said, "This meal will go down in the history books."

Before we sat down, Mama fixed two big plates. She said, "Take this supper to Mr. Lincoln and his son. I bet they're hungry."

Mr. Lucas Lincoln took the plates. He said, "That fried chicken smell was romancing my nose something fierce. We weren't expecting supper, but we sure are grateful."

Later, he brought the plates back, washed and dried. I heard him talking to Pap.

"Thank you, sir. Everything was fit for a king, everything except those biscuits."

Pap said, "Oh?"

Mr. Lincoln said, "Those biscuits were fit for a king AND a queen."

Pap was still laughing about it when he told Mama.

Love,
Teddy

Name_____ Date_____

Reading Short Response Questions for the Letter of April 27, 1892
Answer the questions below, and be sure to use complete sentences.

1. Describe the wagon, the equipment, and the parts the wagon makers used.

_____

_____

_____

_____

2. Why did Teddy say, **"Jubilation!"** when she found out it would take two days to fix the wagon?

_____

_____

_____

_____

3. Describe the afternoon the children and Miss Melman spent at the swimming hole.

_____

_____

_____

_____

4. What did Mr. Lucas Lincoln mean by, **"Those biscuits were fit for a king AND a queen."**

_____

_____

_____

_____

_____

April 28, 1892

Dear Martha,

Today was our last day at the spring. I'm going to miss this place.

First thing this morning, I milked Girlie. She's been giving a lot of milk lately. I give her and our oxen big buckets of spring water morning and night. During the day, Pap stakes them all out in a field of clover. But at night, he brings them back to our wagon. Two nights ago, Captain Walsh heard a panther! We've not actually seen a panther, but we don't want to risk our animals being out there with one. I even make sure Ethelbert is with me at all times when the sun goes down. Last night, he heard something in the woods, and he growled.

Speaking of Ethelbert, I haven't told you that he's practically well. He's almost as healthy and perky as Dr. Zoren's other dog. Mama and I feed him scraps, and she pours any leftover bacon grease on his food. She gives him some of Girlie's milk every morning. I brush his fur each day with the currycomb, and it's beginning to shine. He walks all the time now. Of course, we're not rolling, but he goes everywhere I go, all around the camp.

This morning, Miss Melman gathered all of us kids together. She said, "The Porters have been through a terrible ordeal. Their wagon is being repaired, but all of their household goods are still in a real mess. Mrs. Porter and the girls are too bruised and sore to do anything. Mr. Porter's arm is in a sling. I think that if we all pitched in for a little while, we could make quite a difference. There'll still be time for swimming this afternoon. What do you say?"

We went through the Porter's household goods and separated all the things that were still usable. We repacked their boxes and refolded their clothes. While we were working, some of the women sewed up the big rip in the canvas, so the men could stretch it over the wooden stays. Travis, Jasper, and some of the other boys went back down the hill and searched for any belongings that had been thrown from the wagon.

I watched Mr. Obadiah and Mr. Lucas working with huge tools. Lucas swings a ten-pound hammer with his giant hands as if it were a toy. Mr. Obadiah took his shirt off while he worked in the heat. I saw long, deep scars on his back. I shuddered. I've never seen anything like it. I wonder how he got those scars.

This afternoon was our last trip to the spring. We played a game where we stand up on each other's shoulders and make a pyramid. I was on the second tier. Sarna Phillips was on the very top. We all yelled, "Look at us!" for folks to see our tall pyramid, but just as they were all turning to look, Sarna fell off and dragged me under with her. Rats!

But I have something astonishing to tell you. I was taking a turn fanning the sand with the slate, and I saw something yellow, something glittery. My heart started beating really fast. At first I couldn't find it, but when the sand settled, I saw it clearly. It was a woman's gold bracelet! I grabbed it and swam to the surface as quick as a wink. It was a gold bracelet with lovely scroll work. I turned it over. On the inside was inscribed, "To Althea Tomlinson from her loving husband, Joseph. How do I love thee? Let me count the ways. August 13, 1862."

I ran to show my treasure to Mama. Soon, folks were crowding around. Everyone wanted to see the gold bracelet that had been found in the springs.

Mama said, "Teddy, this was given during The War Between the States. You have found someone's treasure! What a stroke of luck."

I was curious about Althea Tomlinson. Who was she? How did she lose her bracelet? Is she still alive? Is Joseph still alive?

I wonder. I wonder.

Love,
Teddy

Name_____ Date_____

Expository Writing Prompt for the Letter of April 28, 1892
Read and answer the following writing prompt.

Expository Prompt: Today Teddy found a gold bracelet in the springs. Think about a time that you found an item or something special that someone had lost. If you've never found anything, think of what you would like to find. Now write an expository piece that explains what you found, how you felt, how someone might have lost it, and what you did with it after you found it. Use many descriptive details, specific emotion words, sentence variety, and as many good writing skills as you can.

_____

_____

_____

_____

_____

_____

_____

_____

_____

_____

_____

_____

_____

_____

_____

_____

_____

_____

April 29, 1892

Dear Martha,

We are rolling again. Mama and I started off driving together. I said, "Mama, who do you think Althea Tomlinson was? How long do you think that bracelet has been down there in the spring?"

Mama said, "There's no telling. Thousands of people must have visited this spring for who knows how many years."

I said, "I bet Althea and Joseph were childhood sweethearts. She cut off part of her hair and wove it into a broach for him to wear when he went into battle, and he gave her this bracelet to remember him by. I bet she cried bitter tears the day she lost this bracelet and knew, at that exact moment, that he would not be coming home from the war."

Mama said, "Next thing we know, you'll be writing novels or plays for the stage."

I said, "Well, don't you think that would be romantic if it was true?"

Mama said, "Romantic? Why is every young girl fascinated with all things romantic?"

I said, "Weren't you romantic when you married Pap?"

Mama said, "I suppose I was. He turned my head, that's for sure."

I wanted to ask her about art school and how she learned to make such fine quilts, but Dylan started howling, and Mama had to go rock him to sleep.

As I drove, I thought about all the exciting things that have happened since we started our journey. I want to remember every detail. I've tried to draw things in my sketchbook. Last night, I drew a picture of Mr. Obadiah Lincoln. He was working, and he had taken his shirt off. I drew the scars on his back and wondered again how a man could have such scars. His son's back was smooth.

We made camp beside a spring. It made me homesick for Fanning Springs. But at least we have good, sweet water to drink. Pap and I filled all the buckets with fresh water. First, we watered the oxen and Girlie and Gabriel. Then, we filled all of our canteens and Mama's water crock. Finally, we filled every bucket and hung them on the sides of the wagon. I covered the buckets with cheesecloth to keep out bugs.

While we were alone, I said, "Pap, how do you think Mr. Obadiah Lincoln got those deep scars on his back."

Pap said, "It was a shameful thing."

I said, "What happened?" Pap took awhile before he answered. I thought he might not have heard me, at first.

Pap said, "For a long time, folks thought they could own other human beings as slaves. If their slaves didn't do what they were told to do or tried to run away, they whipped them to within an inch of their lives."

The horror of it made me sick. I'd heard about slavery, but seeing Obadiah's scarred back made it real. Pap said, "Human beings were bought and sold like cattle. Children were taken away from their parents and sold to other plantations. It was a cruel, evil practice. But men did it because it helped them get rich. That's one of the causes of The War Between the States."

I said, "Did anyone try to help them?"

Pap said, "Some did. My grandmother helped those who ran away. She left food on a tree stump out by her cornfield for those who were trying to escape. They traveled at night and navigated by the North Star. There were slave catchers out looking for runaways, but they never suspected my grandmother because she was so poor herself."

I wanted to hear more, but Mama needed me to rock Dylan. He has cried all afternoon and into the evening. I rocked him and sang. Mama thinks he might have a fever. I bet he's teething again.

Love,
Teddy

Reading Extended Response Questions for the Letter of April 29, 1892
Answer the questions below. Be sure to use complete sentences, reasons, and details.

1. Mama said to Teddy, **"Next thing we know, you'll be writing novels or plays for the stage."** Explain why she said this.

_____

_____

_____

_____

_____

_____

_____

_____

_____

2. In her sketchbook, Teddy drew the scars she noticed on Mr. Obadiah Lincoln's back. Where did the scars come from? How did this make Teddy feel?

_____

_____

_____

_____

_____

_____

_____

_____

_____

April 30, 1892

Dear Martha,

Something is terribly wrong.

Our baby, Dylan, cried and screamed all night. His fever is worse, and he can't keep anything down. The poor little thing is sweaty and restless. Mama stayed up with him for hours. Pap took over in the middle of the night and said, "Let me walk with this boy." Pap walked and walked, up and down the trail, but it didn't do any good.

About sunrise, Mama went to Mrs. Carter's wagon to see if she had a remedy for Dylan's fever. Mrs. Carter was gone to Miss Emily's wagon because little Lucy is sick with the same thing. By breakfast time, Miss Essie Mae Pitts came to tell us that her husband and daughter were sick. We were trying to gulp down some coffee and cornbread when several other folks sent word that their families had the sickness, too. I can tell from the looks on the grownups' faces that they are frightened. I can't help but worry.

Captain Walsh heard tell of it and came to talk with Mrs. Carter.

I couldn't hear what they were saying, but they looked very serious. Captain Walsh sent word that we would stay in camp and not drive today.

All day, Mama and I have taken turns bathing Dylan with cool water. We tried feeding him chicken broth, but he can't keep it down. Now, he turns his head when we try to give him anything to eat or drink. He is very weak. I gave him Veronica to hold, and she is in his arms.

Other people on the train are getting sick. Everyone is talking about it. Mrs. Carter begged Captain Walsh to send to the nearest town for a doctor, so he asked Pap to go.

Pap saddled Gabriel.

Mama said, "Dalton, our boy is bad off. Bring the doctor as quick as you can."

Pap leaned over and kissed Dylan's forehead.

I don't know where he is headed, but I saw him study the map with the captain, and then he took off at a gallop.

Sickness and fever are right here among us. I hope Pap gets back soon with the doctor.

Our baby is so sick.

Love,
Teddy

Grammar Questions for the Letter of April 30, 1892
Circle the letter of the correct answer.

1. What punctuation mark should go at the end of this sentence?
   Our baby, Dylan, cried and screamed all night
   A. period
   B. question mark
   C. comma
   D. quotation mark

2. In the following sentence, what kind of word is *Pap*?
   I hope Pap gets back soon with the doctor.
   A. verb
   B. adjective
   C. noun
   D. proper noun

3. In the following sentence, what tense is the verb *saddled*?
   Pap saddled Gabriel.
   A. present
   B. past
   C. future
   D. verb

4. In the following example, what kind of words are *sickness* and *fever*?
   Sickness and fever are right here among us.
   A. compound verb
   B. prepositions
   C. compound subject
   D. compound nouns

5. Which one of the following sentences has correct usage of apostrophes?
   A. I couldn't hear what they were saying.
   B. I could'nt hear what they were saying.
   C. I couldnt' hear what they were saying.
   D. I 'couldnt hear what they were saying.

6. Teddy writes, **"We were trying to gulp down some coffee and cornbread when several other folks sent word that their families had the sickness, too."**
   What part of speech is *gulp*?
   A. a strong verb
   B. a weak verb
   C. a noun
   D. an adverb

May 3, 1892

Dear Martha,

I have the worst news to tell you. It is even hard for me to write the words. It has taken me days just to get up the courage to tell you.

My little brother died three days ago.

How can this be true? I want it to be a dream I can wake up from, but it is not. It is real.

Mama was in the wagon rocking Dylan, and I heard her cry out. I went in to see if she needed me to take over, and she said, "Our little angel has slipped away."

At first I didn't understand. But I watched Mama put him down on the pallet, and he was as still as can be. I felt like my heart would break. I sank right down to my feet and put my head in my hands.

Pap returned with the doctor, and Mama ran to him. They held each other and cried. I've never seen Pap cry before.

I thought I would die from sadness, but Ethel came and put his head in my lap. He licked my hand. Somehow I think he knew about Dylan.

Pap and Mama decided they would bury Dylan on the land on the other side of the spring. Even as I heard them talking, I thought, no! How can this be? They can't be talking about Dylan. Not my baby brother.

I was crying in the hammock under the wagon, alone except for Ethel curled up next to me. Mama found me. She knelt down and put her arms around me. For a long, long time she just held me.

Finally, Mama said, "Teddy, today we must all be very brave. Today, we must do a hard thing."

She and I dressed Dylan in his good clothes, the same clothes he wore when we were in Meridian and had our picture taken. The day he held a balloon and waved at the steam engine.

Pap built a little box. Mama padded the box with cotton and lined it with white satin from her wedding dress. It was beautiful. Dylan looked like an angel.

I said, "I want him to have Veronica."

Mama said, "Are you sure?" I nodded. I didn't want him to be alone.

We buried our baby across the spring. Pap made a wooden sign to place above the grave.

It said:

> *Dylan Luke Bodain*
> *1890-1892*
> *Son of Dalton and Grace Bodain*
> *Brother to Theodosia Bodain*
> *Little Lamb at Rest*

That was the hardest day of my life. But today, three days later, there are already 12 more graves across the spring.

The wagon train has been hit by yellow fever.

Love,
Teddy

Narrative Writing Prompt for the Letter of May 3, 1892
Read and answer the writing prompt below.

Narrative Prompt: You can imagine how Teddy felt at the loss of her brother, Dylan. All of us go through times of loss. It could be the loss of a family member or the loss of a beloved pet. It could be the loss of a best friend who had to move away. It could even be the loss of not getting the position on the team you dreamed about having or the part in the play you desperately wanted. Think about a time you experienced loss. Now write the story of a time you lost something precious to you. Be sure to give plenty of descriptive details. Tell how you felt. Tell how you were able to get over your sadness and move on. Now share your paper with another writer, and help each other.

_____

_____

_____

_____

_____

_____

_____

_____

_____

_____

_____

_____

_____

_____

_____

_____

_____

_____

May 4, 1892

Dear Martha,

Miss Melman came to see me today. She didn't even look like herself. She was wearing one of the calico work dresses Miss Emily made for her, and her hair was down. I was lying in the hammock under the wagon. Ethel was curled up beside me. I knew someone was there because I saw his tail begin to wag.

Miss Melman said, "There you are."

I was glad to see Miss Melman, but seeing her made me have a huge lump in my throat. I didn't want to tell her about Dylan. I didn't want to tell how we had buried him above the spring bank. The thought of talking about it made my head hurt something fierce. But I didn't have to say anything. Miss Melman knelt down on the dirt and wrapped her arms around me. She squeezed me tight. I didn't want to cry, but the more she held me, the more I felt like letting go of my tears.

I can't remember crying that hard. I cried for everything: missing you, having to sell Jester and Jingo, losing my baby brother, and burying him with Veronica. Miss Melman kept her arms around me.

After the longest time, she said, "Tears are good. Don't try to stop them. Years ago, when my sweetheart died, I thought I would never stop crying."

I said, "You had a sweetheart? I thought you were an old—" I stopped, ashamed at what I had almost said. I could feel my face getting warm from blushing.

She laughed. "An old maid?" She handed me her handkerchief. "I know. I'm sure it looks that way. But I had a sweetheart once. I was engaged to be married."

She stopped to open the gold locket she wore around her neck. It held a picture of a man. "His name was Edward. Edward James Hudson."

I said, "What happened?"

Miss Melman said, "He died. Suddenly. Our wedding was just three weeks away."

I wiped my eyes with her handkerchief.

Miss Melman said, "Right now your heart is broken. You've lost your little brother, and that is about the worst thing that could happen to anyone. But you are strong. You will go on. I know you, Teddy Bodain, and you will find a way."

This afternoon, I picked wildflowers. Miss Emily gave me a blue satin ribbon, and I tied it around the flowers. I asked Pap if he would take me and Mama across the spring to put them on Dylan's grave.

We stood looking at the grave. I put the flowers beneath the sign Pap had made. Mama and I both needed our handkerchiefs. Pap put one arm around me and one arm around Mama.

He said, "We've had a hard loss. But we'll get through this. We've got each other. We're still the Bodains." I don't know why, but that made me feel better. We're still the Bodains.

Now, we're back at our wagon, and I'm going to put all of my letters together so Miss Melman can mail them for me. Debbie Goguen made a big pot of stew, and she's invited us and Miss Melman over for supper. I'm so glad Mama and I won't have to cook tonight.

This was another sad day.

Love,
Teddy

Name_____ Date _____

Writing Questions for the Letter of May 4, 1892
Circle the letter of the correct answer.

1. Read the following sentence from Teddy's letter today:
   This was another sad day.
   This sentence is an example of what type of good writing skill?
   A. transitional phrase
   B. persuasive writing
   C. descriptive writing
   D. conclusion

2. Read the following sentence from Teddy's letter today:
   She squeezed me tight.
   The word *squeezed* is an example of what type of good writing skill?
   A. onomatopoeia
   B. strong verb
   C. specific emotion word
   D. transitional word

3. Read the following sentence from Teddy's letter today:
   "An old maid?"
   This sentence is an example of what type of good writing skill?
   A. strong verb
   B. persuasive writing
   C. dialogue
   D. juicy color word

4. Read the following sentence from Teddy's letter today:
   After the longest time, she said, "Tears are good."
   The words *After the longest time* are an example of what type of good writing skill that we
   should include in our writing?
   A. grabber
   B. zinger
   C. specific emotion word
   D. transitional phrase

5. Read the following sentence from Teddy's letter today:
   **Now, we're back at our wagon, and I'm going to put all of my letters together so Miss Melman
   can mail them for me.**
   The words *Now we're back at our wagon* are an example of what type of good writing skill?
   A. grabber
   B. zinger
   C. specific emotion word
   D. transitional phrase

May 5, 1892

Dear Martha,

Yellow fever. I hate those two words. They have brought sickness and death into our lives. Almost every family has lost someone. New people come down with the fever every day. More have died.

For the past two days, I have helped Mama and Mrs. Carter tend to the sick. There is so much work to do—chores everywhere—and so few people to do them. Someone has to cook, so folks can eat. Someone has to tend to the stock and bring them water. The weather has turned warm, so folks have made pallets out under the shade trees, so the sick can catch a fresh breeze that might bring relief to their fevers. Some folks have jaundice with the sickness. I didn't know what that meant, but Miss Melman said it is when your liver isn't working well, and you turn yellow.

The doctor that Pap brought could do little to help us. As a matter of fact, he told Pap he had sick folks in town that he had to get back to because yellow fever has also hit the town. The doctor said he would send the militia to help us. We need help in the worst way.

I don't understand this yellow fever. Where does it come from? How do we get it? Some folks die from it, and some folks don't. Why did my baby brother have to die? What will happen to our animals if we all get it? What will happen to Ethelbert?

Mama and Mrs. Carter and some other women have to bathe those with yellow fever and change their clothing. Mrs. Lark has a wash pot boiling with rags and clean linens for the sick.

Today, I had to do something to be useful to keep me from being so sad. I racked my brain about how I could help, then I had an idea. I borrowed Mrs. Pitts' big pot and filled it half full with clear water. I cut up potatoes, onions, carrots, and some of our jerky. I added salt and pepper, several handfuls of barley, and a bay leaf. The pot was heavy! Travis Lark helped me lift it up and hang it on the tripod over the fire.

While we were working, we didn't talk much, other than about the soup we were making.

But when the soup came to a boil, Travis said, "I'm sorry about your baby brother."

I said, "Me, too."

I let the soup boil all afternoon. While it boiled, I made several skillets of cornbread and cut them into wedges. Travis helped me gather all the bowls and spoons we could find. As folks came by, we gave them a bowl of soup or delivered some to their wagon or to the pallets under the shade trees.

Folk said, "This is all I've had to eat today," or "This soup will do my wife good." I'm glad I can help. I can't just sit around while people are sick or dying.

Pap came to eat supper with us around the campfire. He said, "Teddy, this might be the best soup I ever put to my lips." That made me happy, but I am tired all the way down to my bones.

Mama isn't feeling well. She hasn't eaten all day. I tried to give her soup, but she shook her head. She has cried over Dylan until she has no tears left. Tonight by the fire, she was shivering.

We are sleeping outside under the stars again. Mama and Pap are lying on a pallet. Ethel and I are in the hammock under the wagon.

I heard Pap say, "We'll get through this. I love you more than the stars are bright."

Mama said, "I love you more than the moon is round."

Pap said, "I love you more than the ocean is deep."

But Mama was asleep and didn't answer.

Love,
Teddy

Class Discussion Questions for the Letters of March 7 - May 5, 1892
Today, instead of doing a writing assignment or a lesson, it's time for something fun:
a good ol' class discussion. Break up into small groups and discuss the following questions.

1. For you, what would be some of the biggest challenges of traveling with a wagon train in 1892?

2. How do chores today compare with chores in Teddy's day?

3. Who is your favorite character so far in the story? Who is your least favorite? Support your choices with examples and mini-stories from the book.

4. Medical care was very different in Teddy's day. What are some of the benefits we have today that Teddy did not have?

5. Today, owning a horse sounds like a neat way to have fun. In Teddy's day, however, people owned horses as a method of transportation. What would be involved in taking care of a horse, so it would stay in good health and be able to take you where you wanted to go?

6. Travis and Teddy are friends and like to do some of the same things. How are their personalities alike? How are their personalities different?

7. What is Teddy's relationship like with Mama? List some examples from the book that support your ideas.

May 8, 1892

Dear Martha,

How can our happy life have turned into a nightmare of yellow fever? Weren't we swimming in the spring just a few days ago? Weren't we singing our hearts out at a whoop-de-doo?

Mama has yellow fever. We were up with her all night. She's burning up with fever and can't keep anything down. I noticed that her face has a yellowish cast.

The militia arrived this morning. They instantly took control. The military doctor told Captain Walsh that there is an epidemic of yellow fever that has hit several towns and many travelers. The towns are under quarantine, and the hospitals are full. The militia has just set up several more quarantine stations within a few miles of here. The doctor gave instructions to his men and told Captain Walsh he would begin seeing patients and recommending evacuations.

The military men began working immediately, like a colony of ants, digging latrines, boiling huge vats of water, and giving out blankets. Some of their cooks set up a kitchen and began preparing food for us.

All day I bathed Mama's forehead with cool rags. Pap fanned her with a palmetto frond and held her hand because the weather was hot and sticky. It is a horrible time to be sick with a fever.

Mama's fever got so high she was talking out of her head. She said, "It's so nice to see you. I've made a fresh fruitcake. Let me slice it and fix you a glass of lemonade."

I thought she was trying to tell me that she wanted some lemonade. I squeezed one of her lemons and made two cups with plenty of sugar. Pap sipped his, but Mama turned her head when I held it to her mouth. I was worried again. Mama needed fluids, but she would hardly drink.

I pictured Mama going to art school. I pictured her making beautiful quilts. Why hadn't I noticed her quilts were beautiful before? I pictured her learning to play the piano, giggling with Miss Melman in the back of the piano wagon.

I said, "Mama, you've got to get well. I haven't heard you play 'Narcissus' yet."

Mama said, "Why, Teddy, Ethelbert Nevin is coming to call this very afternoon. I'll play 'Narcissus' for him, and you can hear me then."

The military doctor came to see Mama. His aide had a clipboard in his hands and was making notes for the doctor. They both wore cloth masks over their noses and mouths. The doctor was kind. He knelt beside Mama and felt her pulse. He lifted her eyelid and said, "Jaundice."

The aide said, "Transfer?"

The doctor nodded. "Right away."

I said, "Where are you taking her?"

The doctor said, "Where we can help keep her hydrated. You can see her in a day or so."

The doctor's aide called out, "Quarantine one, two, or the Plum's farm quarantine, wherever they have room."

I held Mama's hand before the wagon left.

Mama opened her eyes and said, "Teddy, you'll be sure to feed the cardinals for me, won't you?"

I said, "Yes, Mama."

She said, "Good. I saw a bright red one just over in that tree. He sang so sweetly. If you look, I bet you'll see his mate. She's never far behind."

The soldiers lifted her gently into the back of the wagon. I covered her with a blanket.

I whispered, "Oh, Mama, please come back to me."

Love,
Teddy

Reading Multiple Choice Questions for the Letter of May 8, 1892
Circle the letter of the correct answer.

1. Teddy said there was an epidemic of yellow fever that had hit several towns.
    Using clues from the reading, what do you think an *epidemic* is?
    A. a certain kind of yellow fever
    B. another disease that makes the yellow fever worse
    C. a cure for yellow fever
    D. when a lot of people are infected with a disease in a short period of time

2. Why was Mama **"talking out of her head"** and telling Teddy things that didn't make sense?
    A. she took some medicine that made her that way
    B. because Mama's fever was so high
    C. she was exhausted from not getting enough sleep
    D. she was chilled from the night air

3. Who did Mama tell Teddy was coming to call that afternoon to hear her play "Narcissus"?
    A. Captain Walsh
    B. Miss Melman
    C. Ethelbert Nevin
    D. Mrs. Carter

4. The doctors who arrived in the town said they were taking Mama to quarantine.
    From clues in the reading, what is *quarantine*?
    A. a place where the sick are taken to separate them from healthy people
    B. a town that was near the Bodain's camp
    C. a city in Florida
    D. a hospital that specializes in yellow fever

5. What did Mama ask Teddy to be sure to do for her while she was away?
    A. make dinner every night for Pap
    B. keep up with her studies at school
    C. feed the cardinals
    D. milk Girlie morning and evening

6. Who lifted Mama into the wagon to take her away?
    A. the doctor and his aide
    B. Pap
    C. Mr. Obadiah Lincoln and his son
    D. soldiers who had come to camp

7. What did Teddy do before Mama was taken away?
    A. She cried because she knew Mama would not come back.
    B. She held Mama's hand.
    C. She gave Mama a redbird.
    D. She gave Mama a book to read.

May 16, 1892

Dear Martha,

My world has turned upside down. In the past two weeks, everything I know has changed. I wish you were here. I need to talk to someone who knows what my life was like before all this happened.

Last week, the day after they took Mama away in the wagon, I came down with yellow fever. It started when I went to the Good's wagon for dinner around their campfire. Pap wasn't feeling well, so he stayed home, and I went alone.

Mrs. Good handed me a plate of rice and beans and a cup of tea. All of a sudden, I started feeling dizzy and hot. I remember someone picking me up, someone holding my head while I was sick, someone putting a cold cloth on my forehead. After that, I don't remember anything until three days ago.

I woke up on a pallet, under some trees, near a big house. All around me were people I didn't know. Sick people lying on pallets. Folks helping. Soldiers carrying people on stretchers. A man sitting by his wife's pallet. She moaned all night long. He held her hand and prayed.

At first, I was confused. I didn't see any of the folks from our wagon train. I thought, am I dreaming? Where are Pap and Mama? Why am I here?

A kind woman came to put a cool rag on my face. When she saw my eyes were open, she smiled.

She said, "So you've come back to us. Try to take a little broth." She held a cup to my lips. The broth tasted good. I was terribly thirsty. I was still too weak to talk, but I wanted to ask about my folks.

I said, "Mama."

She seemed to know what I was talking about because she said, "We sent for your people. We had some trouble finding them, but they should be here tomorrow."

That made me feel better. I fell into a deep sleep.

The next day, the same kind woman said, "Your family is here." I was so glad.

She brought a man and a woman to see me. The woman had red hair and green eyes. I wondered who they were. I stared at them. They stared back.

I said, "Where's Mama?"

The kind woman said, "Honey, here are your people. Don't you recognize them?"

I was confused. Why was she talking nonsense?

She tried again. "These are the Tomlinsons, your people."

The Tomlinsons? My people? I didn't understand.

She said, "When your fever was high you talked and talked about Althea and Joseph Tomlinson. This is Althea's daughter, Alice. We sent for them over in Gainesville."

The woman with the green eyes said, "What is your name, dear?"

I said, "Theodosia Bodain."

She said, "How are you related to Althea Tomlinson? I'm her daughter."

I knew the name Althea Tomlinson from somewhere, but where? Althea Tomlinson. Althea Tomlinson. Suddenly, I remembered. I took the bracelet off and held it up. "I found this in the spring."

The woman with the green eyes read the inscription on the inside. She said, "Well, as I live and breathe! This is Mother's bracelet! She lost it years ago, when I was just a little girl. This is most amazing."

She looked at me with pity. "I'm sorry we're not your family, but my mother will be so happy to have this back. She's wondered about it for years."

I don't know why, but I snatched the bracelet from her and put it on my arm. I said, "You can't have it. I found it, and now it's mine. Finders keepers, losers weepers."

Mama would have been so ashamed.

Love,
Teddy

Reading Short Response Questions for the Letter of May 16, 1892
Answer the questions below, and be sure to use complete sentences.

1. Why has Teddy's world turned upside down?

_____

_____

_____

_____

2. Explain how the people with yellow fever were comforted and soothed.

_____

_____

_____

_____

_____

3. Why did the kind woman send for the Tomlinsons?

_____

_____

_____

4. What did Teddy end up doing with Althea Tomlinson's bracelet?

_____

_____

_____

_____

May 17, 1892

Dear Martha,

I'm still in the quarantine hospital, if you can call it that. About 40 of us are on pallets under some shade trees in a big field. I found out the nice woman's name is Mrs. Plum, and she lives here in the big house. She brought a soldier to see me this morning. He had a stack of papers.

He said, "I'm here to help you. I understand you are looking for your father and mother."

I said, "Yes. Dalton and Grace Bodain."

He said, "Any brothers and sisters?"

Mrs. Plum whispered, "She lost a brother to the fever."

The man looked through his sheets of paper. He said, "Bodain, Bodain, Bodain," and ran his finger down the list. "No Bodain." He made some notes and promised to see what he could find out.

Mrs. Plum brought me some soup and said, "Eat, child. You need strength."

I said, "I don't know why I kept the bracelet. I don't usually act like that."

Mrs. Plum said, "You've lost a lot. I'm sure you just want to hold on to the things you have."

As I ate, I wondered what had become of Mama and Pap. Why weren't they here? Why weren't they looking for me? Is Mama still sick? Has Pap come down with the fever?

I looked around for anyone I knew, anyone from our wagon train. I asked a girl in the next row if she knew where the people were from the wagon train.

She said, "They could be anywhere. So many people are sick, they just put you wherever there's room. I heard there was a wagon train, but I have no idea where all the sick folks were taken."

Someone called out, "Did you say wagon train? There's a woman here by me who was with the wagon train. She's mighty sick, though."

It was Miss Essie Mae Pitts. She was on a pallet three rows over. I made my way over to her and knelt down. "Miss Essie Mae, it's Teddy Bodain. Have you seen my parents? Do you know what happened to my parents? I've been sick, and I don't know where they are."

She was pale and weak. She opened her eyes just a little. She said, "Who are you looking for?"

I said, "Dalton and Grace Bodain."

She said, "Their daughter is sick. They took her away in the wagon. The mama was bad off. Mr. Bodain, he got the fever, too. Poor family. Lost their baby, they did."

I tried to be patient. I said, "Where did they take them, Miss Essie? Where did they take Dalton and Grace Bodain?"

Her fever must have been up because she said, "I make a great pound cake. Would you like a slice? Help yourself, honey. Be sure to get the recipe before you leave."

I crept back to my pallet and lay down, trying not to cry from frustration.

Great buckets of butterbeans. Mama and Pap are both sick. Where are they? Do they know where I am? And where is Ethelbert?

My head hurt, and I felt as weak as a kitten.

Love,
Teddy

Name_____ Date_____

Expository Writing Prompt for the Letter of May 17, 1892
Read and answer the following writing prompt.

Expository Prompt: Teddy is in a quarantine hospital all by herself. Think of a time that you may have been all alone. Now write an expository piece, and explain why you were by yourself. Remember to explain how you came to be by yourself, what you did while you were alone, specific emotions that you felt, and so forth. Use as many good writing skills as you can. Be sure to include a beginning, a middle, and an ending. Share your paper with another reader. Share ideas.

_____

_____

_____

_____

_____

_____

_____

_____

_____

_____

_____

_____

_____

_____

_____

_____

_____

May 19, 1892

Dear Martha,

Yesterday, the soldier came back and brought a clerk from the yellow fever quarantine office.

Mrs. Plum introduced him.

The clerk said, "You are looking for a Mr. and Mrs. Bodain from the wagon train?"

I was so scared, I just nodded. I noticed Mrs. Plum came and stood by my side.

The clerk said, "I am sorry to tell you, but a Mr. and Mrs. Bodain from the wagon train expired two days ago." He shuffled through his papers and checked his watch.

Expired?

Mrs. Plum said, "Teddy, I'm sorry, but your parents passed away." I stared at her.

The clerk said, "Passed away means died." He sounded impatient.

I don't know why, but it was like a string of firecrackers went off in me all at once.

I screamed, "I know what 'passed away' means! Do you think I'm dumb just because I'm a kid? You can't keep records worth beans! You don't even know where all the wagon train people are! My baby brother passed away. He was just two years old! You didn't know him! We had to bury him on the spring bank! I know what 'passed away' means!"

The clerk and the soldier backed away.

I was still yelling for Mama and Pap when Mrs. Plum handed me a cup of water.

She said, "Drink this, honey. This will help you feel better."

I said, "My mama and pap are dead?"

She said, "I am so sorry."

I thought about Mama and Pap. I needed them. How could they be dead?

Mrs. Plum must have put sleepy drops in the water because I was soon floating. I was dreaming, but it was as if I was awake at the same time. I dreamed of flying kites with Minnie and Travis and Jasper. I saw Travis cut my line, and I watched The Florida Belle float up into the sky. We laughed and laughed and laughed. I called to Travis, "Minnie and I will pay you back. Just you wait and see!" He laughed like only Travis can laugh. I felt the sun shining on my face.

I saw us jumping off the rope swing right over the deepest part of the spring and dog paddling to the side of the swimming hole to climb out and do it all over again. I felt the splash of the cool water.

I saw the fiddlers and the banjo players playing to beat the band as folks danced and sang at the whoop-de-doo. I saw Miss Melman waltzing with Captain Walsh. I saw the Carters and the Larks. I saw folks from the other wagon train. Who did we meet?... The Bodains... The Bodains... The Bodains.

I woke with a start. It was early morning. Birds were chirping in the trees. I sat up on my pallet.

Something caught my eye. Something red. A redbird. A cardinal! He flitted from the oak tree to a bush near my pallet. He looked at me, cocking his head to one side and then the other. He opened his throat and sang a joyful little jingle. A few seconds later, his soft brown mate joined him on another branch.

She looked at me with bright eyes, as if she was trying to tell me something. I knew it right then. The Bodains the soldier talked about are not Mama and Pap. They are the Bodains we met when our two wagon trains joined up. It has to be.

Mama and Pap are alive. I just know it.

Love,
Teddy

Name_____   Date_____

Reading Extended Response Questions for the Letter of May 19, 1892
Answer the questions below. Be sure to use complete sentences, reasons, and details.

1. Mrs. Plum put sleepy drops in Teddy's water, and she began to dream. Describe her dream.

_____

_____

_____

_____

_____

_____

_____

_____

_____

2. When Teddy woke from her dream, something red caught her eye. Describe what she saw. What did this mean to Teddy?

_____

_____

_____

_____

_____

_____

_____

_____

_____

May 20, 1892

Dear Martha,

All day today, I thought about Mama and Pap. Where are they? Maybe they think I'm dead. Maybe they're sick themselves. Maybe they're with the wagon. Why aren't they looking for me?

When I woke up from a nap late this afternoon, the girl in the next row came over. She said, "They came while you were asleep. I heard them say something about an orphanage."

I said, "I'm not an orphan! My parents are alive!"

She looked puzzled. "Didn't they tell you your parents are dead?"

I said, "Yes, but that's because they don't know about the other Bodains. We met some people not too long ago. They were named Bodain, too, and they were traveling with a wagon train."

She said, "Some other Bodains?"

I said, "And I saw a redbird—a cardinal—and his mate. They came to my pallet and sang for me. That is Mama's favorite bird. I think Mama and Pap are alive."

She made a face. "You saw a redbird, and now you think your mama's alive?

I said, "I know it sounds crazy." I looked at her. "Do you think it sounds crazy?"

She said, "Yes, it sounds crazy." She smiled. "But yes, they might be alive. There's a chance. But if you want to go while the getting's good, if you don't want to end up in an orphanage, you better get out of here soon. They come and take children away when they haven't got any folks."

Great buckets of butterbeans!

She said, "Hold on," and was gone for a few minutes. When she came back, she handed me a little bundle tied with a bandana.

I said, "What's this?"

She said, "I scrounged a few things from here and there. Some of these folks aren't going to make it, and where they're going, they won't need it. This should do you for today."

I said, "Thanks."

She said, "Mrs. Plum and her helpers are getting ready to serve supper. This would be a good time to hit the road and not be seen. Go on. If anyone asks, I'll cover for you."

It felt strange to just walk away from the quarantine area and the lady who had helped me. I had nothing but the clothes on my back and a single bundle wrapped in a bandana. Where would I go? Where would I sleep? How would I find my parents?

I felt helpless and more alone than ever in my life. I trembled from head to toe.

Then, Miss Melman's words came to me: *I know you, Teddy Bodain, and you will find a way.*

You will find a way. You will find a way.

The sun was setting. I walked quickly out from under the trees, across the field to the lane in front of the big house. I walked and walked, following the road. It led to the edge of town, and I began to see more houses. One of them had a hammock in the back yard. The light was fading, so I don't think anyone saw me. Here in the hammock, I opened the bandana. There is an apple, a ham sandwich, and a hard-boiled egg. I am so hungry I could eat a buttered skunk!

I thought about the girl who gave it to me. She helped me, and I don't even know her name.

Love,
Teddy

Grammar Questions for the Letter of May 20, 1892
Circle the letter of the correct answer.

1. Which one of the following sentences has the correct use of apostrophes?
   A. Maybe theyr'e sick themselves.
   B. Maybe the'yre sick themselves.
   C. Maybe theyre' sick themselves.
   D. Maybe they're sick themselves.

2. When Teddy told the girl that she was not an orphan and that her parents were alive, the girl looked puzzled. What does the word *puzzled* mean when used in this way?
   A. surprised
   B. confused
   C. angry
   D. excited

3. Which of the following examples has the correct use of commas?
   A. When, she came back she handed me a little bundle tied with a bandana.
   B. When she came back she handed me a little bundle, tied with a bandana.
   C. When she came back, she handed me a little bundle tied with a bandana.
   D. When she came back she handed me, a little bundle tied with a bandana.

4. Which of the following words is spelled correctly?
   A. hammock
   B. hammuck
   C. hamock
   D. hammack

5. Where do the quotation marks go in the following example?
   A. "I said, What's this?"
   B. I said, "What's this?
   C. I said, "What's this?"
   D. I said, What's this?"

6. The girl who helps Teddy said, **"I scrounged a few things from here and there. Some of these folks aren't going to make it, and where they're going, they won't need it."**
   When used this way, what does the word *scrounged* mean?
   A. looked for
   B. took things from other people
   C. gave away
   D. stopped

7. Teddy says she is so hungry she could **"eat a buttered skunk."** What is this an example of?
   A. using an idiom to make her writing colorful
   B. dialogue
   C. a strong verb
   D. onomatopoeia

May 21, 1892

Dear Martha,

Today, I found out, by listening to other people's conversation, that there is another quarantine station two miles out on the other side of town. Mama and Pap might be there.

As I walked through town, my stomach was growling. I ate all my food last night. I should have saved something for breakfast. I walked past houses, and I smelled coffee and frying bacon. I passed a fruit stand. There were oranges! Sweet, juicy oranges. I passed a bakery, and the smell almost knocked me out of my shoes. The window was filled with rolls and loaves of bread and buns.

I didn't have any money, but I was so hungry, I stopped in. I asked the baker, "Sir, do you have any deliveries I could make? You wouldn't have to pay me in money. All I need is a slice of bread."

He said, "Sorry, we have a delivery boy." My shoulders sagged.

I said, "Thank you, anyway. I'm going to the other side of town, so I thought I'd just ask."

As I was leaving, he called, "Well, it might make a good impression on Mrs. Jenkins if I got her bread to her a little early. The delivery boy was late yesterday."

He handed me two loaves wrapped in white paper and tied with a string. He said, "And this is for you." He folded down the top of a paper sack and handed it to me.

I said, "Thank you," and started to leave.

He said, "Mrs. Jenkins is the last house on this road before you leave town. Big white house with green shutters." He looked at me over his glasses. "I hope I'm making a good decision to trust you. You won't eat Mrs. Jenkins' bread, will you?"

I said, "No, sir. I'm trustworthy."

When I got to Mrs. Jenkins' house, she tipped me for delivering the bread. I didn't want to take it, but she said, "Nonsense. I tip Jack Taylor, and he's always late." She gave me two cents! I tied them in my bandana. Two cents will buy some food. Two cents. All I have to my name.

I had to walk slow because I am weak from having yellow fever. But all the walking I've done these past weeks on the trip has strengthened my legs. I got to the quarantine camp and went to see the clerk.

I said, "I am looking for my parents, Dalton Luke Bodain and Grace Alice Bodain."

He checked his list, just like the other clerk had done, and said, "No, sorry. No Bodains. We have a Bordeaux and two Bordens but no Bodains."

I asked him if I could look for folks from our wagon train to see if they had any news about Mama and Pap. I told him I had already had the fever and was over it, otherwise he wouldn't have let me in.

He said, "You may look for 15 minutes. These are fever victims, and they need their rest."

I looked up and down the rows. I spotted Mr. Lowe, Jasper's father. He was very weak, very sick.

"I think they took your pap over to quarantine one," he said. "I don't know about your mama."

I said, "Where is everyone else from our train? The captain? Miss Melman?"

He said, "Don't know. Been sick for a week."

I said, "Where is our wagon train?"

He said, "Three miles east of here, but if there's no one living in your wagon, it's likely to have been impounded. I heard talk of it today. Yep, you better head east if you want the train."

The sun rises in the east and sets in the west, Mama said. I started walking east.

As I walked, I opened the bag the baker had given me, hungry for the slice of bread. But instead of the bread slice, there were three jelly doughnuts. I've never had a jelly doughnut before, but if I live long enough, I'm going to eat 10,000 more.

When I got to our camp, most of the wagons were gone! What can happen next?

Love,
Teddy

Writing Questions for the Letter of May 21, 1892
Circle the letter of the correct answer.

1. Read the following sentence from Teddy's letter today:
   As I walked through town, my stomach was growling.
   The words *As I walked through town* are an example of what type of good writing skill?
   A. persuasive writing
   B. descriptive writing
   C. transitional phrase
   D. grabber

2. Read the following sentence from Teddy's letter today:
   I passed a bakery, and the smell almost knocked me out of my shoes.
   The phrase *and the smell almost knocked me out of my shoes* is an example of what type of good writing skill?
   A. descriptive writing
   B. persuasive writing
   C. onomatopoeia
   D. transitional phrase

3. Read the following sentence from Teddy's letter today:
   I've never had a jelly doughnut before, but if I live long enough, I'm going to eat 10,000 more.
   The words *but if I live long enough* are an example of what type of good writing skill?
   A. strong verb
   B. persuasive writing
   C. transitional phrase
   D. simile

4. Read the following sentence from Teddy's letter today:
   He handed me two loaves wrapped in white paper and tied with a string.
   This sentence is an example of what type of good writing skill?
   A. beginning, middle, and ending
   B. conclusion
   C. simile
   D. writing with details that you can picture

5. Read the following sentence from Teddy's letter today:
   He handed me two loaves wrapped in white paper and tied with a string.
   The words *handed, wrapped,* and *tied* are examples of what type of good writing skill?
   A. persuasive writing
   B. strong verbs
   C. similes
   D. dialogue

May 22, 1892

Dear Martha,

I slept under the stars last night. There were still soldiers about, but no one noticed me.

I spent the morning looking around and realized what a mess I'm in. I'm tired, I'm hungry, and I have no place to go. My parents aren't here. Most of the wagons are gone, and the few that aren't have no people in them. Everyone has just disappeared!

There is no sign of Girlie or Jeb and January or Ethelbert. When I thought about Ethelbert, my heart sank. He found me, and now I've lost him. Where in the world is he? Does he have any food or water?

I asked one of the soldiers, "Where is everyone?"

He said, "The wagon train headed on. The folks who were well felt they needed to get out of harm's way with this epidemic. You can't blame them."

I said, "But where is our wagon? My mama and pap had yellow fever and—"

He said, "So they were fever victims, eh? Then, your wagon is most likely impounded down at the quarantine stockade. We moved wagons all day yesterday. We have a few more to move today. They're empty. Folks are either dead or too sick to protect their own stuff. The U.S. government has to do it for them." He snapped the suspenders on his uniform.

I said, "Where did you move our wagon? It isn't here."

He said, "It must be at the quarantine stockade about four miles that way." He pointed. "But they're not going to let you go in there. The court has to decide who those things go to. Death certificates have to be verified. Next of kin have to be notified and so forth."

I said, "My parents are not dead."

He said, "Then, they'll be able to claim their things. But they aren't about to let a young girl near those wagons. They're government property until a proper claim has been filed. I'm sorry, but that's just the way it is. It's out of my hands."

I felt like I had been punched in the stomach.

He must have seen how upset I was because he said, "I'll tell you what I can do. I can feed you before I send you on your way." That was the best news I'd had all morning.

The cook at the chow wagon was not too happy about it, but the soldier stayed with me to make sure I got plenty. I went through the chow line and piled sliced beef, green beans, coleslaw, corn on the cob, a big chicken leg, and two rolls on a plate. I tore into that food like my life depended on it. The soldier said, "Are you sure you're not an orphan?"

I said, "I'm sure."

He laughed and said, "Then, you eat like a boy." I put the two rolls and the chicken leg in my pockets, thanked him, and headed on my way.

He called, "I'm sorry about your wagon. If it's impounded, there's nothing I can do about it."

I walked the four miles to the quarantine stockade. It's surrounded by soldiers guarding people's belongings. There are many wagons in the stockade. Some are covered wagons, like ours, and others are just plain wagons. They are lined up in several rows. Unfortunately, most covered wagons look a lot alike. But if I can sneak in there, I could find our wagon because of Mama's artwork. If the soldiers spot me, they might arrest me since I'm not supposed to be there, so I'm staying out of sight.

I found a little clump of bushes near an oak tree where I can rest and not be seen. Late this afternoon, I ate the chicken leg and the two rolls. When it's dark, I'm going to find our wagon and get what I can.

Love,
Teddy

Persuasive Prompt for the Letter of May 22, 1892
Read and answer the following prompt.

Persuasive Prompt: Teddy had to be on her own for a long time. Pretend you lived back in Teddy's day, and you have to be on your own for weeks without your parents. What skills would you need? Persuade us that you have the skills it would take for you to live on your own in the woods. For instance, one skill might be the ability to build and start a campfire. Explain each skill, describe it in detail, and give us reasons that would convince us that skill would be helpful. Write so we can picture what you are writing about in "mind movies."

_____

_____

_____

_____

_____

_____

_____

_____

_____

_____

_____

_____

_____

_____

_____

_____

_____

_____

_____

May 23, 1892

Dear Martha,

Tonight was one of the scariest nights of my life.

The soldiers in the stockade built campfires and ate supper. I watched them through the bushes. There were eight or ten of them, and after they ate, they started a card game. While they were busy, I snuck around to the side. One soldier walked back and forth, guarding the wagons. When he walked the other way, I slipped in beside the rows of wagons.

I walked as quietly as I could, trying to find our wagon. Each time the guard turned and walked back, I hid. I made my way to wagon after wagon, looking for Mama's artwork.

At last I saw it: the last wagon in the last row. The soldiers were having an argument.

One soldier said, "Pistachios ARE nuts, I'm telling you."

Another soldier said, "And I'm telling you there's no such thing. I think YOU'RE nuts!"

While they were arguing, I ran forward and hid by our wagon. There was Mama's artwork. Mama. The thought of her made my heart ache. I climbed onto the frame and slipped inside. It was dark, dark.

I felt my way to the candle stubs I used to keep for writing. I felt a book of matches. I found my copy of Little Women and stood it on end. I lit the candle behind the book so the flame was barely visible.

The first thing I saw, when my eyes adjusted, was a fancy envelope with my name on it. It was a note from Miss Melman! My hands were shaking as I tore it open.

"Dear Theodosia, I'm hoping you are alive. Your father was taken away sick. I'm sorry, I don't know where. The soldiers were going to impound Girlie and Gabriel, so I took them with me. You can have them back when you get settled. Captain Walsh took Jeb and January for safekeeping for your father. I'm sorry, but I couldn't find Ethelbert anywhere. I'm going on with the wagon train to St. Augustine, to The Sheridan School for Girls. Please come see me. Remember, no matter what you face, you are Teddy Bodain, and you will find a way. Love, Miss Melman"

I don't know how long I sat there, but my cheeks were wet with tears. I heard the soldiers talking and realized I had to hurry. I gathered a few things to take with me: a change of clothes, my colored pencils, my sketchbook, my slingshot, and some jerky. Oh, and some fishing line and hooks. I bundled my belongings in the bandana.

What I really needed was under the wagon in the secret compartment. I was headed for the door when I stepped on one of Dylan's toys. It made a loud noise. I froze, hoping the soldiers weren't paying attention. I heard someone coming. It was the guard. I blew the candle out and crouched down behind the sugar barrel. My heart thundered in my chest.

The guard stopped outside our wagon. He called, "Anyone there?" He climbed up on the frame. I held my breath. He slipped inside, feeling around in the darkness. I thought he would discover me any second, but as he walked through the wagon, he put his hand on the envelope with the fake rattlesnake fangs. I didn't even know it was there. The paperclip fangs went off with a loud, "Z-z-z-z-z-z-z-z!!!" It scared him and me, both. He backed out fast and jumped to the ground.

When he hit the ground, one of the soldiers called, "Find something?"

The guard said, "There's a rattlesnake in this last wagon."

The soldier called, "Shoot him in the morning when you can see."

I put my hand over my mouth and laughed till I almost fell over.

You've got to love Miss Melman!

Love,
Teddy

Reading Multiple Choice Questions for the Letter of May 23, 1892
Circle the letter of the correct answer.

1. How did Teddy know which wagon was hers as she searched among all the impounded wagons?
   A. because of the color of the canvas
   B. because one of the wheels had a broken spoke
   C. because the rear of the wagon had the word Bodain written on it
   D. because of Mama's artwork

2. Who was the letter from that Teddy found in the wagon?
   A. Mama and Pap
   B. Miss Cassie Melman
   C. Captain Walsh
   D. her best friend, Travis

3. What did Teddy step on that made a loud noise and sent the guard running to check her wagon?
   A. the envelope with the fake rattlesnake fangs
   B. a mouse
   C. one of Baby Dylan's toys
   D. Pap's harmonica

4. What did the soldier think was in the wagon when he heard the loud, **"Z-z-z-z-z-z"**?
   A. a rattlesnake
   B. a leak in the roof
   C. someone hiding
   D. a scarlet king snake

5. What did Miss Melman say she did with Girlie and Gabriel?
   A. sent them to the quarantine camp with Pap
   B. left them with a family back at the creek where Baby Dylan was buried
   C. took them with her to St. Augustine
   D. Miss Melman didn't say what happened to them

6. Where did Miss Melman say she was going to teach school?
   A. back to Mississippi
   B. Sarasota, FL
   C. Orlando, FL
   D. St. Augustine, FL

7. What book did Teddy stand on end to hide the light?
   A. *Tom Sawyer*
   B. *Little Women*
   C. *Oonawassee Summer*
   D. *Huckleberry Finn*

May 24, 1892

Dear Martha,

I stayed inside the wagon when the guard left. I had to wait until things calmed down. I found as much food as I could in the dark and stuffed myself. I brushed my hair with Mama's hairbrush and braided my hair into braids again. I rested on the pallet. I filled my pockets with lemon drops. I found Mama's neck pouch where she kept her money when she used to sell eggs back in Salter's Grove.

When I thought it was safe, I lit the candle again. I had to see in order to write to Mama and Pap. I wrote quickly.

> "Dear Mama and Pap,
>
> I know you are alive even though they say you are dead. I took the land deed because they might sell this wagon before you get here, and no one knows about our secret compartment but us. I took some of the money. I left the rest for you because you will need it to travel. Miss Melman has Girlie and Gabriel. Captain Walsh has Jeb and January. If I don't find you in the next few days, I'll go to our kinfolk, Daniel Bodain.
>
> Love, Teddy
>
> P.S. Mama, I saw a red cardinal."

After I wrote the letter and folded it carefully, I put it in an envelope and left it for them just like Miss Melman had left the one for me. I pictured Mama and Pap finding the letter and then coming to find me. I pictured all of us laughing and hugging and feeling safe again.

I climbed quietly down and found the secret compartment under the wagon. I eased it open and felt inside for the folded land deed. I felt the cool metal of my grandfather's watch. I slipped the deed, the watch, and twenty dollars into the neck pouch and closed the secret compartment.

Just then, I heard a soft whimper. It was coming from right there beneath the wagon. I listened again. It was coming from inside the hammock. I reached my hand in and felt something furry.

Ethelbert!

I was so surprised, I almost called out his name. My sweet Ethel was guarding our wagon, waiting for me to come home. He found me for the second time. His whimpers turned from pitiful to joyful.

Before I could stop him, he barked, a loud happy bark.

One of the guards called, "What's that?"

Another soldier said, "It's probably that dog that's been hanging around begging. When you shoot that rattlesnake, please put that dog out of his misery, too."

We had to get away! We were both in danger! I hung the neck pouch around my neck, took up my bundle, and slipped away into the woods. Ethel followed.

When we had walked far, far away, I sat down and wrapped my arms around his neck.

I said, "Ethelbert! Good dog! You loyal, brave dog!" He whined and whined, trying to tell me what a rough time he'd had of it.

I shared my jerky with him. He gobbled it greedily.

I said, "You're hungry." I thought of how confusing and terrifying the past two weeks must have been for him. I wonder if anyone has fed him. I wonder if he thought he had been abandoned. I wonder if anyone has been cruel or mean to him.

I buried my face in the fur of his neck. "I won't leave you again," I said.

Ethelbert will help me find Mama and Pap. I know it.

Love,
Teddy

Name_____ Date_____

Narrative Writing Prompt for the Letter of May 24, 1892
Read and answer the prompt below.

Narrative Prompt: Teddy found a huge surprise when she reached her hand into the hammock and found her dog, Ethelbert. Imagine how she felt after finding her beloved dog. Pretend you come home from school one day, and on the front step you find a brown wicker basket covered with a blue fuzzy blanket. You slowly reach your hand inside and find the best surprise ever! Think about what this surprise could be. Now write a story, and tell all about this surprise, how it makes you feel, and how this surprise could change your life. Use descriptive words as you write, so your reader can picture each detail in a "mind movie."

_____

_____

_____

_____

_____

_____

_____

_____

_____

_____

_____

_____

_____

_____

_____

_____

_____

_____

_____

_____

May 27, 1892

Dear Martha,

For the past three days, I've looked for Mama and Pap everywhere. I've walked until I have blisters on my feet. I've been to all three quarantine stations. No one remembers Grace or Dalton Bodain. Folks are so busy taking care of the sick, or burying the dead, that no one pays much attention to paperwork. I went to the hospital in town. They said they didn't allow patients from any of the wagon trains. I checked with the sheriff, the preacher, and the undertaker. I checked at the telegraph office and at the school. Most of the time, when I ask for help, people end up sending me somewhere else.

This afternoon, Ethel and I bought our dinner. I'm trying to make my money last. I bought an orange for two cents, a roasted turkey leg for a dime, and a big baked potato for a nickel. Oh, I splurged and bought a giant dill pickle for a nickel, too. And some milk! I forgot that. I bought a little bottle of milk for a nickel.

Anyway, I had seen a grassy field out behind the feedstore, and we went there to eat our supper. There's a spring nearby, and Ethel likes to drink from it. When I saw it earlier, the field was empty, except for a few geese. But this afternoon, there was a GIANT piece of colored cloth spread out across the field.

A woman was fussing with the cloth, tugging and pulling it. She had gray, curly hair and wore trousers, like a man, and a vest. She was spreading the cloth this way and that way, talking to herself. Ethel and I watched her while we ate. She was a curious sight.

After we ate (I shared everything with Ethel except the orange and the pickle), I asked the woman what she was doing with the brightly colored cloth.

She said, "Have you heard of a hot-air balloon before?"

I said, "Well, I saw one in a picture book once, but it was blown up."

She made a face and said, "Well, this one would be blown up, except it has a huge rip in it, and it's going to take me seven forevers to sew it up by myself. That means I'm off schedule and can't leave in the morning. There's an epidemic here, and I'd like to do more traveling before I catch my death of the fever."

I said, "Which way are you headed?"

She said, "Here and there."

I said, "Anywhere near Micanopy?"

"That depends on which way the wind is blowing."

I had an idea. I said, "I'll help you sew up your rip if you let me and my dog go with you."

She looked at Ethel and frowned. She shook her head.

"I don't take dogs."

I said, "Too bad. I'm handy with a needle."

She looked me over. She said, "Where are your parents?"

I said, "I don't know. They had the fever, and I've been looking

for them ever since. I've looked just about everywhere. We have some kinfolk near Micanopy, so I guess I'll go there."

She said, "Does your dog stink?"

I said, "That depends on which way the wind is blowing." That made her laugh.

We sewed up the rip all afternoon. We used special needles and stitched each seam a certain way. I tried to sew carefully because Dr. Winklepleck—that's her name—said our lives depended on it. She also said Ethel and I could sleep in the back of the feed store.

"My brother, Carl, owns this feed store. There's some hay in the back and some blankets that might be comfy. Get some sleep. I'll be back to fill the envelope at six o'clock in the morning, and we'll take off."

Great buckets of butterbeans! What have I gotten myself into?

Love,
Teddy

Reading Short Response Questions for the Letter of May 27, 1892
Answer the questions below, and be sure to use complete sentences.

1. Teddy has been looking for her parents for three days. Where did she go to search for them?

_____

_____

_____

_____

2. Teddy said she **"splurged"** on something? What did she mean by that?

_____

_____

_____

_____

3. Teddy watched a woman fussing with a giant cloth while she and Ethel ate dinner. Why did she say the woman was a **"curious sight"**?

_____

_____

_____

_____

4. When Teddy said, **"That depends on which way the wind is blowing,"** to what was she referring?

_____

_____

_____

_____

_____

May 28, 1892

Dear Martha,

Today was a day I will never forget.

I woke up to a strange whooshing sound. Dr. Winklepleck and some of her friends were out in the field filling the balloon with hot air. They had tied a large, rectangular basket underneath. The basket was on its side, but as the balloon filled with hot air, it stood up. The basket was tethered to the ground, so it couldn't float away. Ethel and I watched, amazed.

Just as the sun was coming up, Dr. Winklepleck called, "Teddy, time to go." Her friends helped me into the basket, which she called a "gondola," and lifted Ethel over the side. Someone slipped a collar around Ethel's neck and tied it to the basket. Dr. Winklepleck got in with a camera and a picnic basket. She called for someone to release the tethers. We floated up!

At first, I was so scared my legs felt like wet noodles. I sunk down to the bottom of the gondola. Ethel whimpered. Dr. Winklepleck said, "You'll get your legs in a minute, Teddy. We're going to ascend slowly, so you can look around. Just think of it. You're getting to see sights most people can only dream of."

I pulled myself up and peeked over the side of the gondola. What I saw took my breath away! The roofs of houses were below us. I could almost touch the spire of the church. The tops of the trees were practically close enough to reach as we floated over them. The town was stirring below, and people shouted when they saw us.

They said, "Look! It's a balloon!" and "Come, quick!" and "Hurry!"

We were close enough to see their faces. I searched everywhere for Mama and Pap. I called, "I'm looking for Dalton and Grace Bodain. If you see them, tell them their daughter has gone to their kinfolk in Micanopy!"

The balloon rose higher as Dr. Winklepleck operated the burner. The people grew smaller and smaller. Soon, I could see all around. I saw orange groves and tomato fields. I saw the quarantine stations. I saw the stockade where our wagon was and saw our wagon there in the last row. We rose higher and began to slowly blow across the sky. I couldn't imagine how high we were. My feet have never been off the ground like that before! I wished with all my heart that you could have been with me, Martha.

The balloon carried us a long way. I studied the sky.

I said, "I believe we are traveling southeast."

Dr. Winklepleck said, "You're good with directions."

She explained that she is a cartographer, which means she is a mapmaker. Can you imagine a woman doing something so—curious? She is also a photographer. While we were in the air, she took some photographs with her camera.

She said, "I've been all over the world, but nothing gives me more satisfaction than ballooning right here in America. From up here, you can see the intense beauty of the landscape. We have a chance to see nature at its finest."

I told her the story of leaving Mississippi, traveling with the wagon train, Dylan dying of the fever, and getting separated from Mama and Pap. She really listened, which is unusual. Lately most adults have brushed me off or sent me somewhere else.

This afternoon, Dr. Winklepleck said, "We'd better descend. We're near Gainesville, and I see a nice pasture to land in." As we floated lower, folks came out of their houses and barns and pointed up at us. When we landed, a farmer and his wife agreed to let us stay at their house for the night. The farmer's wife, Mrs. Green, is making fried chicken for supper tonight.

Jumping jubilation!

Love,
Teddy

Expository Writing Prompt for the Letter of May 28, 1892
Read and answer the following writing prompt.

Expository Prompt: Teddy has just enjoyed a unique experience, floating in a hot-air balloon. Think of something unusual that you have not done before, but you would like to do. Now write an expository piece, and explain what unusual thing you would like to do. What are some things about it that would be fun and adventurous? How would you prepare to do it? Be sure to include specific details, clear-cut reasons, and good descriptions.

_____

_____

_____

_____

_____

_____

_____

_____

_____

_____

_____

_____

_____

_____

_____

_____

_____

_____

_____

_____

_____

May 29, 1892

Dear Martha,

The Greens are great folks. They live on a farm outside of Gainesville. They're the family who invited us to stay with them last night. They saw our balloon as we landed in their field and came running to help us. Folks came over from other farms, too, to watch us land. They had never seen a balloon with a basket under it float down from the sky. Neither had I!

The Greens have four daughters: Sylvia, Betty, Carlene, and Molly. Carlene, who has curly, black hair, is my age, and I slept in her room. She's so pretty! She shares a room with Molly, so all three of us slept in their big bed. They wanted me to tell them all about my journey, but I was too tired.

Dr. Winklepleck slept in the guest room. The bedspread and the curtains are pink, and the wallpaper has fancy roses on it. On the dresser is a matching pitcher and face bowl.

This morning, Mrs. Green, Sylvia, and Betty made a big breakfast. It was the first time I've sat down to a table since we left Salter's Grove. It made me homesick for Mama. She would have loved Mrs. Green and the beautiful plates on the table. We had hotcakes, sausage, strawberries, hash brown potatoes, and orange juice. I ate like there was no tomorrow.

Mr. Green said, "Ladies, I'd love to stay, but I've got to get out to the fields. Make yourselves at home. Kate will take good care of you."

Mrs. Green said, "Teddy, tell us all about your journey. Dr. Winklepleck tells us you've been through a great ordeal."

I was full of good food, and a whole audience wanted to hear my story. I took my time. So much has happened, I had to think of which details to tell. I told everything I could think of. When I got to the part about Dylan, we all cried. I didn't mean for it to happen. It just did.

Carlene said, "And you left Veronica in his arms?"

Betty said, "You poor dear."

Sylvia said, "And you believe your parents are alive?"

Molly said, "Well, I'm glad the big balloon came out of the sky and brought you to us."

Mrs. Green begged me to stay with them for a few weeks to get my strength back.

She said, "Next week, we'll be traveling to Sarasota to visit the shore. You could go with us."

The girls got excited. Carlene practically jumped up and down. I thought about Mrs. Green's offer. It was tempting to say yes. Who wouldn't want to stay in their beautiful home and eat Mrs. Green's tasty cooking? And the shore! I haven't seen the ocean yet. The thought of it was almost overwhelming. It is so nice to have a family that welcomes me. I've been so lonely and scared without Mama and Pap. For days I've slept on hammocks and hay and under trees. Sometimes, I've had food and sometimes I haven't.

Dr. Winklepleck said, "It might be a good idea, Teddy. The Greens seem like such nice people."

I wanted to say yes, but I couldn't. I said, "I would love to stay with you, but I must find our kinfolk in Micanopy. That's the only way I know for Mama and Pap to find me. They must be worried sick."

This afternoon, Carlene and I played outside with Ethelbert and Carlene's dog, Freddy. She and I bathed the dogs and scrubbed them with a brush and a bar of soap. Mrs. Green gave me an old brush, and I brushed Ethel in the sunshine until his fur was as soft as silk. He lay on his back and fell asleep.

Tonight, Mrs. Green came in Carlene's room to sit with me. She said, "We can take you to Micanopy the day after tomorrow in the buggy. Would that be all right? We want to make sure you get there safely." Carlene and I have another day together! Jubilation. It's so good to have a friend again, but she'll never take your place, Martha. You're still my best friend.

Love,
Teddy

Reading Extended Response Questions for the Letter of May 29, 1892

Answer the questions below. Be sure to use complete sentences, reasons, and details.

1. Teddy thought that the Greens were great folks. Describe the Greens through the eyes of Teddy.

_____

_____

_____

_____

_____

_____

_____

_____

_____

_____

2. Mrs. Green invited Teddy to stay with the family. How did Teddy feel about this offer? What did Teddy decide to do?

_____

_____

_____

_____

_____

_____

_____

_____

_____

_____

May 30, 1892

Dear Martha,

Today, Carlene and I went out to the fields with her father. Mr. Green is interested in the fact that Pap is going to farm. He asked, "Where is his land?" and "What does he plan to grow?"

I said, "His land is down south, somewhere below Lake Okeechobee. I don't know what he plans to grow, but in Mississippi, we grew cotton and corn."

Mr. Green's face lit up. He said, "I'm a cotton farmer, too. But I tell you what. You tell your daddy he might be interested in two things he could do well with in Florida: cattle and tomatoes. The farmers in north Florida who are into cattle are making heaps of money. Folks are wanting to move the citrus industry down south, on account of the cold snaps freezing their trees. Your pap might consider citrus, but it takes three to five years before you get a cash crop when you start out."

I listened carefully to what Mr. Green was saying, so I could tell Pap later.

Mr. Green said, "Let me tell you a thing or two about tomatoes, Teddy. They are going to be a popular crop. Good for you. Hearty. The railroad is coming in this year. Mark my words: tomatoes and cattle. That's the ticket."

Just before noon, we said goodbye to Dr. Winklepleck. We helped her spread her balloon envelope out on the grassy field and smooth out the wrinkles. We fastened the gondola to the envelope and turned it on its side. Then, we carefully tethered the gondola to the ground.

As Dr. Winklepleck was filling the envelope with hot air from the burner, we gathered around.

Mrs. Green said, "Amanda, you're welcome to stay."

Dr. Winklepleck said, "Thank you for your impeccable hospitality. I don't know when I've ever tasted better fried chicken in my life. However, I have a friend who is also a cartographer. She went on a map-making expedition with me to the Florida Keys, two years ago. She's been asking me to visit in June. That's two days from now. The wind is blowing to the south. I'm hoping the balloon will blow me close enough, so I can see her for a few days. If not, I'll have another unexpected adventure."

I said goodbye to Dr. Winklepleck. She said, "Teddy, I'm happy our paths crossed. Thank you for helping me sew up my ruined envelope."

I said, "Thank you for taking me with you in the balloon."

Before she left, Dr. Winklepleck took our picture. Then she hugged me and Ethelbert. "He doesn't stink," she said. "Even when the wind isn't blowing." A few minutes later, we watched her float gently up, high over the pasture, and then away. We waved until she was out of sight. I tried to memorize that picture in my mind, so I can sketch her in my sketchbook.

Speaking of sketchbooks, I showed Carlene all my drawings. I was a little nervous about it at first, but she liked my pictures. I showed her the gold bracelet. She made me tell her all about Althea Tomlinson. I was ashamed to tell her that I met her daughter and refused to give back the bracelet, so I skipped over that part.

Mrs. Green gave me some new clothes. They're not really new, but they're new to me. She gave me bloomers, a pretty pink gingham dress, and a white pinafore to go over the top of it. She gave me stockings and a comfortable pair of shoes. Tonight, I took a bath and scrubbed myself from head to toe. Betty brushed my hair until my scalp tingled and rebraided my hair. I brushed my teeth and laid out my clothes and my gold bracelet. I don't want to leave, but I feel ready.

Carlene, Molly, and I are all in the big bed. They watched me sketch the balloon sailing into the sky. I will hate to say goodbye to the Greens. They've become like my own family, almost.

Love,
Teddy

Grammar Questions for the Letter of May 30, 1892
Circle the letter of the correct answer.

1. Which example has the correct use of capitalization?
   A. Mr. green's face lit up.
   B. mr. Green's face lit up.
   C. mr. green's face lit up.
   D. Mr. Green's face lit up.

2. Which of the following words is spelled correctly?
   A. interested
   B. intersted
   C. enterested
   D. interestid

3. Which of the following examples is correct?
   A. Mrs. Green said, Amanda, you're welcome to stay.
   B. Mrs. Green said, "amanda, you're welcome to stay."
   C. Mrs. Green said, "Amanda, you're welcome to stay."
   D. Mrs. Green said, "Amanda you're welcome to stay."

4. Which word is the subject of the following sentence?
   The railroad is coming in this year.
   A. railroad
   B. The
   C. year
   D. is

5. Which word is the verb in the following sentence?
   Then, we carefully tethered the gondola to the ground.
   A. Then
   B. carefully
   C. tethered
   D. gondola

6. Why did Teddy capitalize the words **"Florida Keys"**?
   A. The Florida Keys is a specific place and proper noun.
   B. She lives in Florida, and she's proud of her state.
   C. The word Florida started the sentence.
   D. The Florida Keys are part of the state of Florida.

7. Dr. Winklepleck says, **"Thank you for your impeccable hospitality."**
   What does the word *hospitality* mean?
   A. staying in a hospital
   B. opening your home and serving your guests
   C. quarantine
   D. becoming friends

May 31, 1892

Dear Martha,

I don't know how to tell you about today, except to say that it didn't turn out like I thought it would.

This morning, Mr. and Mrs. Green and Carlene and I drove to Micanopy in their buggy. They have two beautiful horses to pull the buggy. The large, thin buggy wheels go much smoother and faster than the ones on our covered wagon. On the way, we sang songs and told stories. Mrs. Green taught us the song "She'll Be Coming 'Round the Mountain When She Comes."

When we got to Micanopy, Mr. Green suggested we go to the post office. He said, "They should know your relatives and tell us where to find them."

The woman at the post office said, "Bodains? There's no Bodains here in Micanopy, but seems like there's a family several miles out of town on the dirt road by the name of Bodain. Only house out there."

We drove down the dirt road. My heart beat quicker every minute. I was going to meet my kinfolk, Pap's cousin, Daniel Bodain. Would he like me? Would he help me until Mama and Pap could find me? The more we drove, the more I hated to leave the Green family, but I knew there was no other way.

We found the place. It was run-down and dirty looking. The porch was sagging, there was trash in the yard, and three kids were running around hitting each other with sticks.

Mr. Green called, "We're looking for the family of Daniel Bodain."

A woman came out on the porch. She looked about Mrs. Green's age. She said, "Who are you?"

Mr. Green said, "I'm Doyle Green. This here is my wife, Kate. We've brought your kinfolk. This is Teddy Bodain."

The woman on the porch said, "Teddy—Bodain?"

I said, "Yes, ma'am. My name is Theodosia, but I go by Teddy."

The woman said, "I'm Verna. We're the family of Daniel Bodain, but I don't know you. How are you related?"

I felt nervous. Her voice made me feel unwelcome. I said, "My pap is the cousin of Daniel Bodain. We came to Florida on a wagon train. My folks got sick, and we got separated. I looked for them for days. I'm sure my pap will come here to try to find me."

She said, "Why would your father come here?

I said, "I have his land deed for safekeeping. I left him a note that said I would try to find you."

Mrs. Bodain said, "Look, I'm sorry about your trouble, but we've got a lot of mouths to feed here. The last thing I need is another—"

I said, "You won't have to feed me. I have some money. A little."

She said, "Money?" Suddenly, she looked interested.

I said, "I had twenty dollars, but I've spent some on food. I have $19.00 and change left."

Mr. Green said, "I don't feel right about this. I think we better take Teddy back with us. Teddy, you can leave a note for your family, telling them where you are."

I wanted to leave with the Greens. Something about Verna Bodain made me uneasy. But I wanted to be sure my parents could find me.

Mrs. Bodain said, "Nonsense. Teddy is welcome to stay with us till her folks come."

I said, "Ma'am, my dog is with me, but he's a good dog. He won't be any trouble."

She said, "Teddy, our home is your home."

I hugged the Greens. Carlene and I tried not to cry. Mrs. Green did cry. She said, "Teddy, if you don't find your folks, you have a family waiting for you. Don't forget that."

When the Greens drove off, Mrs. Bodain turned to me. She said, "Let's have that money."

The kids quit staring at me and started hitting each other again. How can I be related to these people?

Love,
Teddy

Name_____ Date_____

Writing Questions for the Letter of May 31, 1892
Circle the letter of the correct answer.

1. Read the following sentence from Teddy's letter today:
   The porch was sagging, there was trash in the yard, and three kids were running around hitting each other with sticks.
   This sentence contains examples of what good writing skill?
   A. similes
   B. details you can picture
   C. transitional phrases
   D. dialogue

2. Read the following sentence from Teddy's letter today:
   I felt nervous. Her voice made me feel unwelcome.
   The words *nervous* and *unwelcome* are examples of what type of good writing skill?
   A. similes
   B. specific emotion words
   C. dialogue
   D. transition words

3. Read the following sentence from Teddy's letter today:
   I don't know how to tell you about today, except to say that it didn't turn out like I thought it would.
   This sentence is an example of what type of good writing skill?
   A. transitional phrase
   B. descriptive writing
   C. grabber
   D. dialogue

4. Read the following sentence from Teddy's letter today:
   Suddenly, she looked interested.
   The word *Suddenly* is an example of what type of good writing skill?
   A. onomatopoeia
   B. dialogue
   C. specific emotion word
   D. transitional word

5. Read the following sentence from Teddy's letter today:
   The kids quit staring at me and started hitting each other again.
   The words *staring* and *hitting* are examples of what type of good writing skill?
   A. strong verbs
   B. similes
   C. transitional words
   D. metaphors

June 1, 1892

Dear Martha,

Mrs. Bodain acts different than she did in front of the Greens. After she took my money, she said, "And keep that dog out of my house. I'll not have a dog in here, do you understand?"

All three of the kids have done something mean since I've been here. The oldest girl, Sissy, said, "Don't think you're sleeping with me. I bet you're stuck up with that pink dress."

Georgie threw corncobs at Ethel. I said, "Don't throw things at him!"

He said, "You better not let him kill one of Mama's chickens. That'll be his last day on earth."

Randy sticks his tongue out at me every time Mrs. Bodain's back is turned. I don't know what she does all day, but it sure isn't cooking, cleaning, or laundry. I think she just yells at the kids.

We ate beans and cornbread for supper. I said, "Where is Mr. Bodain?"

Mrs. Bodain said, "He had to make some deliveries over to Ocala. He'll be back."

After supper, she seemed a little friendlier. She said, "Teddy, come in here and tell me about your family. We need to get to know one another." When I sat down, she said, "You can call me Cousin Verna."

She asked me lots of questions, all about Mama and Pap and our plans. I told her about Dylan, all of us having the fever, and getting separated. She seemed interested in every detail. When I told her about taking the land deed out of the wagon, she said, "You are a smart girl. Who knows where that wagon will end up? Now, the deed is safe, with you."

I felt proud of the fact that I had rescued the deed. I said, "I keep it in a pouch around my neck. When Mama and Pap come for me, we'll travel down to our land and start a new life."

She said, "I'm glad you kept it safe. May I see it?"

I said, "I guess so."

I unfolded the land deed, and Verna studied it. She said, "Forty acres of Florida farmland. Won't that be nice for your pap."

After the kids went to bed, a man I'd never seen before rode up on a horse.

Cousin Verna said, "Oh, let me tell Daniel you're here. He'll be so tickled." She ran out to meet him. I sat there, wondering what he'd be like, hoping he would like me and I would like him.

Daniel Bodain came in and shook my hand. He said, "Hello, Teddy. I'm your dad's cousin, Daniel Bodain." He had long hair and piercing blue eyes. I noticed a long white scar that ran from his eyebrow down to his ear. He didn't look anything like Pap, but he seemed nice enough.

We talked for a while. Cousin Verna repeated lots of the details about our family that I'd told her earlier. She said, "Grace and Dalton got separated from Teddy, and she thinks they'll come for her here."

He said, "Teddy, I'm sure you're right. They'll show up sooner or later."

I hoped it was sooner. I don't want to stay here any longer than I have to.

I slept on a pallet on the back porch. Ethelbert slept next to me.
I was so tired, I fell asleep right away, but later that night, I had a nightmare. I dreamed Cousin Verna and Cousin Daniel were talking.

She said, "The deed is made out to Dalton Bodain."

He said, "So?"

She said, "So—Dalton Bodain is probably dead."

He said, "What if he's not?"

She said, "No one knows what Dalton Bodain looks like. If someone gets there first and hands in that land deed, that someone could become the owner of 40 acres of Florida farmland."

I woke up sweating. Great buckets of butterbeans! Thank goodness it was only a dream.

Or was it?

Love,
Teddy

Persuasive Writing Prompt for the Letter of June 1, 1892
Read and answer the following prompt.

Persuasive Prompt: Teddy has just arrived at her cousins' house. She is not sure she likes it there. After reading today's letter, give convincing arguments of why you would NOT want to stay with Verna and her family for any length of time. Give detailed reasons and examples that would convince us you are right. Read your paper quietly. Add any details you may have left out.

_____

_____

_____

_____

_____

_____

_____

_____

_____

_____

_____

_____

_____

_____

_____

_____

_____

_____

_____

_____

June 2, 1892

Dear Martha,

I woke up early and fed Ethel some leftover cornbread from last night's supper. I had saved my piece, so Ethel could have it. I was pretty sure Cousin Verna wasn't going to feed a dog, so I hid it in the pocket of my apron. This morning Ethel gobbled it up. I straightened my pallet and swept the back porch with an old broom I found in a corner.

I didn't feel like playing with the kids. I hated the thought that we were even cousins. What would I do all day? I said, "Cousin Verna, I saw some blackberry bushes along the edge of the woods behind your house. Would you like for me to pick a bucket of blackberries for you? My mama taught me to make a real tasty blackberry cobbler, and I'd be happy to make one for you."

Cousin Daniel said, "I know I would like some blackberry cobbler."

Cousin Verna said, "Well, it's nice to have someone who offers to help around here. Teddy, the blackberry bushes are full of briars. Why don't you change your clothes, so you won't mess up your dress?" She gave me one of Sissy's old raggedy dresses. "You can change in my room. Lay your things across my bed, so they'll stay nice." I changed into the dress and lay my clothes on her bed.

I took the big bucket and walked back to where I'd seen the blackberry bushes yesterday. Ethel came with me. I'm sure he wanted to stay as far away from Georgie and those corncobs as he could get. The bushes were filled with berries. The light ones were sour, but the darkest ones were as sweet as sugar. I stuffed myself. I picked and picked. I needed more berries to fill the bucket, so I kept going to bushes that were farther away.

Suddenly, a boy stepped out on the path. I was so surprised I almost dropped the bucket. Ethel growled. I stared at the boy. He looked familiar. Had I met him somewhere before? He was about my age.

I said, "You scared me."

He said, "Who are you?"

I said, "Who's asking?"

He said, "I'm Daniel Bodain. What are you doing in that house?"

I was confused. I said, "You can't be Daniel Bodain. I met Daniel Bodain last night. He's a grown man, and he lives in that house."

He said, "Well, you're wrong. I don't care who you met."

I said, "Liar, liar, pants on fire. Nose as long as a telegraph wire."

The boy said, "Who are you calling a liar? Daniel Bodain is my name, and Daniel Bodain was my pap, and he's been dead for six months."

I'm sure my mouth was hanging open. I said, "Then, who is that man back at the house?"

He said, "Probably Verna's new husband, Jimbo Dudd. She was my stepmother. I took to the woods a few days ago because I won't live there anymore. I stood it as long as I could. She's mean, and her kids are even meaner. She's nothing to me now that my pap is gone."

I was more confused. I said, "But she told me that man is Daniel Bodain."

He said, "Well, that wouldn't be the first time she's lied."

My head felt like it was spinning. I said, "Why would she lie to me?"

He said, "Probably because you've got something she wants." I stood staring at him. He said, "I know you don't believe me. But you better watch out. Those people will steal you blind."

And then, just like that, he was gone.

Great buckets of butterbeans. Who is lying? Who is telling the truth?

Love,
Teddy

Name_____ Date _____

Reading Multiple Choice Questions for the Letter of June 2, 1892

Circle the letter of the correct answer.

1. What did Teddy go out to pick for Cousin Verna?
   A. blueberries
   B. raspberries
   C. oranges
   D. blackberries

2. Who startled Teddy and Ethel while they were out picking fruit?
   A. Georgie
   B. a young boy
   C. Cousin Verna
   D. Sissy

3. Who is Jimbo Dudd?
   A. the boy Teddy met on the road
   B. Pap's cousin
   C. Cousin Verna's husband
   D. a man who drove by in a buggy

4. What did Daniel tell Teddy about Verna and Jimbo?
   A. that they are thieves and she better watch out for them
   B. that they are liars
   C. that they are not really related to her pap
   D. all of the above

5. What did Teddy save from supper the night before to feed Ethel in the morning?
   A. some jerky
   B. a bone from her chicken leg
   C. some leftover cornbread
   D. she was so hungry she didn't save anything for Ethel

6. Why did Teddy change into one of Sissy's old dresses?
   A. because she didn't like the dress Mrs. Green had given her
   B. because the other girls were jealous of her pink dress
   C. because she had dropped some soup on her pink dress at dinner
   D. to prevent her dress from being ruined by the briars on the blackberry bushes

7. What did Teddy say when she thought Daniel was not telling the truth?
   A. "Liar, liar pants on fire. Nose as long as a telegraph wire."
   B. "I'm going to tell on you. You'll never lie again."
   C. "I knew you couldn't tell the truth! You're not a Bodain."
   D. "Ask me no questions. I'll tell you no lies."

June 3, 1892

Dear Martha,

I'm in terrible trouble!

Yesterday, after I picked the blackberries, I helped Cousin Verna wash the stacks and stacks of dirty dishes that lay all around the kitchen. Then, I mashed the berries with sugar, strained the juice, and made a blackberry cobbler for supper. After we ate, I helped Sissy do the dishes. When the others went to their rooms, I lit a candle stub, so I could write a letter to you. When I finished writing, the house was dark and silent, like everyone was asleep. I went out on the back porch.

I thought about the boy in the woods for the hundredth time. Why would he make up a story like that if it wasn't true? But why would Cousin Verna and Cousin Daniel lie to me?

I don't know what made me do it, but I crept around to Cousin Verna's window. She and Cousin Daniel, or Jimbo, or whoever he is, were talking softly. I listened.

She said, "She keeps it around her neck. She won't take it off."

He said, "Then, let's all go to the swimming hole tomorrow. She'll have to take it off then. I'll get it while she's swimming with the kids."

Fear washed over me. I reached for the pouch around my neck.

She said, "Her parents probably died of the fever. They won't miss the land. This is our big chance."

He said, "What will we do with the girl?"

She said, "They have orphanages for kids with no parents, don't they?"

He said, "But she'll tell them that her parents are alive."

She said, "Who are they going to believe: her or us? They won't believe a kid. Besides, she's had the fever herself. We'll say she's not in her right mind after losing her folks and being so sick."

He said, "Verna, you are a genius. This will be as easy as falling off a log."

She said, "One more thing. Take that mangy dog off and get rid of him, permanently. Do it first thing in the morning before the girl gets up. I don't want him hanging around here eating my food or killing my chickens."

I ran back to the porch. My heart was pounding. I was shaking from head to toe.

I tried to calm down. I knew we had to get away. I looked at the sky. The stars were bright. I found the Big Dipper and the North Star. I thought, if the slaves could do it, so can I.

I bundled my things up in the bandana and felt for the pouch around my neck just to remind myself that it was safe.

Ethelbert and I set out into the night, as quiet as two mice. I found the road and headed back toward Micanopy, just barely able to see the way. We walked and walked. I was tired, but we couldn't stop.

My heart was heavy with fear when I thought about what I'd heard at the window. Why would folks want to steal something my pap had worked so hard for? What made me feel worse was that there was no one I could go to. The Greens would be at the beach in Sarasota, and I didn't know how to get in touch with them. Who else would believe the word of a kid over two adults? The only thing I could do was run away.

We finally came to the edge of town. I wanted to wait until daylight, so I could leave a message for Pap and Mama at the post office, in case they came there for directions, like I had. I looked for a place for us to sleep. There was a wagon parked under an oak tree. It was filled with freshly ginned cotton. I helped Ethel over the side and then climbed in. In two shakes of a lamb's tail, the two of us were fast asleep.

Love,
Teddy

Name_____   Date_____

Narrative Writing Prompt for the Letter of June 3, 1892
Read and answer the prompt below.

Narrative Prompt: Teddy picked blackberries and made a cobbler. Think of a time when you made something. Now write a narrative piece and tell about the time you made this item, being sure to include all the juicy details of what you made and how you went about making it. Reread your paper carefully, and add a few more writing skills to make your paper exciting and interesting.

_____

_____

_____

_____

_____

_____

_____

_____

_____

_____

_____

_____

_____

_____

_____

_____

_____

_____

_____

_____

June 4, 1892

Dear Martha,

Early this morning, a voice woke me up. It said, "I told you those people weren't any good."

It was the boy from the woods. I said, "Would you quit scaring the daylights out of me?" I felt sore from head to toe, my head ached, and I was hungry. Now, this kid was pestering me.

He said, "Well, who are you? You never did tell me your name."

I said, "And I'm not going to. I don't even know who you really are. How do I know I can trust you? You might be working with those people to trick me." The thought of that house, of those kids, of those voices in the night, filled me with dread.

He said, "I told you. I'm Daniel Bodain."

I glared at him. "I'm looking for Daniel Bodain, the grown man."

He said, "And I told you, my pap died last November. Just after Thanksgiving. He got pneumonia, and that was it."

I felt frustrated. I said, "I don't believe you."

That made Daniel mad. He said, "Alright, don't believe me then. I don't care two hoots in a holler if you believe me or not."

I said, "You don't have any idea what I've been through."

He said, "You? You don't have any idea who I am or what I've been through. You don't know what it's like. You have a family. What have I got? Nothing." His eyes snapped anger as he spoke. Martha, this kid was RILED UP.

He started off down the road, kicking a fat stick that lay in his path.

I watched him leave, wondering. He looked so familiar. Who did he look like? Had I met him before? Where had I seen his face?

I remembered Mama showing me something once. She kept it in a tiny velvet box. It was a picture of Pap as a boy. That was it. The same eyes. The same chin.

The boy looked like Pap.

My heart almost skipped a beat.

I called, "Daniel!"

He said, "What?" and turned to look at me.

My voice was soft when I asked, "Are you sure you're not related to that woman?"

He said, "My mama died when I was little. Pap married Verna last year, a few months before he died. She came with those three Philistines. They're not related to me, thank goodness. I don't have any family, period, at least none that I know of."

I said, "I think you do."

He said, "Do what?"

I said, "Have a family."

He looked curious. "How so?"

I said, "My name is Teddy. Teddy Bodain. You do have a family. You and I are cousins."

Love,
Teddy

Name_____ Date_____

Reading Short Response Questions for the Letter of June 4, 1892
Answer the questions below, and be sure to use complete sentences.

1. Teddy said, **"You don't have any idea what I've been through."** What did she mean by this?

_____

_____

_____

_____

_____

2. What made Daniel kick a fat stick that was in his path?

_____

_____

_____

_____

3. What led Teddy to realize Daniel looked like Pap?

_____

_____

_____

_____

4. In talking to Daniel about having a family, what did Teddy mean when she said, **"I think you do."**

_____

_____

_____

_____

June 5, 1892

Dear Martha,

Daniel looked absolutely astonished. He said, "You think we're cousins?"

I said, "I know we're cousins. If your dad was Daniel Bodain, he was my pap's cousin. That makes you and me cousins."

He said, "I've got a cousin? And it's you?"

I said, "Well, I'm not that bad."

He said, "Where is your pap?" He squinted at me.

I said, "That's what I'm trying to find out." I told him the quick version of who we are, where we came from, and what we are doing in Florida.

"So I've got family?" He smiled for the first time. I smiled back.

The sun was getting brighter. People were out and about. I pictured Jimbo and Verna discovering I was gone. I said, "Daniel, I've got to get out of here. Those people are going to be looking for me."

He said, "What's your plan?"

I tore out a sheet of paper and wrote a quick note.

"Dear Mama and Pap, your cousin, Daniel Bodain, is dead. The people who live in his house are bad. They are liars, and they want to steal your land deed. I'll try to keep the deed safe until you find me. Miss Melman is going to a school in St. Augustine. The Sheridan School for Girls. She'll know where I am.

Love, Teddy

P.S. Ethelbert is with me. So is my cousin, Daniel Bodain. He's 11 years old."

I went to the post office. Daniel waited outside with Ethelbert.

The same woman who had helped me before was just opening the door.

I said, "May I buy an envelope, please, and a stamp?" I paid with the two pennies the woman had tipped me for delivering her loaves of bread. Now, I was totally broke, but I had to mail the letter.

I sealed my letter in the envelope and put the stamp on the outside. I addressed the letter to Dalton and Grace Bodain, General Delivery, Micanopy, Florida. I said to the woman, "My parents, Dalton and Grace Bodain, might come looking for me. If they do, would you please give them this letter?"

She said, "I'll make a note of it. "

I went back outside and told Daniel, "I've got to get out of town. Jimbo wants Pap's land deed."

We walked around the corner from the post office. The streets were busy with people. Suddenly, Daniel pulled me into the dry goods store. He said, "Look. Across the street."

I looked out the window. It was Jimbo. He asked a woman something, and she shook her head. He looked straight over at the window, and I could swear he saw us. We ducked down. I peeked down the road at the wagon where Ethel and I had slept. A man was loading more cotton.

Daniel and I snuck out the back door of the dry goods store, behind the oak tree, and behind the wagon. The man loading the cotton was big and muscular and reminded me of Lucas Lincoln. His skin was the color of coffee grinds.

He said, "Are you the kids who slept in my wagon?"

I said, "We need to get out of town. A bad man is looking for us. Would you help us?"

The man looked back toward the busy street. Jimbo was headed our way. The man frowned.

He said, "Get in the wagon on the far side. Cover yourself with cotton as best as you can." Daniel and I scrunched Ethel down between the two of us.

As the wagon rolled through town, the driver sang a sad song.

"When the great big river meets the little river, follow the drinking gourd."

Love,
Teddy

Name_____ Date _____

Expository Writing Prompt for the Letter of June 5, 1892
Read and answer the following writing prompt.

Expository Prompt: A man with a cotton wagon helps out Teddy and Daniel in the story today. Think of reasons that explain why it is important to help other people. Now explain why being helpful is important to you and the people in your life. You can include a mini-story of a time you helped someone or someone helped you. But remember: your job is to explain why being helpful is important! Be sure to include vivid reasons, good descriptions, emotion words, and other writing skills that make your paper enjoyable to read.

_____

_____

_____

_____

_____

_____

_____

_____

_____

_____

_____

_____

_____

_____

_____

_____

_____

_____

_____

June 6, 1892

Dear Martha,

We rode in the cotton wagon for what seemed like forever. Daniel, Ethel, and I were so tired that the gentle rocking of the wagon lulled us to sleep.

The driver's voice woke us. He said, "You must like cotton because this is the second time today you've been sleeping in my wagon." He smiled. "I'm Joe."

I said, "Thank you for helping us."

He said, "Well, this is as far as I go. Where are you headed?"

I said, "I'm not really sure. I don't know where my folks are. We got separated. But I do know someone in St. Augustine. Or at least she will be in St. Augustine sometime. She was with a wagon train."

Joe said, "If someone is looking for you, they'll probably stay on the main road. See this trail?" He pointed to a path where the grass had been worn down. "Follow that trail. You'll come to a cabin on a spring, way down yonder. That's where Wanda Watson lives. Tell her Joe sent you. She'll treat you right."

Joe climbed into the wagon. He said, "It's not much, but here's two carrots. They were going to be for my mules, but I'll get them something else." We thanked him for the carrots and waved as he drove off.

I said, "Daniel, you don't have to come with me. Here's your carrot if you want to go off on your own. They're not very big, but they're better than nothing."

He said, "Where else have I got to go? It's safer if we stick together. Besides, we're both Bodains." Hearing him say that reminded me of Pap. I was glad that Daniel wanted to come with me. Traveling alone could be scary and dangerous, especially at night. And, after all, Daniel is my cousin.

We set off down the trail.

Daniel said, "Teddy—how'd you get a boy's name?"

I said, "It's really Theodosia, but everyone calls me Teddy."

While we walked, we told each other everything we could think of about our families. Daniel's mama died when he was young, so he doesn't remember much about her. His pap, Daniel Bodain, was a carpenter. He grew up in north Florida. He remembered going to a family reunion one time when he was a boy but never knew his relatives after that. Daniel is 11, going on 12. One year older than me. That made me remember my birthday. I'd completely forgotten that I was about to turn 11.

I said, "What day is today?"

He said, "I don't know. Thursday? Friday?"

I said, "No, I mean what calendar date." I tried to remember. Hadn't Dr. Winklepleck said something about June being two days away?

Daniel said, "Why?"

I said, "Because my birthday is June 4th. But I think it's passed now. So much has happened, I forgot my own birthday."

He said, "How old are you?"

I said, "I'm 11. I've been 11 for days, and I didn't even know it."

He said, "Happy birthday. That means—we're both 11, for now."

We found the cabin late this afternoon. A woman came out to see us.

I said, "Joe sent us." She looked at me in my dusty, dirty dress, with my bundle tied to a stick. She looked at Daniel, who looked like he hadn't seen the inside of a bathtub in weeks and wasn't too friendly with barbers, either. Then, she looked at Ethelbert. His head drooped, and his tail hung between his legs.

She said, "If Joe sent you, then you're in the right place. Do you like fried fish?"

Daniel and I said, "Yes!" at the same time.

She said, "Then, what are we waiting for? Let's go fishing."

Love,
Teddy

Name_____ Date _____

Reading Extended Response Questions for the Letter of June 6, 1892
Answer the questions below. Be sure to use complete sentences, reasons, and details.

1. What kind of man was Joe? Describe the ways in which he helped Teddy and Daniel.

_____

_____

_____

_____

_____

_____

_____

_____

_____

2. Joe suggested that Teddy and Daniel follow a trail until they came to Wanda Watson's cabin. When they arrived, what happened? Why do you think Wanda welcomed Teddy and Daniel?

_____

_____

_____

_____

_____

_____

_____

_____

_____

_____

June 7, 1892

Dear Martha,

Miss Wanda Watson is a whirlwind. She's the sun coming out on a cloudy day. She's a cool drink of water when you're hot and thirsty. She's as old as the earth. No kidding. She must be about 90 years old.

Yesterday, right off the bat, she took us fishing in the spring by the cabin. We used bamboo poles, like Pap and I did before. Daniel was handy with a fishing pole, I might say. Wanda (She doesn't like "Miss Wanda") gave us slices of stale bread, and we made dough balls for bait. Boy, do fish love dough balls.

We sat on big, flat rocks right on the edge of the spring. The sun was low in the afternoon sky.

Wanda said, "It's suppertime. Pull 'em in." And that's what we did. We caught lots and lots of fish. Every time we pulled one in, Daniel yelled a big, "Woo hoo!" and Wanda shouted, "Yee haw!" Daniel and I were so busy, we didn't notice that Wanda had made a fire, right there on the spring bank. She melted grease in the biggest skillet I've ever seen. I bet she could have fried three dozen eggs in that thing. She made a big pot of grits and set them to boil.

When Daniel and I had a pile of warmouth perch, bluegill, and trout, Wanda called, "Okay, Teddy. Come clean your fish. Daniel, you keep fishing. Boys can eat a heap o' fish."

I said, "I don't have a knife, Wanda."

I thought she'd say, "I'll clean them for you," but she didn't. She pulled a pocket knife out of her apron and handed it to me. "That belonged to my son, Samuel. He cleaned many'a fish with it."

I'd watched Pap clean fish. It couldn't be that hard. I said, "I hope I do it right. I've seen my pap do it."

Wanda said, "Hunger is the best teacher there is."

I took a deep breath and began cleaning. It really isn't hard. You just have to remember all the steps: scales, head, belly, entrails, bloodline. Then, they're ready to fry up in the pan!

I took the fish to Wanda in a bucket. I said, "They're scaled, cleaned, and I buried the heads and guts."

She was surprised. "With you wearing that pink dress, I figured you for a city girl that got herself lost. Now, I'm thinking you're a country girl with a good head on her shoulders. Somebody has taught you right." Her face was the kindest, sweetest face I'd ever seen.

Daniel came to help. He said, "I caught eight more and put them on a line."

Wanda said, "The two of you have some right handy skills. Wash your hands in the spring, dredge the fish in this cornmeal, then fry them up, nice and brown."

By the time we got back from washing our hands, the grease was sizzling hot. We used a long fork to lay the fish in the skillet. Mmmmm. There is no better smell than frying fish—frying fish you caught yourself.

While we fried the fish, Wanda mixed eggs and buttermilk in with the rest of the cornmeal and added some onion and green peppers. I said, "What is that for?"

She said, "I'm making us some hush puppies. You can't eat fried fish without hush puppies."

By the time I dished up the grits and heaped our plates with fish, my mouth was watering. Daniel's stomach was growling, and Ethelbert was whining and about to pester me to death. Wanda threw us each a hush puppy. They practically melted in our mouths they were so good.

She said, "See? See how you hushed? Even the puppy." We all laughed.

Before we ate, Wanda said, "Let's thank the Good Lord." Daniel and I bowed our heads. Wanda prayed nice and loud. "Lord, please help these two runaway children. Thank you for this food. Give us a night of rest and good weather. Amen."

In my mind I prayed, "And keep Mama and Pap safe, wherever they may be."

Love,
Teddy

Name_____ Date_____

Grammar Questions for the Letter of June 7, 1892
Circle the letter of the correct answer.

1. **"Miss Wanda is a whirlwind"** is an example of what kind of writing skill?
   A. simile
   B. onomatopoeia
   C. prepositional phrase
   D. metaphor

2. Which of the following words is spelled incorrectly?
   A. trout
   B. nife
   C. sizzling
   D. buttermilk

3. What should go at the end of this sentence?
   Do you know how to clean fish
   A. a question mark
   B. an exclamation point
   C. a period
   D. a quotation mark

4. **"Hunger is the best teacher there is"** is an example of what?
   A. transitional phrase
   B. metaphor
   C. simile
   D. onomatopoeia

5. Which of the following examples correctly uses capitalization?
   A. "And keep mama and pap safe, wherever they may be."
   B. "And keep Mama and pap safe, wherever they may be."
   C. "And Keep Mama and Pap safe, Wherever They May Be."
   D. "And keep Mama and Pap safe, wherever they may be."

6. When you take the period out from between the following two sentences, what are you left with?
   Daniel's stomach was growling, and Ethelbert was whining and about to pester me to death Wanda threw us each a hush puppy.
   A. a compound sentence
   B. a run-on sentence
   C. a descriptive sentence
   D. a phrase

June 8, 1892

Dear Martha,

   After supper, Wanda told us a story.

   Sitting near the campfire, we were surrounded by twinkly fireflies. Daniel and I reached to catch them in our hands.

   Wanda said, "The firefly didn't always have a light, you know. Once upon a time, he was just a simple beetle. Each day he slept, but at night, he flew down to the river and sat on the bank. There he cried because there was nothing special about him.

   "'Ah, me! The butterfly is beautiful. The ladybug has spots. The mantis prays, the centipede has 100 legs, and the cricket sings for all to hear. But there is nothing special about me. I am just a beetle. No one takes notice of a simple beetle.'

   "In those days, the panther was the ruler of all the creatures. All the animals came to him for advice because he was wise and true. Not a night passed that he wasn't visited by the black bear, the white-tail deer, the grass snake, the pelican, the eagle, or other creatures.

   "One evening, when the firefly was crying by the river, the alligators came to the surface of the water to gossip. They took no notice of the firefly because he was just a simple beetle.

   "The smallest alligator said, 'Tonight, I will eat a catfish. I will lie still on the bottom, and when the catfish swims close, I will catch him by the whiskers.'

   "The other alligators nodded their heads and said, 'Good.' They snapped their jaws in delight.

   "The middle-sized alligator said, 'Tonight, I will eat a turtle. When she swims to the log, I will catch her by the leg.'

   "The other alligators nodded their heads and said, 'Good.' They snapped their jaws in delight.

   "The largest alligator said, 'A catfish and a turtle might be a fine meal for you, but tonight, I will dine on panther.'

   "The other alligators said, 'How can this be?' because they knew that the panther was wise, but fierce.

   "The largest alligator said, 'I will wait quietly below the surface of the water. Only my eyes will be peeping up at the top. When the panther comes to drink by moonlight at the water's edge, I will leap out and seize him by the tail.'

   "The other alligators thumped their tails and said, 'We will watch to see what comes to pass.'

   "Now, the firefly, who was only a simple beetle, knew that someone had to warn the panther. If he had been a butterfly, or a ladybug, or a mantis, or a cricket, the alligators would have noticed him. But he was only a simple beetle, so off he flew, unnoticed, to warn the panther.

   "The firefly flitted up into the trees, up to the highest branches, where the panther was meeting with the raccoon, the osprey, and the squirrel. He flew to the panther's ear and whispered, 'Great panther, tonight the largest alligator is laying a trap for you. As you go to the river to drink by moonlight, he will be hidden under the water. Only his eyes will be peeping up at the top. When you bend to lap the water, he will leap out and seize you by the tail.'

   "The panther said, 'Who is this that warns me? Who is this that saves my life?'

   "The firefly said, 'It is only I, a simple beetle. I am sorry I am not beautiful like the butterfly. I do not have spots, nor 100 legs, and alas, I do not sing.'

   "The panther said, 'Why do you envy what others have? I will reward you with something all your own. From this moment on, early in the evening, you will blink a twinkly light to remind all the creatures that you saved the great panther's life. And, as for the alligator, starting tonight, his eyes will shine and gleam as a warning to all creatures that he is hiding below the surface, ready to leap out and seize them.'

   "The alligator, who heard the commanding voice of the panther all the way from the river, growled and sunk into the watery depths. But the firefly smiled and fluttered down into the trees and bushes, blinking his yellow-green glimmer for all to see.

   "And that is how the firefly got his light."

   It was such a good story. Wanda Watson might be the best storyteller in the whole, wide world. Martha, I wish you could have been here, too.

   Love,
   Teddy

Writing Questions for the Letter of June 8, 1892
Circle the letter of the correct answer.

1. Read the following sentence from Teddy's letter today:
   After supper, Wanda told us a story.
   The words *After supper* are an example of what type of good writing skill?
   A. grabber
   B. transitional phrase
   C. strong verb
   D. simile

2. Read the following sentence from Teddy's letter today:
   'When you bend to lap the water, he will leap out and seize you by the tail.'
   The words *bend, lap, leap,* and *seize* are all examples of what type of good writing skill?
   A. similes
   B. onomatopoeia
   C. metaphors
   D. strong verbs

3. Read the following sentence from Teddy's letter today:
   "In those days, the panther was the ruler of all the creatures."
   The phrase *In those days* is an example of what type of good writing skill?
   A. grabber
   B. transitional phrase
   C. strong verb
   D. simile

4. Read the following sentence from Teddy's letter today:
   "The other alligators said, 'We will watch to see what comes to pass.'"
   This sentence is an example of what type of good writing skill?
   A. grabber
   B. specific emotion words
   C. dialogue
   D. voice

5. Read the following sentence from Teddy's letter today:
   'I will lie still on the bottom, and when the catfish swims close, I will catch him by the whiskers.'
   This sentence is an example of what type of good writing skill?
   A. transitional words
   B. details you can picture
   C. similes
   D. onomatopoeia

June 9, 1892

Dear Martha,

After the storytelling, the fire burned low. Crickets chirped in the bushes, and frogs croaked down by the river. We heard the sad, lonely call of the whippoorwill.

Wanda said, "Let's make up your pallets because, by the looks of you, you two could fall asleep standing up in the middle of a tornado. I don't have much for a pallet, but I think these quilts will do."

We spread the quilts down and wrapped up in them. Wanda said, "That's good. Right near the fire. This smoke will keep the skeeters away." Daniel lay on one side of the fire, and I lay on the other.

We thanked Wanda for everything: fishing, supper, the story, and putting us up for the night.

She said, "I should thank you for the good company. It gets lonesome out here. You children have made me forget that I'll be 92 years old, come September. I've outlived everyone: my husband, my son, and I don't know how many dogs and cats. Now, have a good night. It will be morning before you know it."

Daniel was asleep before Wanda made it into her cottage. I looked at him across the fire. It was still amazing to me that I was looking at my cousin. Daniel and I are family. I have lost my baby brother, my parents are missing, but I am not alone. I have a cousin. Daniel's parents are dead for sure, but now he has me.

The next morning we slept late. I woke to the smell of bacon frying. Wanda was making breakfast.

She said, "We've got to talk. Come eat, and then I need to ask you two a few questions."

Daniel and I ate like bears coming out of hibernation.

Wanda said, "I don't need to know why you're running or where you're running to. But the trail you came in on dead ends at this spring. I have an old jon boat I don't use anymore, and it's still sound. It's propped up by that tree. I oil the bottom a few times each year just in case someone might need it. And now, someone does. It has two poles that would be about right for the two of you and two oars. If you follow this spring, you'll come to the Ocklawaha River. Take that south. When the river forks, bear right, or west. That river, the Silver River, will lead you to Silver Springs."

I said, "Wanda, we're not running away because we've done something wrong."

She said, "Oh, I know that. A guilty conscience always shows."

I said, "A bad man is after something I have. Something my pap worked hard for. I'm trying to keep it safe."

Daniel said, "He married my stepmother after my pap died. They're both bad news. I'm running away with Teddy because I don't have any other place to go and because we found out we're kin."

I said, "Cousins. We're both Bodains."

Wanda smiled. "That's nice. It's always good to have family. I miss my family. Everyone wants to live a long time, but life is only special when you share it with folks you love. I hate to see you go, but if someone is following you, it might be best for you to pack up and head down the spring."

I didn't want to leave Wanda. But the thought of Jimbo finding us made me agree that we had to go. We didn't want to take her boat, but she insisted. "What am I going to do with a jon boat? I'm too old to pole it, and I can fish right here in the spring if I get hungry. I'm staying put right here. You take it, and use it however it helps you."

She packed us a sack of food and some matches. She gave Daniel a pair of boots. The ones he owned had holes in the soles and were too small. She gave me the pocketknife that had belonged to her son, Samuel. When I gathered my belongings, she said, "Teddy, if you're on the run, that pretty dress might call attention." She helped me put on a pair of overalls and an old shirt. "We'll have to roll up the cuffs, but these will help you blend in."

Being with Wanda was almost as good as being with Mama. Almost.

Love,
Teddy

Name_____ Date_____

Persuasive Writing Prompt for the Letter of June 9, 1892
Read and answer the following prompt.

Persuasive Prompt: Teddy, Daniel, and Ethelbert are still running from Jimbo. Pretend you are running away from Jimbo, and you have a choice to use a mule or a jon boat. In your opinion, what would be the best way to get away from Jimbo? Use convincing reasons why your choice is the best. Which one is fastest? How far can you go? Before you write, think through all the possible reasons your choice is best. Convince us that you know how to get away from him and how to keep him from getting the best of you. When you finish, compare your ideas with another writer. Help each other improve your arguments and give each other ideas.

_____

_____

_____

_____

_____

_____

_____

_____

_____

_____

_____

_____

_____

_____

_____

_____

_____

_____

June 10, 1892

Dear Martha,

I told Wanda, "I've never done this before. Pole a jon boat, I mean."

Wanda said, "Learning is half the fun. You'll figure it out. I'm going to miss you two. Come back sometime. I'd love to know you got to where you're going." She waved, and we waved back.

The spring was slow moving, so it gave me a chance to learn how to pole. Daniel had poled before, but I had to learn how to stand in a boat, balance, and pole at the same time. The trick was to stick the pole down in the mud, shove forward, pull the pole out, and start all over again. Daniel poled on one side, I poled on the other. With two of us, it wasn't too bad. The jon boat surged ahead steadily and silently.

The sky was as blue as Mama's eyes. All around us, trees rustled their leaves. Turtles stretched out on flat rocks or fallen logs, taking in the sun. Butterflies opened and closed their wings. I saw the same kind of bird I had seen in the swamp. I said, "I've seen that kind of bird before. What is it called?"

Daniel said, "That's an anhinga. Some folks call it a snake bird. See that pointy beak? That's how he gets his dinner."

I said, "How does he do that?"

Daniel said, "Look! There he goes. You'll see."

The anhinga flew straight up, turned, headed down to the water, and folded his wings back. Chung! He knifed through the water like a fish. I watched, but he didn't come up.

I said, "Is he drowning?"

Daniel said, "He's fine. Just watch."

I had to wait a minute or two, but the anhinga finally surfaced. His beak had speared a shiny, wriggling fish.

Daniel said, "Now, see what he does." The anhinga tossed his beak, and the fish flew up into the air. The anhinga caught it, and tossed it up, again and again. He finally caught the fish head first. This seemed to be what he was waiting for. He swallowed the fish whole. We watched as the bulging lump of fish slid down the anhinga's long, crooked neck.

I shook my head. "Amazing."

We poled the boat until we began to notice the current picking up. The spring widened and turned. We were in the river. It wasn't a huge river but bigger than the spring. The bad thing was that we had to pole against the current. Who ever heard of a river flowing north?

Daniel said, "We can still pole, but let's keep to the bank. The river gets faster and deeper in the middle. If we need to paddle, we've got oars."

I said, "How did you learn all this?"

Daniel said, "Pap. He loved doing things, going places, learning stuff, teaching me."

I said, "I bet you miss him."

Daniel said, "He was all I had."

I thought about how much Daniel knew about living outdoors on his own. I felt kind of dumb when I compared myself to him. I planned to pay attention and learn as much as I could.

The mosquitoes started biting. He poled to the riverbank and said, "Let's mud up."

I said, "Let's what?"

He scooped up a handful of wet mud. "Skeeters can't bite through this."

We covered ourselves with a thin layer of river mud on our arms, necks, hands, and faces. If we didn't look a sight! Ethel looked at me like I had gone crazy. I thought, I wish Martha could see me now.

Teddy Bodain, Queen of the Mud.

Love,
Teddy

Reading Multiple Choice Questions for the Letter of June 10, 1892
Circle the letter of the correct answer.

1. What kind of boat did Wanda give to Teddy and Daniel?
   A. a canoe
   B. a skiff
   C. a jon boat
   D. a sailboat

2. What kind of bird did Teddy and Daniel watch dive for a fish?
   A. an anhinga, or snake bird
   B. a heron
   C. an osprey
   D. a pelican

3. Who did Daniel say taught him so much about the outdoors?
   A. Cousin Verna
   B. Jimbo Dudd
   C. a former slave
   D. his pap

4. What did Teddy and Daniel do to keep the mosquitoes from biting them?
   A. They found a fort and went inside for the night.
   B. They covered their bodies in mud from the river.
   C. They lit a fire on the boat.
   D. They covered themselves with a large cheesecloth that Teddy had.

5. How did Teddy and Daniel make their boat go?
   A. They used long poles.
   B. They used a sail.
   C. They had a motor.
   D. They lay on the back of the boat and kicked their legs.

6. Who else was on the boat with Teddy and Daniel?
   A. Wanda
   B. Joe, the cotton wagon man
   C. a stranger they met on the riverbank
   D. Ethelbert

7. How blue does Teddy say the sky was?
   A. as blue as the Mediterranean Sea
   B. as blue as cobalt
   C. as blue as Mama's eyes
   D. as blue as Pap's work shirt

June 11, 1892

Dear Martha,

Sometimes, we took turns poling, sometimes we had to row.

I said, "We're like Tom and Huck."

Daniel said, "Who?"

I said, "Tom Sawyer and Huckleberry Finn. You know, from the book Tom Sawyer. Did you ever read it?"

Daniel said, "No, Pap's job kept us on the move a lot. I never did get much schooling."

I thought about Miss Pedigrew and our school in Salter's Grove. I thought about Miss Melman and the wagon train school. I wondered what it would be like to not have any schooling.

I said, "But you know so much, Daniel. You're smart about a lot of things."

Daniel said, "But not the things that would help the most."

I said, "What do you mean?"

Daniel said, "Did you ever wonder why I didn't run away before now, I mean, as miserable as that place was?"

I said, "Yes. I can't imagine you living in that place. I wanted to leave the first day."

Daniel said, "I wanted to run. I wanted to run in the worst way. But I can't read. I don't even know how to read my own name. I can't read the name of a town or a map or directions. How far would I get?"

Now, it was my turn to pole over to the riverbank. The shore was flat and wet with mud. I ripped a long, thin branch off a dead bush and wrote in the mud: DANIEL BODAIN.

Daniel said, "What are you doing?"

I said, "See these letters? That is your name, Daniel Bodain." I handed him the stick. "Now, you copy it underneath. It's not hard."

I thought he might be embarrassed for me to be his teacher, but he was happy I was willing to teach him. He copied his name and said, "I remember some of my letters. There's a D in my first name and my last name and an A and an I, too. I just have trouble remembering what all they say. Their sounds, I mean. I know the letters have sounds that form words. You'll have to help me, Teddy."

We must have stayed there on that bank for an hour. Before we left, Daniel could write his own name and read two whole sentences:

Daniel and Teddy Bodain are cousins.
They are running away from Jimbo Dudd.

We were so excited we started shouting and laughing. Ethelbert barked and chased his tail. That made us laugh even harder. Daniel used the stick to draw a face next to the name, Jimbo Dudd. The man's head had long hair, just like the real Jimbo. At that moment, we thought we were the two smartest kids who had ever lived. We danced and laughed and acted like two whippersnappers. But the truth is, we were just full of ourselves, and it was all a lot of monkey business. Don't you like to act like that, sometimes?

Martha, I realized that Daniel and I are both teachers. Neither one of us is dumb. We both have things to learn, that's all. Daniel is teaching me things about living outdoors, and I am teaching him how to read. It's kind of nice, helping each other learn.

I miss Mama and Pap. I miss my little brother, Dylan. I miss Miss Melman, Minnie, and Hallie. I miss Travis Lark. And of course, I miss you, Martha, but it sure is nice to have a cousin.

Love,
Teddy

Name_____ Date_____

Narrative Writing Prompt for the Letter of June 11, 1892
Read and answer the prompt below.

Narrative Prompt: Teddy and Daniel are learning that they both have something they can teach the other. We all have things to learn, and we all have things we know well that we can teach to others. Think of a time you helped teach something new to someone else. Now write the story of the time when you taught a skill to someone. Use specific details so that your reader can form a "mind movie" while reading.

_____

_____

_____

_____

_____

_____

_____

_____

_____

_____

_____

_____

_____

_____

_____

_____

_____

_____

_____

_____

June 12, 1892

Dear Martha,

I don't know when I'll get to mail your letters because I don't have any money, but I'm going to keep writing like I promised.

When the sun was sinking low in the sky, we decided we better find a place to camp. At the bend of the river, there was a little clearing on the shore with an orange grove and several oak trees.

I said, "This would be a great camp. We can eat oranges, and it will be easy to find firewood."

Daniel said, "You're right, but what else? Why is this a good place to camp? There's something important, something you can't ever forget. If you grew up in Florida you'd look for it, first off."

What was he talking about? I looked more carefully, squinching my eyes. "I don't know," I said.

He gave me a hint. "The shore is much higher than the river. Why is that important?"

The shore is much higher than the river. I snapped my fingers. "Alligators!"

Daniel said, "You're learning the outdoor ways, Teddy. Soon, you won't need me." He faked a heart swoon. "Your poor old cousin will be left to linger and die—all alone." I love his sense of humor.

I realized I never wanted to be left alone again, now that I'd found my cousin. I didn't want to be corny and say it out loud, but I thought, we are family. We need each other. We belong to each other. You know how boys hate that stuff. So I said, "Keep teaching me stuff. I want to know everything there is to know about living outdoors when I get back with Mama and Pap."

Daniel got quiet. He never says much when I mention getting back with Mama and Pap. It's strange. Does he think they won't accept him? Does he think I'm wrong and they're really dead?

Ethelbert jumped out of the boat and scrambled up the bank. He loves to run and jump and chase squirrels and act crazy when we stop. As usual, he went sniffing all around the orange grove, barking and snuffling and digging around in things.

Daniel said, "Why don't you get a fire going? I'll go get us some supper."

Right off, I looked around to make sure the ground was dry and smooth and didn't have any anthills. Then, I used a piece of wood to scrape out a site for our campfire. I gathered kindling, sticks, and some bigger pieces of wood. I got rocks from near the river and made a ring around our campfire. I laid out some matches Wanda had given us and started a fire.

The trees were loaded with ripe oranges. I picked an armful and brought them back to our camp. I found a big, flat rock, washed it in the river, and put it near the campfire. I used the flat rock as a table and cut the oranges in half with my pocketknife. The handle was worn from years of use, but the blade was sharp.

Daniel wasn't back yet, so I got out some fishing line, a hook, a sinker, and found some crickets for bait. By the time he got back with a fat rabbit, cleaned and ready to cook, I had caught three fish, cleaned them, and buried the entrails. He grinned. "The Bodains are eating high-on-the-hog tonight." He showed me how to find a long branch to hold over the fire to cook the rabbit and some for the fish. We ate our meal, "drank" our oranges, and I peeled off strips of rabbit and fish for Ethel, who was making a pest out of himself by whining for food. I was sorry I didn't have any of Wanda's hush puppies to give him! We laid out our feast, lapped up every little scrap, and licked our fingers.

We didn't have any blankets, so I spread out my pink dress to lay on and gave Daniel my pinafore.

I said, "It's not a blanket, but at least your face won't be in the dirt." We built up the fire to burn during the night to keep animals away. Daniel lay on his side of the fire, I lay on mine. Ethel curled up beside me. I thought how lucky I am. I have Daniel, and I have Ethelbert.

All is well, for now.

Love,
Teddy

Name_____   Date_____

Reading Short Response Questions for the Letter of June 12, 1892
Answer the questions below, and be sure to use complete sentences.

1. Explain what made Teddy and Daniel's campsite such a good place to spend the night.

_____

_____

_____

_____

2. What does Ethelbert like to do when Teddy and Daniel make camp for the night?

_____

_____

_____

_____

3. What did Teddy do with the big, flat rock she found?

_____

_____

_____

4. What did Teddy do back at camp while Daniel went to get them some supper?

_____

_____

_____

_____

June 13, 1892

Dear Martha,

Can you imagine what it's like to wake up, and your dog is GONE? Yep, that's what happened, alright. Ethelbert was nowhere to be seen. At first I thought he was just off snuffling in the orange grove. But he never came back, even when I called him. Ethel has never wandered off before. Daniel went immediately to the riverbank to look for alligator tracks, but there weren't any.

We called and called and searched the orange grove. By this time, I was beginning to panic. I said, "Daniel, I cannot continue without Ethel. I won't leave him."

Daniel said, "We're not going to leave him. He's a dog. He's probably off exploring or chasing squirrels." I got my slingshot from my bundle, and Daniel got his. He grinned.

We walked through the orange grove. Daniel cut a long, leafy branch and held it out in front of us, waving it to the left and then to the right. I said, "What on earth are you doing?"

He said, "I'm saving your life, Teddy Bodain. An orange grove is filled with the biggest spiders you've ever seen. They're called banana spiders. They won't kill you, but they'll scare you to death. At night, they build their webs from tree to tree. Without this branch, you might run right into one."

I shivered. You know how I hate spiders. From then on, I walked behind Daniel. Just to be sure, I picked up a few pebbles along the way. If I was going to be attacked by spiders, I wanted to be ready.

When we had walked almost to the end of the grove, we heard voices. They were coming from a clearing up ahead. Someone, a man, was talking.

He said, "Well, if this isn't my lucky day. They say the chickens come home to roost, but in my case, it's the dogs. Look what I found."

A dog whimpered. I knew that whimper! It was Ethelbert.

A woman's voice said, "Xavier, let him go."

By this time, Daniel and I were almost to the clearing. I saw the red and yellow wagon. Dr. Zoren was holding Ethelbert by the scruff of the neck. He said, "Get my cage."

Without warning, I burst out into the clearing, angrier than I'd ever been. I shouted, "Get your hands off my dog." Ethel twisted his neck, trying to get away.

Dr. Zoren said, "How dare you! Who are you to come into my camp using a demanding tone?"

He peered at me, as if trying to remember where he had seen me before.

I repeated, "Get your hands off my dog!"

Dr. Zoren said, "You are mistaken. This is my dog."

I said, "The constable gave him to me! He is MY dog."

Daniel grabbed Dr. Zoren's arm and said, "Mister, if you know what's good for you, you better give us this dog back." The next thing I knew, he was switching Dr. Zoren with the leafy branch. Dr. Zoren bent forward, trying to get away from the branch, but still holding on to Ethel's neck.

I reached for my slingshot and one of the pebbles. When Dr. Zoren bent over, I put a pebble in the sling, pulled it way back, and aimed for his behind.

Dr. Zoren screamed, "OWWWWW!!!!!" With one hand, he grabbed his rear. With the other, he tightened his grip on Ethel. Ethel squealed.

At that exact moment, the biggest banana spider you've EVER SEEN, jumped from the branch to Dr. Zoren's face. Martha, I have never heard anyone scream that loud while beating himself in the face with both hands. Ethelbert, Daniel, and I ran back to our campsite, doused our campfire with water, and jumped in the boat. Ethel sat in my lap, shaking. It wasn't until we were at least a mile away that Daniel and I started laughing.

A banana spider saved our sweet Ethelbert. What a day.

Love,
Teddy

Expository Writing Prompt for the Letter of June 13, 1892
Read and answer the following writing prompt.

Expository Prompt: In the letter, Teddy admits that she is afraid of spiders. Think of something that frightens you or might frighten you. Now explain what frightens you. Be sure to include what it is, why it frightens you, and the specific emotions you feel. You may include a mini-story of how this has frightened you in the past and how you got through your experience. But remember: your job is to *explain*. Include a beginning that introduces the topic, a middle that presents all the details, and an ending that tells the reader the most important thing you want him to remember.

_____

_____

_____

_____

_____

_____

_____

_____

_____

_____

_____

_____

_____

_____

_____

_____

_____

_____

_____

June 14, 1892

Dear Martha,

Finally, we came to Silver Springs, right on the river. We needed food and other things, but we didn't have a penny. We tied up Wanda's boat and tried to think. We needed money bad.

I said, "I know you've seen this bracelet that I wear every day, but I can't sell it."

He said, "Did your mama give it to you…or…your granny?"

I said, "No." For some reason, I didn't want to tell the story of Althea Tomlinson and her husband.

He said, "I wouldn't ask you to sell it. It's about the prettiest thing I've ever seen. What about the boat? Wanda said to use it however it would help us." We needed money. We needed food.

I said, "Try to get some money for the boat. I'll go look to see if we can find work."

We agreed to meet at noon, when the sun was straight overhead. The town seemed friendly enough. I walked to the feed store, the dry goods store, and the dentist. No one had any work. There was a cafe, and the smell of the sausage and chicken they were grilling out back made my stomach rumble.

But what I saw in the window of the cafe was worse than being hungry. There was a poster in the window with an artist's picture of a girl and a boy. The girl had braids and looked something like me. She was wearing a gingham dress. The boy had shaggy hair and looked a little like Pap when he was a boy. The poster said, "Two runaway children. Sought by their heartbroken parents. Please notify Jimbo and Verna Dudd in Micanopy."

I wanted to run and hide. I looked around for Jimbo Dudd. Was he here? Was he watching me? Would the sheriff recognize us and put us in jail until he could return us to Jimbo and Verna?

Daniel found me. He had a proud grin on his face and $15 in his hand.

He said, "Look what I got for the boat."

I said, "Great. Look what I found." I pointed to the poster.

He said, "Why do I get the feeling that poster has something to do with us?"

I remembered he couldn't read well. I read, "Two runaway children. Sought by their heartbroken parents. Please notify Jimbo and Verna Dudd in Micanopy."

Daniel said, "Uh-oh. Now, what?"

I said, "We can't think when we're this hungry. Let's get something to eat, and then we can come up with a plan. We'll have to spend carefully. This money will have to last."

We bought three big sausages at the cafe, one for each of us and one for Ethel. Ethel woofed his in three bites, then looked at me with begging eyes. The cook had a big ham bone and sold it to us for three cents, so Ethel settled down happily to eat his bone. Daniel and I each got an ear of corn to go with our sausages. My stomach growled noisily.

We felt much better after we had eaten. I said, "We've got $14.57 left. Let's go to the store and buy what we need to get us through another day or two. Then, we'll get out of town."

When we got to the store, Daniel pointed to a poster in the window. He said, "Looks like a circus. What does it say?"

I read aloud, "Ringling Brothers United Monster Shows, Great Double Circus, Royal European Menagerie Museum, Caravan, and Congress of Trained Animals. Here For Two Days. Now Hiring Boys. Must Be 12 or Older."

Must be 12 or older?

I looked at Daniel with my I've-got-an-idea look. I said, "Could I pass for 12?"

Daniel said, "You could pass for 12, but you couldn't pass for a boy."

I said, "Want to bet?"

Love,
Teddy

Reading Extended Response Questions for the Letter of June 14, 1892

Answer the questions below. Be sure to use complete sentences, reasons, and details.

1. As soon as Teddy and Daniel arrived in Silver Springs, they knew they needed to earn some money. How did they do this? Why was money so important to them?

_____

_____

_____

_____

_____

_____

_____

_____

_____

_____

2. When Teddy and Daniel went into the store, Daniel spotted a poster in the window. Why was this poster so significant to Teddy and Daniel? What will Teddy and Daniel do with the information they saw on the poster?

_____

_____

_____

_____

_____

_____

_____

_____

_____

June 15, 1892

Dear Martha,

At the general store, we bought cheese, pickles, hard-boiled eggs, apples, carrots, jerky, a bar of soap, two work shirts, a pair of overalls, underwear, a hat, a bandana, socks, a comb, and a bottle of black hair dye. Daniel said, "What is hair dye?"

I said, "You'll find out in a few minutes."

We had $5.22 left. I put it in the neck pouch. There was a bathhouse where you could pay to take a bath for ten cents. The woman in charge wasn't too friendly. I asked if she had some scissors I could borrow. She said, " I don't have any scissors you can borrow, but I have some scissors you can rent." She charged us another ten cents to rent the scissors, but we needed them, so we didn't have any choice.

Right away, I took Daniel out to the backyard. I said, "They're looking for a girl and a boy. You're going to cut my hair, so I'll look like a boy. Then, I'm going to cut your hair and dye it black, so you look like a different boy."

Daniel went crazy. "I don't know how to cut your hair. And you don't know how to cut my hair. And I ain't dyeing my hair black!" He glared at me.

I said, "Then, we'll have to split up. They're looking for a girl and a boy. There's a picture of us on the poster, remember? Who knows how many posters are up in this town and other towns. We could be picked up by the sheriff at any moment. Jimbo himself might be here. Verna, too."

Daniel said, "What style do you want?"

I sat on a wooden box and pulled it up close to the window, so I could see my reflection. I said, "There's nothing to it. Cut my braids off, and we'll even it up." Daniel cut my braids off in two seconds. I shook out the rest of my hair, and he cut it even across the bottom. I said, "We better go a little shorter." He cut more off. I looked at my reflection, turning this way and that. I parted my hair and combed it to the side. I said, "That does it."

Daniel sat on the box, so I could cut his hair. I'd seen Mama cut Pap's hair many'a time. The problem was, I couldn't get the comb through Daniel's hair. I said, "You're going to have to bathe first and shampoo your hair. It's in knots, and I can't get the comb through it." I handed him the soap, and he went off to bathe while I waited with Ethel. When he came back, he was all scrubbed and clean. I combed his wet hair and starting cutting.

I smiled. "Terrific. Look how good you look."

He looked at his reflection and felt the sides and bottom of his hair.

I said, "I read the directions for the hair dye while you were in the tub. Work this into your hair, wait ten minutes, and then wash it off. Oh, and be sure to scrub it off your hands as soon as you've finished working it into your hair, so it won't stain your hands."

Daniel practically shouted, "I have to take another bath?" The woman charged us another dime for Daniel's second bath. He came back about half an hour later. He looked like a totally different kid, one with short, black hair. This time he was wearing his new shirt and overalls.

He said, "Not bad, huh?"

I said, "Not bad. I wish Wanda could see you now."

He grinned. "I wish she could see YOU. You look like a boy, for true. And you don't even have to change your name 'cause Teddy is a boy's name." It was true. Wanda would have loved the adventure of it. I put the hat on my head. It felt strange not to feel braids hanging down.

I counted our money. "We have $4.82 left. That won't go far." I divided up our things and bundled them in our bandanas. Daniel cut two new sticks and tied a bandana to the end of each one.

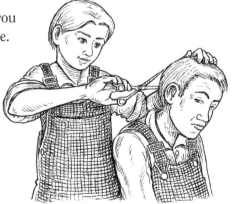

We slung the bundles over our shoulders and headed off for the circus.

Love,
Teddy

Grammar Questions for the Letter of June 15, 1892
Circle the letter of the correct answer.

1. In the following sentence, which word is incorrect?
   "I read the directions for the hair die while you were in the tub."
   A. were
   B. directions
   C. in
   D. die

2. Where do the quotation marks go in the following dialogue?
   A. I said, "You'll find out in a few minutes.
   B. I said, "You'll find out in a few minutes."
   C. I said, You'll find out in a few minutes."
   D. "I said, You'll find out in a few minutes."

3. In this sentence, the words *cheese, pickles, hard-boiled eggs,* and *apples* are examples of what?
   At the general store, we bought cheese, pickles, hard-boiled eggs, and apples.
   A. adverbs
   B. dialogue
   C. items in a series
   D. conclusions

4. Which sentence has the correct use of commas?
   A. "There's a picture of us on the poster, remember?"
   B. "There's a picture of us, on the poster, remember?"
   C. "There's a picture, of us on the poster, remember?"
   D. "There's a picture of us on the poster remember?"

5. Which of the following words is spelled incorrectly?
   A. dyeing
   B. underwear
   C. sissors
   D. reflection

6. Teddy writes, **"I shook out the rest of my hair, and he cut it even across the bottom."**
   What kind of sentence is this?
   A. a compound sentence
   B. a run-on sentence
   C. a descriptive sentence
   D. a transitional sentence

7. Which word is spelled correctly?
   A. adventer
   B. advenature
   C. advencher
   D. adventure

June 16, 1892

Dear Martha,

Daniel and I walked toward the edge of town, where they had set up the circus. We knew we were there when we saw an enormous, striped tent. It looked almost big enough to cover a small town! We heard music, loud clapping, and laughter coming from inside.

We walked around back to see if we could find where they were hiring folks. A man with a big straw hat saw the two of us standing there looking like we didn't know anything.

He shouted, "You two! Lend a hand with this ostrich!"

We jumped right over there and helped him load the gigantic bird into a cage. Martha, you won't believe it, but that bird was the size of a full-grown man. It was so big it looked like you could ride it. It had a fat, feathery body and a long, long neck. The bird's eyes made it look very intelligent, and they had long lashes above and below them.

When the ostrich was safely in its cage, the man with the straw hat wiped his brow with his red bandana handkerchief. He said, "Are you on the show?"

We said, "No."

He said, "You want jobs, don't you? Better see Pete over at the red wagon." He walked us over to Pete, who was counting money and smoking a cigar. Pete didn't look up from his work.

The man in the straw hat said, "Pete, I've got two First-of-Mays for you."

Pete said, "You boys got folks?"

I said, "It's just the two of us. We're cousins."

Pete said, "Cousins? Can cousins travel wherever we go?"

I said, "Yes. But I have a dog that's got to come with me."

Pete said, "A dog?"

I said, "Yes, sir."

Pete said, "Keep him away from the lion cages. A dollar a week, plus food. Take it or leave it."

Daniel said, "When do we start?"

Pete said, "Ten minutes ago. Elmer will show you the ropes."

Elmer turned out to be the guy in the straw hat. He said, "Boys, you'll be watering the animals. But be careful. The last two First-of-Mays got eaten by a lion."

I looked at Daniel. His eyes got big.

Elmer said, "That was a joke. You'll be responsible for bringing water to all the cages, morning and night. You eat after every animal has been watered. You sleep after every animal has been watered. Got it?"

I said, "What do we do in between?"

Elmer said, "You obviously haven't hauled water for circus animals. In between, you rest. Hungry? Come with me. I'll show you the chowhouse."

We followed him. Elmer said, "What are your names?"

Daniel said, "I'm Daniel, and this is Teddy."

I said, "And this is Ethelbert."

We passed a pretty woman with long, dark hair, practicing a balancing act on a jumbo-size rubber ball. Elmer said, "Sabrina, these are the new First-of-Mays, Teddy, Daniel, and Ethelbert."

Sabrina said, "Howdy, boys. Welcome to the show."

Howdy, boys? BOYS. I had passed as a boy. Jubilation!

Love,
Teddy

Writing Questions for the Letter of June 16, 1892

Circle the letter of the correct answer.

1. Read the following sentence from Teddy's letter today:
   We heard music, loud clapping, and laughter coming from inside.
   This sentence is an example of what type of good writing skill?
   A. persuasive writing
   B. descriptive writing
   C. transitional phrases
   D. similes

2. Read the following sentence from Teddy's letter today:
   "In between, you rest."
   The words *In between* are an example of what type of good writing skill?
   A. simile
   B. strong verb
   C. persuasive writing
   D. transitional phrase

3. Read the following sentence from Teddy's letter today:
   We passed a woman with long, dark hair, practicing a balancing act on a jumbo-size rubber ball.
   This sentence is an example of what type of good writing skill?
   A. persuasive writing
   B. transitional phrase
   C. details you can picture
   D. metaphors

4. Read the following sentence from Teddy's letter today:
   He shouted, "You two! Lend a hand with this ostrich!"
   These sentences are examples of what type of good writing skill?
   A. similes
   B. dialogue
   C. persuasive writing
   D. transitional phrases

5. Read the following sentence from Teddy's letter today:
   It had a fat, feathery body and a long, long neck.
   This sentence is an example of what type of good writing skill?
   A. simile
   B. metaphor
   C. strong verb
   D. details you can picture

June 26, 1892

Dear Martha,

Do you know how many buckets of water you have to haul to water all the animals in a circus? I haven't been able to write for a while. There just hasn't been time. I don't even know what town we're in. We pack up and move every night to a new town. Besides, my hands were too sore to do anything but pick up the next bucket of water. Every muscle in my body aches.

Our day starts at five o'clock in the morning. We go to the water wagon and start filling and hauling buckets. We go to each cage and fill the animals' water troughs with a funnel that sticks through the bars. When we first started hauling, we only had the wire handle on each bucket to hold onto. The second day, I found a rubber hose someone had thrown away. Daniel and I cut the hose into lengths, slit each piece with my pocketknife, and fit them over the wire handles. Our "handles" make the buckets much easier to carry.

Elmer said, "You boys know how to use your noggins."

The animals that need the most water are the elephants. They drink so much they have their own water wagon. That means we don't have to haul it as far, but we have to haul a lot of it. The elephants are all girls, even though they're referred to as "bulls." Elmer said the circus doesn't keep male elephants because they're too dangerous. The elephant trainers are Suzanna and Massimo, and they are from Italy. Suzanna wears elegant costumes and rides on the elephants' backs.

She said, "You two are certainly better than the last water boys. They tried to give my girls dirty water, and they were always late. And I have seen you rub their trunks and bring them extra fruits."

Four days ago, Daniel and I were watching Massimo train Linda and Donibelle, two Indian elephant babies. Suzanna said, "If you boys want to earn a little 'cherry pie,' you could start helping me get the elephants' costumes on for the matinee in the afternoons."

I said, "Cherry pie? I love cherry pie."

Suzanna laughed at me. "In the circus, 'cherry pie' means extra pay for extra work."

So now, we help her and Massimo put the headpieces on the elephants and fasten them each day. You can't imagine how smart these animals are.

Massimo says, "Left up!" and they pick up their left feet. Massimo says, "Around the world!" and they spin around in a circle. Massimo says, "Line grip!" and they line up and grab each other's tail with their trunks. The first elephant in the line is always the matriarch, Babbette. The others line up behind her, from tallest to smallest, all the way down the line to Linda and Donibelle, the baby elephants. When the audience sees the little ones, they clap harder and laugh at how cute they are.

We eat in the chowhouse. Daniel and I are always the last to eat. The food is good, and they want the workers to eat plenty, so we can work hard. We each sleep in a "possum belly," a storage shelf under the wagons. We go to sleep to the smells and snorts and trumpets and growls of animals. The lions roar all night, but the loudest animal of all is the peacock. Have you ever heard a peacock's cry? It gives me the willies, as Jasper Lowe might say.

The circus performers keep to themselves and don't mix with the work crew.

Elmer said, "It's unusual for Suzanna and Massimo to even associate with the likes of you two."

The performers who work the midway have their own group, too, and they're friendlier with the work crew. I met a man whose entire body is covered in hair—including his face! I met a fire eater, a sword swallower, a woman whose neck is ten inches long, covered in brass coils, and Lena, the alligator woman.

Love,
Teddy

Name_____ Date_____

Persuasive Writing Prompt for the Letter of June 26, 1892
Read and answer the following prompt.

Persuasive Prompt: Teddy and Daniel are busy hauling water at the circus. When Massimo, the elephant trainer, says, **"Left up,"** the elephant picks up its left foot. When he says, **"Around the world,"** the elephant spins in a circle. Pretend you are the world's best animal trainer. Give yourself a fabulous trainer's name, and think of a specific animal you have trained. Now write an advertising flyer that would convince people to come watch your show. Give us enough details of what you and your animal can do so that we want to buy a ticket to your big performance.

_____

_____

_____

_____

_____

_____

_____

_____

_____

_____

_____

_____

_____

_____

_____

_____

_____

_____

_____

June 27, 1892

Dear Martha,

Yesterday afternoon, Suzanna and Massimo were training the elephants. Suzanna said, "Teddy, Daniel, would you like to ride an elephant in the Spec?" We were astonished. The Spec is the grand entrance into the Big Top at the start of the circus. She said, "You'll have to practice with the girls. They seem to like you. The Ringlings like for our entrance to be a big production. I think it would add flair."

Massimo called Saba for me. He said, "Saba, trunk down!" Saba knelt down and curled her trunk around to the side. Massimo said, "Step on. Don't be afraid. She'll do the work. You just hold on." I stepped on Saba's trunk and held on. She raised me up. Massimo said, "Now, climb up on her neck, nice and easy." And just like that, I was up on her neck. It's the highest I've ever been, except for the balloon ride.

Massimo led Saba around, so she could get used to me, and I could get used to her. After a while, he said, "Now, Teddy, you do it alone. The elephants have done the Spec hundreds of times, so all you have to do is sit up there and look like you know what you're doing." I rode Saba around the empty ring until I felt comfortable. Massimo seemed impressed. "I think you've got it."

Suzanna said, "Hold on to her headdress with one hand, Teddy. Use your other hand to wave to the crowd." Soon, Daniel was doing the same thing on Denise, a pretty elephant with long eyelashes. The two of us couldn't quit smiling. I almost had to pinch myself to see if I was dreaming. What would Mama think?

Suzanna took us to Marie, the costumer. "Do you have something these boys could wear? They're going to ride Saba and Denise in the Spec." Marie found two costumes that looked somewhat near our sizes. She pinned the places that were too big, so she could sew them. The shirts are made of shiny blue material with spangles and sequins sewn across the front. The black trousers are full and gathered at our ankles. She gave us each a pair of pointy shoes with tassels on the toes and bright red satin turbans. Daniel and I looked at ourselves in Marie's full-length looking glass.

Suzanna clapped her hands and said, "They look so handsome."

Daniel said, "How in the world did we go from living in the woods to this?"

When she left, Marie said, "Handsome—and pretty." She looked at me. "I've been a costumer for thirty years. If you're a boy, I'll eat my hat."

I felt like someone punched me in the stomach. If Marie turned me in, we'd have to leave the circus. I said, "I have to look like a boy. I have to."

Marie said, "I think you'll fool everyone else. But honey, I do this for a living." She gave me a look. "Relax. I know everyone's secrets around here, and I know how to keep my mouth shut."

Tomorrow is our first performance. We will do two shows each day, a matinee and the "big show," which means the evening show. In between, ticket holders visit the midway, buy food, play games, and walk by the animal wagons. The minute we finish the big show, we start packing up to move to the next town.

Another good thing happened that we weren't expecting.

Three more boys joined as First-of-Mays, so Suzanna arranged for Daniel and me to work only with the elephants from now on.

She said, "No more carrying water for the other animals: only our girls. You'll cut up their fruit and vegetables, and help Massimo bring their hay. Afterward, you'll have to take a bath by one o' clock and change into your costumes." I couldn't believe our good luck!

Daniel whispered, "A bath every day? Are you kidding?"

Massimo said, "From now on, you'll be considered performers. Beginning performers—performers who are still working for their keep—but you won't be with the work crew. You'll bunk in the costume wagon instead of the possum's belly. Three dollars a week?"

Great buckets of butterbeans. We are performers!

Love,
Teddy

Reading Multiple Choice Questions for the Letter of June 27, 1892
Circle the letter of the correct answer.

1. What is the name of the elephant that Teddy rode?
    A. Denise
    B. Linda
    C. Saba
    D. Donibelle

2. While Teddy was riding on the elephant's neck, what did she hold onto, so she wouldn't fall?
    A. the elephant's headdress
    B. a rope that was tied around the elephant's head
    C. a muzzle that was in the elephant's mouth
    D. the elephant's trunk

3. At the circus, who was the first to figure out that Teddy is really a girl?
    A. Suzanna
    B. Marie, the costumer
    C. Massimo
    D. Charles Ringling

4. Now that they are performers, how much money will Teddy and Daniel be making per week?
    A. 1 dollar each per week
    B. 2 dollars each per week
    C. 50 cents each per week
    D. 3 dollars each per week

5. How often do Teddy and Daniel have to take a bath now that they are performers?
    A. every day
    B. every other day
    C. once a week
    D. once a month

6. Where will Teddy and Daniel sleep, now that they are performers?
    A. in the horse barn
    B. with the elephants
    C. outside the Big Top
    D. in the costume wagon

7. What is the **"Spec"**?
    A. the grand entrance into the Big Top
    B. a tiny little rock stepped on by an elephant
    C. a pair of glasses used by a clown
    D. the man who collects the ticket money

June 28, 1892

Dear Martha,

Why does trouble always come?

Today was the big day Daniel and I were starting as performers. Just before two o' clock, Massimo led the elephants down the midway to the ring doors, the canvas curtains that lead to the Big Top. Daniel rode Denise, and I rode Saba. The band played "Entrance of the Gladiators."

Everything went swell with the elephants. My face beamed and I grinned from ear to ear when I entered the ring on Saba's back. Massimo led the way, followed by Babbette, with Suzanna on her back. As I rode past the crowd, I smiled and waved to all the little kids.

As we went around the ring for the second time, to give folks their money's worth, a kid threw an apple at one of the elephants. The ringmaster said, "Son, don't do that!" and I looked to see who had done it. It was Verna Dudd's boy, Georgie! There sat Jimbo, Verna, and the rest of the family.

Massimo gave the signal for the elephants to stop. Saba stopped right in front of Jimbo and Verna! My heart felt like one of the clowns was pounding on it with his bigger-than-life hammer.

Massimo called, "Company, down!" The elephants knelt, and that was my signal to stand up and wave. The crowd clapped like they'd seen something glorious. Jimbo and Verna were staring right at me, but they didn't seem to recognize me. I had to force myself not to jump off Saba's back and run away. All I could do was act like I was a performer who had been doing this all my life.

As Daniel and I stood on our elephants' backs, the ringmaster called, "Massimo and Suzanna and the amazing Tornecki Brothers!" Who? No one had told us that we were now the "Tornecki Brothers."

We rode the elephants back out of the ring, so Suzanna could perform her tricks with Babbette.

As soon as Daniel and I were alone, I said, "We've got trouble. Jimbo is here. Jimbo Dudd."

Daniel said, "Jimbo Dudd? Are you sure?"

I said, "You know the kid that threw the apple at Mindy? That was Georgie."

All the color drained out of Daniel's face. He said, "Did he recognize you?"

I said, "I don't think so. I don't know for sure, though."

Between the shows, Marie came to see us. She waited until Suzanna and Massimo weren't around. She said, "I thought you'd want to know. Someone's snooping around, asking questions out on the midway. They're looking for two runaways, a boy and a girl."

I sank right down to my feet and sat there with my head in my hands. I said, "They can't find us. He's trying to steal my pap's land. They want to put us in an orphanage."

Marie said, "I don't think they'll get any information here. Circus folks don't talk to townies. I just came to warn you."

Daniel said, "We'll run away again if we have to, Teddy."

The thought of running away again filled me with sadness. Today, I had ridden an elephant. Today, I had been a circus performer.

Suddenly, we heard a commotion. We looked out at the midway. One of the monkeys had escaped from its cage. It jumped from wagon to wagon, then leaped to the top of the lemonade stand. A crowd had gathered to see the naughty monkey run from his keeper. The monkey leaped on a dog's back and tried to ride him like a horse. This made everyone laugh so hard that some were almost falling down.

Jimbo, Verna, and the kids were in the crowd. Georgie threw peanuts at the dog. Then, he pulled on Jimbo's arm and whispered something in his ear.

Daniel pointed. The dog was Ethelbert.

Love,
Teddy

Name_____ Date_____

Narrative Writing Prompt for the Letter of June 28, 1892
Read and answer the prompt below.

Narrative Prompt: Teddy and Daniel are performers in the circus. Think of a time you were in a performance. This could be something real, drawn from your own life, or an imaginary performance you wish you could have. Now write the story about the time you performed. Use all your creativity skills and your vivid imagination. Describe as many of the details as you can, so we can imagine just what it was like.

_____

_____

_____

_____

_____

_____

_____

_____

_____

_____

_____

_____

_____

_____

_____

_____

_____

_____

_____

_____

June 29, 1892

Dear Martha,

Daniel and I had remembered to disguise ourselves, but we had forgotten that someone might recognize Ethelbert. Oh, Martha! Why didn't we think of that?

Thank goodness the circus was leaving town that evening. Daniel and I fed Ethel and hid him in the costume wagon. We finished the second show, changed into our work clothes, and tried to stay out of sight as we helped Massimo and Suzanna get the elephants back in their wagons and ready to roll.

Just before we left, I heard a familiar voice coming from the other side of Saba's cage. It was Jimbo Dudd! He was talking to Massimo in an ugly tone. I crouched down out of sight.

Jimbo said, "They think I'm too dumb to follow their tracks, but they can't fool old Jimbo Dudd. I saw their writing on the riverbank. There's two of them, a boy and a girl. She took off with something that belongs to me." Listening to Jimbo's lies made my heart ache. Liar, liar, pants on fire!

Jimbo said, "I know they're here. My boy saw their mangy dog."

Massimo said, "Please leave this area immediately. My elephants don't like strangers, especially men. My wife has told you that we haven't seen the persons you speak of. There are only ourselves here and our nephews, the Tornecki Brothers."

Jimbo wouldn't leave. "What are their names?"

Massimo said, "Their names are none of your business. But since you persist in being rude, their names are Vincelli and Gordamo. Now, if I have to ask you to leave again, I'll have you thrown out."

Jimbo said, "It's a free country. I'll leave when I'm good and ready."

All this time, Saba had been drinking water, sucking it up in her trunk and squirting it into her mouth. Now, she raised her trunk and blew a blast of water at Jimbo Dudd. His face turned a deep, angry red, and he left in a huff, dripping water and cursing.

Massimo looked at Saba and laughed. He said, "You are a smart girl, Saba! You are the smartest girl."

I was shaking from fear, but I couldn't wait to tell Daniel what Saba had done to Jimbo.

Massimo turned the corner and almost ran into me. He looked at me with his kind eyes.

I said, "It's not true, you know. He's trying to steal something from me that belongs to my pap."

Massimo said, "Teddy, I know you are a good kid."

I said, "How do you know, Massimo?"

He said, "The elephants told me." I looked puzzled.

He said, "Elephants have a sixth sense. They only trust people who are trustworthy."

I said, "Can I stay? Can Daniel stay?"

He said, "No, I am sorry. There is no job for Teddy and Daniel here."

My heart skipped a beat.

Massimo said. "Their jobs have been taken over by Vincelli and Gordamo, the Tornecki Brothers."

In my relief, I threw my right hand in the air like a salute to the crowd.

I shouted, "Non te la prendere!" an expression Suzanna and Massimo use all the time.

He smiled and said, "Sta facendo il pappagallo!"

Five minutes later, we were on the roll. Every mile took us farther away from Jimbo Dudd.

Love,
Teddy

Reading Short Response Questions for the Letter of June 29, 1892
Answer the questions below, and be sure to use complete sentences.

1. What happened to cause Teddy's heart to ache?

_____

_____

_____

_____

2. Describe what Saba did that made Jimbo Dudd finally leave.

_____

_____

_____

_____

3. Massimo told Jimbo Dudd that his nephews, the Tornecki Brothers, were with him. Why did Massimo say this? Who are the Tornecki Brothers?

_____

_____

_____

_____

4. Massimo said, **"Teddy, I know you are a good kid."** Explain how he knew this about her.

_____

_____

_____

_____

_____

June 30, 1892

Dear Martha,

The circus is headed to Jacksonville. We are going there for the Fourth of July celebration. Every day, we stop in little towns along the way to set up the Big Top. As we come to a town, the workers set up the tent using some of the elephants to help pull up the big poles that hold up the tent. The poles are actually ship masts, so they are tall and extremely strong.

While the workers are setting up, the performers parade through the town with the animal wagons, the clowns, and the elephants. Daniel and I are getting good at riding Denise and Saba in the parades. The ringmaster leads the way, and we invite all the onlookers to come to the circus that afternoon. When I am on Saba's back, I am at least ten feet up in the air, so I can see everything happening below.

We are getting to know the circus, which is quite fascinating. The clowns have their own society. They work and practice and eat together, along with their trained dogs. They have many props, like their highchair, their giant baby bottle, their fake mirror, and the huge bed they all pile into at the end of their act.

The acrobats start their daily practice every morning as soon as the Big Top is set up. They make sure their ropes and trapezes are all safe. Then, they dust their hands with powdered rosin to make sure they can grip without slipping. They leap off the platform, swing out, flip, and catch each other by the ankles.

The animal trainers have their own areas to set up and practice with their animals. The elephants always have their own place, apart from the other animals. I guess elephants are so big they make other animals nervous. Suzanna and Massimo have been with the Ringling Brothers Circus a long time, so they are very important to the circus. Sometimes, Massimo has to demand things, like fresh water and better fruits and vegetables to help the elephants. He is also very careful about who can come close to the elephants.

He warned, "No one goes near the elephants except for the four of us. Do you understand?"

We passed another spring the other day. This one was shallow and clear and bright, bright blue. We didn't have a show the next day, so we stopped the wagons to allow the elephants to take a bath. It was a sight I will have to draw in my sketchbook!

Massimo led Babbette, and she led the other elephants down to the spring. She looked at the water, turning her head this way and that, and then stepped in. It was an extra hot day, and I know the elephants were miserable in the heat. When Babbette felt the cool water, she trumpeted loud and long, calling the other elephants to join her. Soon, they were in the water, rolling and blowing and snorting.

Massimo gave me and Daniel some long brushes with wooden handles. He spoke to Babbette, and she rolled over on her side. She was so big that half of her was sticking up out of the water. The three of us crawled up on her side and scrubbed her with the brushes. She loved it! After a while, Massimo told us to get down, and he gave another command. Babbette rolled over on her other side, and then looked at Daniel and me as if to say, "Well, get busy scrubbing this side!" We spent several hours scrubbing elephants. Their bodies are immense! Titanic! Colossal! Gargantuan!

While they were in the water, Suzanna asked some of the workers to shovel out their cages and wash them down with buckets of fresh water. They formed a bucket brigade. About 40 men lined up from the springs to the elephant wagons. They passed the full buckets from man to man until they reached the wagons. The last three men splashed the buckets of water into the wagons, washing them down.

Suzanna called, "Thanks, guys. Next time you get paid, expect some cherry pie!" They cheered. Circus men love BOTH kinds of cherry pie!

Daniel and I are glad to be somewhere where we feel like part of a big family.

Love,
Teddy

Expository Writing Prompt for the Letter of June 30, 1892
Read and answer the following writing prompt.

Expository Prompt: The circus is headed to Jacksonville for the Fourth of July holiday. Think of a holiday or special day that is your favorite. Now write an expository piece, and explain all about your favorite day. Be sure to introduce the topic in the beginning. In the middle, include all the details and descriptions you can think of. Help us picture the many things that happen on your special day. Include foods, family customs, ways you celebrate, and who you celebrate with. When you come to the ending, include the most important thought you want the reader to remember.

_____

_____

_____

_____

_____

_____

_____

_____

_____

_____

_____

_____

_____

_____

_____

_____

_____

_____

_____

July 1, 1892

Dear Martha,

Today, our wagons were traveling through the pine forests. It reminded me of when our wagon train had passed through the pine forests of Alabama, and that made me miss Mama and Pap and how our life had been. I was riding up front with Massimo. We rode without talking, most of the time.

Suddenly, Massimo said, "Look at the trees." He pointed with his chin. All the pine trees had little buckets hanging on them. Someone had made cuts in the trees—cuts that looked like a big V in the bark.

Massimo said, "They are making turpentine. Smell it?"

He was right. Soon, I began to smell the aroma of turpentine. You know, the clear liquid you soak your paintbrush in when you're painting the house or painting your fence? Massimo said they use it when they build ships, too. Something about making them waterproof. Anyhow, turpentine smells peculiar.

The road opened to a camp in the woods. Rows and rows of tiny houses, all identical, lined the way. Children were running around playing EVERYWHERE. When they saw us, they stopped and stared like they were seeing the most astonishing thing they had ever seen. I'm sure they were. It's not every day a circus drives through the woods. The funny thing was, one second kids were laughing and shouting to each other, and the next second, they were completely silent. They stared with wide eyes as we drove by.

Most of the women's hair was bound up in bandanas or turbans. Their feet were bare. Many of them carried two, or even three, babies on their hips. They were as curious as the children.

The turpentine camp was just past the cabins. There was a company store, a big turpentine still, and sweating, muscled men working. When they saw our wagons, they came running, shouting questions:

"Did that lion come from Africa?"

"What do your elephants eat?"

"Could that tiger eat me? I bet he could!"

"Mister, is that a monkey?"

I asked Massimo about the workmen.

"Distilling turpentine is how they make their living. It's dangerous, hard work. Did you see that store back there?" He pointed over his shoulder. "Well, that's a company store. They let you buy on credit, then they let you buy a little more. Soon, you 'owe your soul to the company store,' as the saying goes. You can't leave or quit work because you still owe the boss man."

We rolled on past the workers, past the still, through the forest. As we were jostling along, glad to be in the shade of the pines, a wagon full of people was headed in our direction. Now, this wasn't just a wagon. This was at least ten times bigger than any wagon I've ever seen, including a circus wagon. It was filled with people, at least 40 men, women, and children. They looked poor and weary and hungry. When they saw us, the driver pulled over off the road, so we could pass. They looked like they had traveled a great distance and were headed to the turpentine camp.

When Suzanna saw them, she said something in Italian to Massimo. They stopped our wagons and pulled over. Massimo and Suzanna brought out washtubs full of fresh, sweet oranges.

I knew they were meant for the elephants' treats, but Suzanna said, "Daniel, Teddy, please help us give these folks something to eat." We gave out oranges to the folks in the wagon.

A man said, "These folks have given us oranges. See, children? Bite a hole in the skin, and then you can work the peel off with your fingers. This is fine eating. Thank you, kindly."

After the oranges were gone, we drove on to join up with our own caravan of wagons.

Love,
Teddy

Name_____ Date _____

Reading Extended Response Questions for the Letter of July 1, 1892
Answer the questions below. Be sure to use complete sentences, reasons, and details.

1. As the wagon came to a camp in the woods, children were everywhere. How did the children feel when they saw Massimo, Suzanna, Teddy, and Daniel? Why did they feel this way?

_____

_____

_____

_____

_____

_____

_____

_____

2. While traveling, Teddy, Daniel, Massimo, and Suzanna came upon another wagon with many people inside. Describe how the people on this wagon looked? Why did they look this way?

_____

_____

_____

_____

_____

_____

_____

_____

July 2, 1892

Dear Martha,

Today is our last day of driving to Jacksonville.

Daniel and I watered all of the elephants early this morning. We drew extra buckets of water, too. Then, we cut up their fruit and vegetables and brought in fresh hay. By eight o'clock, we were finished and could eat breakfast, but no matter how hard we try, we're always the last to eat. Circus folks get up before the crack of dawn! Of course, when we're cutting ripe watermelon for the elephants, we might snitch a few pieces for ourselves. I'll never tell! Ha ha!

Daniel and I rode together all day on the platform right behind Babbette's wagon. It looked like a good place to work, and Daniel wanted to get back to his reading and writing. I wanted to get caught up in my sketchbook. We gave Babbette a handful of ripe bananas, so she would know we meant her no harm. I had to ask Massimo's permission for us to sit there. Elephants are funny about their territory.

We sat on the platform with our backs next to the door of Babbette's cage. Ethel lay down beside me and put his head in my lap. Daniel and I reviewed the letters of his name, the sounds he has learned, and some of the basics about reading and writing. While Daniel practiced, I flipped through the pages of my sketchbook. I hadn't looked at it in weeks! It was like taking a journey back to the beginning of our trip.

Could I be the same kid who left Mississippi this past February? So much has happened. So much has changed. I looked at the sketch I had made of the white heron. It seemed like I had drawn it 100 years ago. And the burlap sack "troll" we shot at with our slingshots. And the scarlet king snake. And the dancing at the whoop-de-doo. And Jeb and January. So many memories, happy and sad…I don't even feel like the same girl.

Of course, I'm not the same girl. I'm now a boy, Teddy Bodain, traveling with my cousin Daniel, who I didn't even know existed before I got to Micanopy and found him. For about the millionth time, I wondered how it would all turn out. Where in the world are Mama and Pap? Will we ever get to our land?

The part about the land is a puzzlement. Pap doesn't work for Mr. Albritton anymore. Junie Loquat's father took over Pap's job when we left. So we can't go back to Mississippi. I don't even know how Mr. Albritton is going to pay Mr. Loquat because he couldn't pay Pap. But what will Pap do if he tries to claim the land and doesn't have the deed? Did I do the wrong thing to take the deed with me? Should I have left it in the wagon? Is Pap somewhere wishing he had the land deed?

Thinking about all of that gave me a stomachache and a headache at the same time. When I turned the page and saw the sketch of Dylan, I had to put my fist to my mouth to keep from crying. I wondered, what will happen to me now? Who else will I lose?

Martha, I couldn't help it. The tears came, and I couldn't stop them. I was embarrassed in front of Daniel. When I tried to cry quietly, I ended up crying louder. I felt stupid and miserable and ashamed.

Daniel said, "It's okay, Teddy. I won't tell anyone. Just tell me. What is it? What's wrong?"

I didn't even know why I was crying. My answer came out so dumb.

I said, "What if there isn't a redbird, Daniel? What if there isn't a redbird to guide us?"

Daniel didn't say anything. Instead he wrote something on his paper and slid it over to me.

He wrote, "Dont wury, Teddy. We will gide eech other."

I dried my tears. Daniel can read and write some, and I taught him how! He still needs help in spelling, but that's what I'm here for. Jumping jubilation!

Today was a good day after all.

Love,
Teddy

Grammar Questions for the Letter of July 2, 1892
Circle the letter of the correct answer.

1. Which of the following words is the subject of this sentence?
   Today is our last day of driving to Jacksonville.
   A. Jacksonville
   B. Today
   C. day
   D. driving

2. Which of the following sentences has the correct use of commas?
   A. The tears came and I couldn't stop them.
   B. The tears came and, I couldn't stop them.
   C. The tears came and I, couldn't stop them.
   D. The tears came, and I couldn't stop them.

3. In the following sentence,
   We gave Babbette a handful of ripe bananas,
   which of the following describes the word *ripe*?
   A. noun
   B. verb
   C. adjective
   D. adverb

4. What punctuation should go at the end of this sentence?
   Are they looking for me and Ethel
   A. a period
   B. a question mark
   C. an exclamation point
   D. a quotation mark

5. Find the verb and its helper in the following sentence.
   We were cutting ripe watermelon for the elephants.
   A. were cutting
   B. ripe watermelon
   C. for the elephants
   D. We were

6. What is missing in the following?
   Daniel and I watered all of the elephants early this morning We drew extra buckets of water, too.
   A. Nothing is missing.
   B. There should be a comma between the word "morning" and the word "We."
   C. There should be a period between the word "morning" and the word "We."
   D. The word "We" should not be capitalized

July 3, 1892

Dear Martha,

We are in Jacksonville. Tomorrow is the Fourth of July. We are here for all of the festivities.

Massimo and Suzanna wanted to be sure the "girls" look their best tomorrow. We scrubbed each elephant, filed her toenails and painted them with lard, and mended their costumes if they needed it.

Suzanna said, "Boys, time for haircuts. I don't want you to look shabby during the parade."

I remembered Daniel's hair dye. It was time to re-do it, or all the black part would be cut off.

I said, "Um, Suzanna. We might have a problem with Daniel's hair."

She said, "Just tell Angelo to dye it black again after he cuts it."

I said, "How long have you known it was dyed?"

Suzanna said, "I'm an Italian. You can't fool an Italian."

Angelo did a good job dyeing Daniel's hair black again and gave us both hair cuts. This time I really look like a boy. I ran my hand through my hair, looking at it from side to side.

Suzanna said, "And don't think you've got me fooled about you being a boy, either."

I said, "Did Marie tell you?"

She said, "She didn't have to. I already told you—you can't fool an Italian."

We wiped down all of the cages, polished the metal trim on the elephants' costumes, and brushed up the plumes on their headdresses.

This afternoon, Daniel and I went to hear John Phillip Sousa's Marching Band. They are here for the big parade tomorrow morning for the Fourth of July, and they are practicing right next to us on the fairgrounds. Daniel and Ethelbert and I sat on the grass and listened to them tune. I've never seen so many different kinds of instruments. There were tiny little silver piccolos, giant tubas and timpani, xylophones, trumpets, trombones, flutes, and every kind of drum you could imagine.

The sound of all the instruments tuning filled us with excitement. I've heard the circus band tune up before, but it was nothing like this!

John Phillip Sousa took the field. All of the instruments came to attention. Wow! He is handsome! He wore a uniform even to practice in. When he raised his hands to direct, all of the musicians raised their instruments. When his hand with the big baton came down, they played!

Tom Harrison, from our circus band, came to sit with us. He called out the names of the marches as they played them: "The Gladiator March," "Semper Fidelis," "The Washington Post," "The Thunderer," "The Liberty Bell," and a new march called "The Beau Ideal." They must call them "marches" because when you hear them, the music is so stirring and patriotic that you feel like marching, yourself.

Afterward, Daniel and I volunteered to help them pack up their chairs and instruments. The drum band still had their drums out. Some of the men said, "Would you boys like to learn how to play the bass drum?" We thought it was for real, but they were just playing a trick. Once we got strapped to the big drum, it was a lot bigger than we were, way too big for us to march and play. We laughed about it and were good sports, so they let us play a little while they stood the drums on the ground.

While we were playing around, guess who came over to speak to us?

John Phillip Sousa.

I was flabbergasted.

He said, "Boys, I need good musicians, not just now, but in the future. Here's a silver dollar for each of you. Remember me when you get good enough to join a marching band."

Great buckets of butterbeans! Only in my life could you scrub elephant cages in the morning, and in the afternoon, meet the most famous musician in the world.

Love,
Teddy

Name_____ Date _____

Writing Questions for the Letter of July 3, 1892
Circle the letter of the correct answer.

1. Read the following sentence from Teddy's letter today:
   Only in my life could you scrub elephant cages in the morning, and in the afternoon, meet the most famous musician in the world.
   This sentence is an example of what type of good writing skill?
   A. takeaway ending
   B. similes
   C. metaphors
   D. transitional words

2. If the author had decided to include the words **"Rat-a-tat-tat-tat"** or **"Boom, boom, boom"** when she described the drums, she would have been using what kind of good writing skill?
   A. strong verb
   B. onomatopoeia
   C. metaphors
   D. similes

3. Read the following sentences from Teddy's letter today:
   John Phillip Sousa took the field. All of the instruments came to attention. Wow! He is handsome!
   These sentences are examples of what very important writing skill?
   A. sentence variety
   B. onomatopoeia
   C. persuasive writing
   D. transitional phrases

4. Read the following sentence from Teddy's letter today:
   I was flabbergasted.
   This sentence is an example of what very important writing skill?
   A. sentence variety
   B. voice
   C. simile
   D. transitional word

5. Read the following sentence from Teddy's letter today:
   The sound of all the instruments tuning filled us with excitement.
   The words *filled us with excitement* are examples of what writing skill?
   A. onomatopoeia
   B. transitional words
   C. specific emotion words
   D. sentence variety

July 4, 1892

Dear Martha,

I don't know if there has ever been a Fourth of July like this one. Not for me, at least.

Jacksonville is filled with people: people who came to see the circus, people who came to see the fireworks display, and people who came to hear John Phillip Sousa and his world-famous band.

This morning was the big Fourth of July parade for the city of Jacksonville. Along with everyone else, our circus and the Sousa marching band marched. Sousa's band was right in front of us, then came the ringmaster, the clowns, all the acrobats, all the animals in cages, and finally, our elephants.

Suzanna led the way, perched on top of Babbette, followed by the rest of the elephants. Daniel and I rode on Denise and Saba, holding on to their collars with one hand and waving to the people with the other. Massimo walked behind us with the babies, Linda and Donibelle. Massimo said he overheard Pete talking with Carl Ringling, and they estimate there were 10,000 people lining the streets of Jacksonville to see us. All I know is, I've never seen so many faces laughing and smiling and pointing.

Right after the parade, they opened the midway, so folks could buy their lunches. They hired extra staff to help with the workload while we are here in Jacksonville. They were up all night making candy apples, caramel corn, popcorn, fudge, corn on the cob, hot dogs, and wagon loads of lemonade.

After folks got their lunches, we started our first matinee performance. Today is a "three-fer," meaning there were so many people, we gave three performances. The performances are each a little shorter than they would normally be, but that's so we can get all the folks in to see the circus.

This evening when we finished, the sun was still shining. Carl Ringling invited all performers to join in a special celebration on the beach. The beach! I have looked forward to seeing the beach since we arrived in Florida. Right near the beach, there was a railroad track set up with a steam engine and a few cars hooked behind it. The mayor of Jacksonville and some officials were standing on a platform next to the train tracks.

The mayor spoke with a megaphone. "Our friend, Henry Morrison Flagler, has already opened up Florida with the railroad. Today, folks can travel from Jacksonville to Daytona Beach. I am happy to announce to you that he is starting a new phase of work on the tracks, and soon we'll be able to travel from Jacksonville to Miami by railroad car!"

The cheering almost drowned out the beginning of John Phillip Sousa's Marching Band. Almost. They started up on a brand new Sousa march called "Manhattan Beach March."

As the song began to play, fireworks exploded into the sky. I had never seen fireworks before, and when they first went off, I was astonished—even frightened. They looked like explosions from an invading army, but they were beautiful. They lit up the night sky, trailing lights in disappearing colors. One after the other, they burst out colors and shapes and sparkles that were almost beyond my imagination.

Sousa's marching band played and played while the fireworks exploded in the sky overhead.

Daniel and Ethel and I sat on the sand, eating hot dogs and drinking root beer. When the band finally started playing "The Star Spangled Banner," everyone began singing. Daniel and I stood to our feet and sang, too, even though we had to struggle with the words.

> *And the rockets red glare. The bombs bursting in air,*
> *Gave proof through the night, that our flag was still there.*
> *Oh, say does that star-spangled banner yet wave*
> *O'er the land of the free and the home of the brave.*

Oh, Martha! I have so much to tell Mama.

Love,
Teddy

Persuasive Writing Prompt for the Letter of July 4,1892
Read and answer the following prompt.

Persuasive Prompt: Teddy and Daniel are in a parade in Jacksonville on the Fourth of July. In the parade, John Phillip Sousa's Marching Band, the ringmaster, the clowns, the acrobats, and all the animals marched. In your opinion, which job in a parade would be the hardest? John Phillip Sousa has to keep all the players in time. The ringmaster has to keep all the circus performers in place. The clowns are able to do just about anything, as long as they keep the crowd laughing. The animal keepers have to keep their animals happy and safe from the crowds. Think of the duties each person needs to accomplish his job while walking in the parade. Persuade the reader which job would be the hardest. Give many convincing, detailed reasons to support your opinion. Use your imagination.

_____

_____

_____

_____

_____

_____

_____

_____

_____

_____

_____

_____

_____

_____

_____

_____

_____

_____

July 5, 1892

Dear Martha,

Today was a free day. After we got our work done, we were free to walk around the town. About four o'clock, Massimo called us to his wagon. He said, "I've asked Pete to have the work crew haul the water this evening, so you don't have to do it."

Daniel said, "That's great, but—why not?"

Massimo said, "Because we're taking you out to supper." He handed us a stack of folded clothes. "Suzanna said you would be able to find something to wear in these. Be ready to leave in 30 minutes, eh?"

Daniel and I raced off to get ready.

When we met to leave for supper, Suzanna said, "I hardly recognize you." She smiled her approval. "Tonight, we want you to see the city. There won't be much time tomorrow. We roll out early."

Massimo said, "Tonight, we eat Italian. My brother, Stefano, owns the best restaurant in town."

We rode in an elegant, open buggy through the town of Jacksonville. It gave us a chance to see the beautiful buildings and homes. The sights were breathtaking.

But the best part was—we got to see the ocean again!

Stefano's Restaurant was built on white sand. Farther out from it, waves crashed, forming a shore. As far as I could see, to the north and the south, was beach. The waves rushed in, becoming only a thin foam by the time they reached my feet. I wanted my sketchbook, so I could draw them.

Massimo pointed. "You see this big ocean? This is the Atlantic. Suzanna and I crossed this ocean by ship all the way from Italy. We were three weeks sailing."

I tried to look beyond the waves and picture the big, vast ocean that brought Suzanna and Massimo all the way from Italy. I felt very small. The world is bigger than I ever dreamed.

Stefano came to greet us with embraces. Massimo introduced us as Vincelli and Gordamo. Stefano instantly began speaking Italian. Massimo said, "They don't speak Italian."

Stefano shook his head, disappointed. "Well, then you better EAT Italian! This is the best Italian food this side of Lago Maggiore!" His waiters brought out platters of food, so many we couldn't keep up with them all. I have never tasted such delicious foods: sausages, peppers, fish, meats, cheeses, and—even octopus.

After the dishes were cleared away, Massimo said, "Teddy, Daniel, we have something to tell you. Tomorrow, the circus will leave Florida. We are headed north."

I thought of Mama and Pap looking for me.

Suzanna said, "We know you are looking for your parents, Teddy. You are welcome to stay with us for the season, but you need to know that our journey will now take us far from Florida, thousands of miles, perhaps."

My heart felt heavy. I said, "I cannot go with you. I must continue to look for Mama and Pap."

Suzanna said, "Daniel? Will you stay with us?"

I held my breath. I know how Daniel loves the circus.

Daniel said, "Teddy and I are family. Family sticks together. Thank you for your offer, though."

Massimo said, "Here is your pay and a little extra Suzanna and I threw in to help you. There is enough for a train ticket to take you from Jacksonville, down south of here. Perhaps you will pick up the trail of your parents." He handed me an envelope. "You are always welcome with us if you come back."

I said, "Thank you. I don't know how to repay your kindness."

Massimo looked at me with his kind eyes. "You are nice to our girls. We are nice to you."

We were all quiet as we rode in the open buggy back to the circus camp.

I will miss Suzanna, Massimo, and especially the elephants.

Love,
Teddy

Reading Multiple Choice Questions for the Letter of July 5, 1892
Circle the letter of the correct answer.

1. What was the name of Massimo's brother who owned an Italian restaurant?
   A. Giovanni
   B. Rossini
   C. Carmelo
   D. Stefano

2. Which ocean does Jacksonville border?
   A. The Gulf of Mexico
   B. The Atlantic Ocean
   C. The Indian Ocean
   D. The Pacific Ocean

3. Why did Teddy and Daniel decide to leave the circus?
   A. They were not being paid enough money.
   B. Teddy was afraid of the animals.
   C. The circus was traveling north, and Teddy needed to stay in Florida to find her parents.
   D. Massimo and Suzanna did not have enough work to keep them.

4. How did Teddy, Daniel, Massimo, and Suzanna get back to the circus from their dinner at the Italian restaurant?
   A. They rode in an open buggy.
   B. They rode on a train from the railroad station.
   C. They walked.
   D. They rode horseback.

5. What did Massimo give Teddy and Daniel to help them on their journey?
   A. a brand new slingshot
   B. a compass
   C. some money
   D. a pocketknife

6. What is one strange thing that Teddy and Daniel were served at the Italian restaurant?
   A. goat cheese
   B. liver and onions
   C. squid
   D. octopus

7. What names did Massimo give to Teddy and Daniel?
   A. Mortimer and Elvis
   B. Vincelli and Gordamo
   C. Luigi and Tomas
   D. Linda and Donibelle

July 6, 1892

Dear Martha,

Daniel and I didn't have long to be sad about leaving the elephants. When we got back to camp last night, Marie and Elmer came to see Massimo.

Elmer said, "He was here again, that troublemaker."

Massimo said, "Who? Which one?"

Marie said, "That townie with the scar. The one who was asking questions about Teddy and Daniel."

Suzanna knew that I would panic. She said, "See, Teddy? Not a minute too soon. Perfect timing."

Massimo said, "He'll be here in the morning trying to find them as we leave."

Suzanna didn't seem worried. "Yes, he'll be here looking for two boys, boys who will be going north with us. But he won't be looking for two girls, girls who are going south on the train."

Daniel said, "Uh-oh." He looked at me. "Two girls?"

Marie said, "You will need my help."

Suzanna said, "Yes. Marie, meet me at the costume wagon. Elmer, can you find me two boys who are roughly the size of Teddy and Daniel? I'll need them for a little while in the morning, about seven o'clock."

Marie and Suzanna began laying out bolts of material and shuffling through patterns.

As they worked, Suzanna asked, "Teddy, did you mention that you know someone in St. Augustine?"

I said, "Yes. Miss Melman lives in St. Augustine. She will help us, I'm sure."

Suzanna said, "Good. Then, this disguise only has to work until then."

Daniel said, "But what about my hair? It's cut really short."

Marie said, "This is a circus, Daniel. We have every kind of wig you could ask for."

Massimo said, "I'll telegraph your Miss Melman first thing in the morning."

I said, "She's at The Sheridan School for Girls. Miss Cassie Melman."

Marie and Suzanna worked quickly, calling in Eleana and Camille to help with the sewing. Marie measured and poked and prodded us to turn this way and that. Daniel and I napped in between fittings.

Early this morning, our "costumes" were ready.

When Suzanna and Marie got through with Daniel, he looked like any other girl you would see on the street, except he was miserable. He rolled his eyes. He twitched. He even moaned.

Suzanna patted his hand and said, "Desperate times call for desperate measures."

When I got my dress on and the wig and the hat Marie had chosen for me, everyone stared.

"Oh, Teddy," Suzanna said. "For the first time, you look like a girl. A pretty girl."

Massimo bundled us off to one of the big wagons while it was still dark. He said, "Whoever comes to get you, call him Uncle and act like you are his family. He will make sure you get to the train station. Leave the rest up to us."

"What about Ethelbert?"

"We've got a plan. You'll see."

About seven o'clock, the door to the wagon opened. It was Carl Ringling, the owner of the circus! He called out, "Come Prissy, come Helen. We're ready to take you to the station." We got into a buggy. A baby's pram was already in the buggy beside us. I looked at it. Inside the pram, in a baby's gown and bonnet, was Ethelbert! Only his furry face showed above the blankets. I had to force myself not to look shocked or laugh out loud.

I said, "Thank you, Uncle. We had a nice time visiting you at the circus."

We drove to the station. He helped us find a seat on the train, lifted the pram up beside us, and put our suitcase on the shelf overhead. He smiled and said, "Now, be good children, and tell your mother hello." Then, just like that, he was gone.

Love,
Teddy

Name_____ Date_____

Narrative Writing Prompt for the Letter of July 6, 1892
Read and answer the prompt below.

Narrative Prompt: Daniel was expected to dress in a costume in order to disguise himself as a girl. Make up a story about a time when you dressed in a costume, whether it was to change your appearance, to trick someone, or to pretend you were someone else. As you write, describe your costume, why you wore it, and what happened in the story that would be interesting for your readers to read about. Be sure to include juicy details, so your reader can form a "mind movie" of your story.

_____

_____

_____

_____

_____

_____

_____

_____

_____

_____

_____

_____

_____

_____

_____

_____

_____

_____

_____

July 7, 1892

Dear Martha,

We left the station this morning, right after Carl Ringling made sure we were safe in our seats, and we had our tickets in hand.

The train started out slow as the steam built up.

chug — chug — chug — chug

But after a few minutes, it picked up speed.

clackety —choo, clackety —choo, clackety —clackety —clackety—choo

Before we knew it, we were whipping along those tracks lickety-split.

Ethel looked at me with wild eyes. He was frightened, and I was afraid he would start howling, but Suzanna had thought of everything. There was a big baby bottle in the pram, and it had milk in it. Ethel couldn't suck it like a baby, but he licked up the drops that squirted out the tip until he was calm and sleepy eyed. I scratched his ears under the baby bonnet. He fell asleep on his back, which is a good thing, because when he falls asleep on his back, he sleeps a long time.

It was also a good thing because the conductor came by and punched our tickets right after Ethel fell asleep. I had turned the pram, so no one could see inside.

Today was my first train ride. The only word that comes to mind is POWER. The train is built of steel and iron and the engine fills a whole car. The train cars are on wheels, but each wheel has a steel arm that pulls it around and then around again and again.

I opened my sketchbook and tried to sketch the scenes I saw from the open window. The sea was calm, so instead of crashing, the waves folded over gently and washed ashore. We passed giant sand dunes, a few beach cottages, and flocks and flocks of seagulls.

Suddenly, the conductor called, "St. Augustine!" and the train began to slow. The steam whistle blew.

Daniel grabbed our suitcase, and I rolled the pram to the exit. A porter lifted it down for me. I couldn't believe it, but Ethel stayed inside.

The platform was filled with people getting on and off the train. Families and friends gathered down at the end.

Daniel hissed at me, "I look stupid, you know."

I said, "No, you don't. You look like a girl."

He said, "What if she doesn't like me?"

I said, "Who are you talking about?"

He said, "Miss Melman. What if she doesn't like me?"

Right then, I saw her. She was wearing a starched skirt and a trim white hat, and she had a gold locket around her neck.

I called, "Miss Melman!"

She came forward and said in a formal voice, "I am so pleased to meet you. I'm Cassie Melman of The Sheridan School for Girls."

I said, "Miss Melman! It's me, Theodosia!"

She frowned. Then, she looked curious. She stepped back and looked at me again as if she couldn't believe her own eyes. Then, Miss Melman's face broke into the biggest smile. She grabbed me in a bear hug and squeezed me like she would never let go.

"You're alive! It's you? I got the strangest telegram from the Ringling Brothers Circus. It said Carl Ringling's nieces would be arriving at the station today and would I please meet their train. I had no idea it was YOU! This is truly a stellar day."

When Ethel heard the commotion, he jumped up and started barking.

Miss Melman said, "Ethelbert?" I'll have to admit, it was strange seeing Ethel in a baby bonnet.

Oh, Martha, I wish you could have been there.

Love,
Teddy

Name_____ Date _____

Reading Short Response Questions for the Letter of July 7, 1892
Answer the questions below, and be sure to use complete sentences.

1. What did Teddy do to hide Ethelbert from people on the train and the conductor?

_____

_____

_____

_____

_____

2. Teddy had her first train ride. Why did she choose the word POWER to describe it?

_____

_____

_____

_____

_____

3. Explain why Daniel said, **"I look stupid, you know."**

_____

_____

_____

_____

_____

4. What made Miss Melman's face break into a big smile?

_____

_____

_____

_____

July 8, 1892

Dear Martha,

Let me continue. I've left you hanging! I could tell that Miss Melman was totally confused. There would be a lot of explaining to do.

I pushed Daniel forward. "Miss Melman, this is my cousin."

Miss Melman said, "She's so pretty! I'm so glad to meet her." She turned to Daniel. "And what is your name, dear?"

I said, "His name is Daniel."

She looked at Daniel's bonnet, hair, and dress and said, "His—name—is—DANIEL? We have some catching up to do."

When we got to Miss Melman's cute little cottage at The Sheridan School for Girls, she said, "I'm a cook now, Teddy, so no talking until I get a good hot meal into you. I know two tired, hungry children when I see them." She made chicken and dumplings, salad, melon slices, and iced tea. We ate out on her porch.

Then, she said, "Now, I want to hear all about it."

Daniel and I spent the next three hours telling her everything that has happened since I last saw her with the wagon train. Every now and then she would interrupt us to say, "It did?" or "You don't say!" or "I can't imagine!" or "Weren't you scared?" Miss Melman is another adult who listens when kids speak. She was interested in everything we talked about.

I told her about the quarantine station, about Miss Essie Mae Pitts, and about Jasper Lowe's pap. I told her about the wagons being impounded and about having to live on my own.

She said, "Goodness gracious, Teddy. You are a brave girl, but this just takes the cake."

I told her about Dr. Winklepleck and the balloon ride and the Green family and Verna and Jimbo and Verna's creepy children. Daniel told her about us meeting in the woods and how we are cousins and why we had to run away together. He told her about Wanda and Dr. Zoren and joining the circus.

Miss Melman said, "So you had to disguise yourself as a boy?" and pointed at me.

When we got to the part of the story about Jimbo Dudd looking for us again at the circus yesterday, Miss Melman said, "So you had to disguise yourself as a girl?" and pointed at Daniel.

Then, she chewed on her bottom lip and squinched up her eyes. She sat thinking, rubbing her thumbs.

She said, "We're going to have to have a plan, yes we are. What Suzanna and Massimo did bought us some time, but sooner or later that ne'er-do-well will turn up here asking questions and looking for you."

Now, it was my turn to ask questions. I said, "What happened when the soldiers took me away?"

Miss Melman told us how the wagon train had to move on to keep more people from getting the fever and dying. She said, "I didn't know what to do, Teddy. I took Girlie and Gabriel with me because I could tie them behind my wagon. We'll go out and see them a little later. I left you a note in the wagon."

I said, "I found it." I felt a lump in my throat thinking about the night I found it. I felt so alone.

She said, "Lots of folks died. We lost 16 people from our wagon train that we know of. There are others that we never heard from once they were taken away." Her voice grew soft. "Teddy, where are your parents? Do you know if they are alive?"

I told her what the man at Mrs. Plum's quarantine station said about a Mr. and Mrs. Bodain dying of the fever. I said, "But I'm sure it's not them. I'm sure they're alive."

I hope she believed me. Mama and Pap can't be dead. Not now, when they are so young. Not now, when we are going to start our new life together. Not now, when I need them so much.

Before bedtime, I showed her the land deed. "See? This is about Pap's land."

Miss Melman read it carefully. "It says your father's land is in Dade county. He's to file his claim at the land office in the county courthouse."

She fixed me a nice warm bath and went to round us up some clothes to wear. I feel like tonight I might be able to sleep without worrying for the first time in a long time. I hope.

Love,
Teddy

Expository Writing Prompt for the Letter of July 8, 1892
Read and answer the following writing prompt.

Expository Prompt: Miss Melman has come to St. Augustine to teach at The Sheridan School for Girls, a school where girls live away from home while they are going to school. Pretend you are a student at a similar boarding school for either girls or boys. Explain what your life might be like living away from your parents. How would you keep in touch? What would life in the dorm be like? What would be the pros and cons of living in a boarding school? First, discuss these things with other writers and share ideas and thoughts. Now, write an expository piece. Be sure you include specific reasons and descriptive details, so we can picture life in a boarding school.

July 9, 1892

Dear Martha,

Last night, while I was in the tub, I could hear Miss Melman talking to Daniel. She said, "I'm happy you came here, Daniel. I'm glad Theodosia has a cousin like you. It's good to have family."

He said, "I'm glad I have a cousin like her. I thought I was all alone. But now I can read and write some." By the time I dried off and changed into the clothes Miss Melman had gathered for me, Daniel was sitting beside her, reading aloud. I listened at the door, unseen.

He read, "Teddy and I poled and rowed the boat up the river. We camped on the riverbank."

She said, "Just like Tom and Huck."

Daniel said, "That's what Teddy said. Who are Tom and Huck again?"

Miss Melman laughed, "They are two kids from the book Tom Sawyer. I was reading it to the kids on the wagon train." Hearing her say that reminded me how much I miss our wagon train school.

That evening, as the sun was going down, we walked along the seashore and picked up shells. It was hard to imagine that this is the same ocean we saw on the Fourth of July in Jacksonville. We found lots of colorful shells. Did you know that tiny little sea creatures used to live in the shells? We found starfish, sand dollars, even coral. Daniel found some colorful, frosty pieces that weren't shells.

Miss Melman said, "That's sea glass. See? Hold it up to the light. Unfortunately, some people throw bottles into the ocean. Those bottles can be a real danger because they almost always end up getting broken. The sea tosses the bits of broken glass to and fro in the waves and on the sand. After a while, it smoothes the edges and frosts it up so that it no longer looks like glass."

Daniel said, "They're pretty. Would you like to have them?"

Miss Melman said, "I'll add them to my collection of sea glass. Thank you, Daniel."

Yesterday, we went to the fort of St. Augustine. Miss Melman's friend, Mr. John Mikelson, took us and was our tour guide. Miss Melman said, "I've just moved here, remember? Mr. Mikelson knows all about the fort, and he was kind enough to agree to take us on a tour."

Mr. Mikelson is handsome! He's tall, with dark brown hair and big brown eyes. He showed us all around the fort. He said, "Teddy, did you know that St. Augustine is the oldest continuously occupied European-established city in the United States?"

I said, "Yes, I did. Wasn't it built by the Spanish?"

He said, "Yes, in 1565. The architecture is called Spanish colonial."

We walked to the Castillo de San Marcos, an enormous Spanish star fort. Mr. Mikelson pointed to the walls and said, "Look carefully at this material." We ran our hands over the stones.

Daniel said, "It looks like shells are in it."

Mr. Mikelson said, "That's right. This is called coquina. It's kind of like limestone, but it's made up of ancient shells that have bonded together. Coquina is rather soft, when it comes to building materials, so the enemy's cannonballs would embed themselves in the wall rather than punching holes through the wall. The star shape of the fort also helped protect them from cannon fire."

We also visited the oldest wooden schoolhouse, built sometime before 1716.

Mr. Mikelson said, "Kids, I'd like you to see Miss Melman's first school."

Miss Melman said, "Tee hee. Very funny. Are you trying to say I'm an old maid?"

Mr. Mikelson said, "On the contrary, Miss Cassie Melman, I might be trying to say you found the fountain of youth."

Martha, I think they were flirting!

Tomorrow, we're going swimming in the Atlantic Ocean!

Love,
Teddy

Reading Extended Response Questions for the Letter of July 9, 1892
Answer the questions below. Be sure to use complete sentences, reasons, and details.

1. Why did Miss Melman compare Teddy and Daniel to Tom and Huck? How did Teddy feel when she heard Miss Melman talking about Tom Sawyer?

_____

_____

_____

_____

_____

_____

_____

_____

_____

_____

2. Describe Teddy's trip to St. Augustine. Paint a "mind movie" of some of the highlights of her visit to this ancient city. You may use the Internet or other resources if you need more information.

_____

_____

_____

_____

_____

_____

_____

_____

_____

_____

July 10, 1892

Dear Martha,

Trouble seems to find me no matter where I hide.

Today, Miss Melman took Daniel and me swimming in the Atlantic Ocean. Right near the water's edge were tiny little houses, called "cabanas," made of cloth. You rent a cabana for the day for a quarter, and that's where you change into your bathing costume.

Daniel and I don't own bathing costumes, so Miss Melman borrowed some for us. We rented a bright, red-striped cabana and took turns changing. When it was my turn, I took off my neck pouch and hid it under my clothes. I'd almost forgotten that I was wearing it, but I'm glad I remembered, because it has Pap's land deed and his father's watch in it. I think seawater would have ruined them, for sure.

I opened the pouch to make sure everything was there: the land deed, the silver dollar given to me by John Phillip Sousa, and Pap's watch that was given to him by his father. For some reason, I opened the watch. On the inside was a picture of Pap's mother, Isabelle, and an inscription.

It said, "To my beloved Dalton: I love you more than the stars are bright, more than the moon is round, more than the ocean is deep. Isabelle"

I realized, for the first time, that Pap's mother must have given the watch to Pap's father. It would have been a long time ago, maybe 30 years, maybe around the time Althea Tomlinson's husband would have given her the gold bracelet. That reminded me. I took off the gold bracelet, so I could put it in the pouch with my other treasures. I held it in my fingertips. I had found the bracelet in the springs. It was a treasure. It showed me how when I search for something and don't give up, I might come across something good.

I thought about Althea Tomlinson. It had been her treasure, too. But I didn't want to think about that, so I dropped the bracelet in the neck pouch, pulled the strings tight, and hid the pouch under my clothes again.

Swimming in the Atlantic Ocean was incredible fun. The beach was filled with people, all having a good time. We looked stylish in our swimming costumes, and I felt proud about that because that's what just about everyone wore. Miss Melman showed us how to jump up high, get on top of a wave, and ride it in, all the way to the shore. When we were hungry, we bought hot dogs and lemonade.

A man and a woman were making saltwater taffy to sell. They made the candy in an enormous copper kettle. After they let it cool for a bit, they gathered it all up together on a marble slab and then began pulling it back and forth with their hands. The brownish candy began to get lighter and lighter, and when they got finished, it was completely white. That's when they added colorings and stripes. They finally cut it and wrapped the pieces in waxed paper. The whole process was fascinating. I wish I had that job.

When we got back to the cabana late in the afternoon, we changed and put on our regular clothes. We were tired, a little sunburned, but very happy.

When Miss Melman went to tip the cabana porter, he said, "Did your husband get his things, too?"

Miss Melman smiled and said, "You must have me mixed up with someone else."

The porter said, "No, ma'am. I don't think so. Didn't you and the children have the last cabana there, the red one? Well, your husband came earlier and asked if he could change, too. He pointed to the kids on the beach and said you were his family."

We looked at each other, puzzled. Was someone playing a trick?
Miss Melman said, "Excuse me, sir. What did this man look like?"

He said, "I didn't pay much attention to his looks. He was in a hurry. Oh—I do remember a scar, a scar he had right here." He pointed to the area between his eyebrow and his ear.

At the word "scar," my hands flew to the pouch around my neck.

I loosened the strings and looked inside.

The land deed was missing! Oh, Martha, what a disaster.

Love,
Teddy

Grammar Questions for the Letter of July 10, 1892
Circle the letter of the correct answer.

1. Which one of the following sentences is correct?
   A. Today, Miss Melman took Daniel and I swimming in the Atlantic Ocean.
   B. Today, Miss Melman took Daniel and me swimming in the Atlantic Ocean.
   C. Today, Miss Melman took we swimming in the Atlantic Ocean.
   D. Today, Miss Melman took I and Daniel swimming in the Atlantic Ocean.

2. Which one of the following words is spelled incorrectly?
   A. inscription
   B. loosened
   C. stylish
   D. eybrow

3. Where do the quotation marks go in the following dialogue?
   A. Miss Melman smiled and said, "You must have me mixed up with someone else."
   B. Miss Melman smiled and said, "You must have me mixed up with someone else.
   C. Miss Melman smiled and said, ""You must have me mixed up with someone else.""
   D. "Miss Melman smiled and said, You must have me mixed up with someone else."

4. In the following sentence, which word is incorrect?
   The brownish candy began to got lighter and lighter.
   A. lighter
   B. brownish
   C. got
   D. began

5. Which word is the subject of the following sentence?
   I dropped the bracelet in the neck pouch.
   A. bracelet
   B. neck
   C. pouch
   D. I

6. What is missing in the following sentence?
   When we were hungry we bought hot dogs and lemonade.
   A. a comma between *hungry* and *we*.
   B. an exclamation point
   C. a verb
   D. a question mark at the end

7. What does the word *inscription* mean?
   A. asking a question
   B. writing that is carved into a surface
   C. a gold bracelet found in the springs
   D. writing that is impossible to read

July 11, 1892

Dear Martha,

I know my letters seem filled with ups and downs, but I want you to know what's going on!

The land deed is gone, and there's no use in wondering WHO took it. The only person who could have stolen it is Jimbo Dudd. Just the thought of that man makes my skin crawl.

Miss Melman questioned the cabana porter. Jimbo had shown up at the beach and had stood in the shade, searching for us. When he finally found us, he came to see the cabana porter. That was about two o'clock in the afternoon, three hours before we discovered it was gone.

I felt like crying. Daniel said, "We are going to get it back, Teddy, I promise you that."

Miss Melman found a policeman and reported the theft. Then, she said, "We need a plan, but first, we need full bellies. You can't think as well on an empty stomach." It was true. We were hungrier than an army.

When we got back to her cottage, I volunteered Daniel and me to make supper while Miss Melman went to get Mr. Mikelson. "He will know what to do," she said.

After supper, we had a meeting. Mr. Mikelson said, "Teddy, this is a terrible thing that has happened, but if it got me an invitation to supper, it might not be all that bad. Thank you and Daniel for a delicious meal." Mr. Mikelson has a gift for looking on the bright side.

Miss Melman said, "Teddy's mama taught her to cook. She's the woman I told you about, John, the woman who taught me to cook."

Miss Melman called him John! Not Mr. Mikelson, but John. JOHN.

Mr. Mikelson said, "Where do you think this Jimbo Dudd will go, Teddy?"

I said, "He wants the land deed, so he can claim Pap's land as his own. I heard him discussing it with his wife, Verna."

Daniel said, "She is one disgusting excuse for a woman, let me tell you. She's a worthless piece of shingle-rot that would steal your clothes and try to sell them back to you."

Mr. Mikelson smiled. "So you're saying you're not too fond of her, Daniel?"

Daniel smiled back. "She's a nasty-tempered, kid-whipping, tobacco-spitting scalawag is what she is, and her cooking is even worse."

We laughed. Mr. Mikelson said, "Well put, Daniel. You do have a way with words."

I said, "Jimbo and Verna talked about going to file the land deed. They said no one would know that Jimbo is not my pap, Dalton Bodain."

Miss Melman said, "That would have to be in Dade County. That's where the deed states your father's land is located. I'm so glad you let me have a look at it."

Mr. Mikelson said, "The county seat of Dade County is Juno. They moved it in '88."

I said, "Then, that's where I'll have to go. I don't know where Pap and Mama are. They may already be down there, or they may be back up in Gainesville in who-knows-what quarantine station, or they may be—" I didn't want to say the word DEAD out loud. "But if Jimbo is going down to Juno to try to file the deed, then I've got to go there and tell those people that he isn't Dalton Bodain."

Miss Melman said, "Teddy, could you wait till the first of August? I could go with you then."

Mr. Mikelson said, "And I have to leave on business to Tallahassee tomorrow morning. If you could wait until the end of next week, I can go with you."

I said, "Thanks for your offers, but I can't wait."

Miss Melman studied my face. "Of course, you're right, dear. Let's see if we can come up with the fastest way to get you to Juno." She got her map of Florida and spread it out on the table.

The four of us put our heads together and studied the map.

Love,
Teddy

Writing Questions for the Letter of July 11, 1892
Circle the letter of the correct answer.

1. Read the following sentences from Teddy's letter today:
   "You can't think as well on an empty stomach." It was true. We were hungrier than an army.
   These sentences are an example of what good writing skill?
   A. sentence variety
   B. persuasive writing
   C. onomatopoeia
   D. transitional words

2. Read the following sentence from Teddy's letter today:
   "He will know what to do," she said.
   This sentence is an example of what very important writing skill?
   A. onomatopoeia
   B. dialogue
   C. transitional sentence
   D. metaphor

3. Read the following sentence from Teddy's letter today:
   "She's a nasty-tempered, kid-whipping, tobacco-spitting scalawag is what she is, and her cooking is even worse."
   This sentence is an example of what very important writing skill?
   A. sentence variety
   B. onomatopoeia
   C. descriptive writing
   D. transitional phrases

4. Read the following sentence from Teddy's letter today:
   The land deed is gone, and there's no use in wondering WHO took it.
   This sentence is an example of what very important writing skill?
   A. onomatopoeia
   B. grabber
   C. simile
   D. specific emotion words

5. Read the following sentence from Teddy's letter today:
   "She's a worthless piece of shingle-rot that would steal your clothes and try to sell them back to you."
   The phrase *She's a worthless piece of shingle-rot* is an example of what very important writing skill?
   A. onomatopoeia
   B. transitional phrase
   C. specific emotion words
   D. metaphor

July 12, 1892

Dear Martha,

Daniel said, "What about the train? Didn't they say the train was going to go all the way to Miami?"

Mr. Mikelson said, "Not yet. As far as I know, it only goes down to Daytona Beach at this point."

I said, "What about a ship? We're right on the seacoast."

Mr. Mikelson said, "Now, that's an idea. Ships leave here daily to go down the coast."

Miss Melman said, "Yes! You can leave in the morning. You can take Gabriel. Once you're there, you'll need some way to travel. A horse would be much faster than traveling on foot."

I said, "Perfect. But do you think they let horses on the boat?"

Mr. Mikelson said, "I don't know why not. I think they take horses and cattle. It's just a one-day sail. You don't even have to spend the night on the ship."

Daniel said, "And Ethelbert?"

Miss Melman said, "There's always the baby pram!" and that made us laugh.

And so we agreed that in the morning, Miss Melman and Mr. Mikelson would take Daniel, me, Ethelbert, and Gabriel down to the dock to put us on a boat for Juno before Mr. Mikelson has to leave town. Miss Melman said, "You children go to bed and get some rest, then. I'll do up the dishes."

Mr. Mikelson said, "I'll help. There aren't too many. Together we'll be done in no time."

I lay on the guest bed and tried to sleep. I was tired, but Miss Melman and Mr. Mikelson were talking softly as they did the dishes. I didn't mean to listen, but I could hear them. Sort of. If I listened hard enough. Okay, I went to the wall and put my ear next to it, but I HAD to know what they were saying.

Miss Melman said, "Do you think they'll be alright?"

Mr. Mikelson said, "Cassie, they're smart kids. They've made it this far. Teddy is right. If she doesn't get down to the land office soon, this Jimbo Dudd might just be able to steal her father's land."

He called her Cassie!

Miss Melman said something I couldn't hear. Then, Mr. Mikelson said, "I hope so, for her sake. But if they're not, then the land should belong to Teddy. Her father worked hard for that land."

Miss Melman said something else I couldn't hear. Mr. Mikelson spoke to her gently. "We will do whatever we can to help them."

Miss Melman said, "Thank you, John. You are so kind."

He said, "Good night, dearest."

He called her dearest!

She said, "Good night."

Then, they kissed. I didn't see them kiss, but I think they kissed, because there was a silent part, and I don't know what else could have been happening. They kissed. I'm sure of it. I hope they kissed.

I am sure Miss Melman thinks he's the cat's pajamas! Mr. Mikelson is handsome and smart and funny and nice. And he seems crazy about her. And he has a good job. And he kissed her, maybe.

But in the middle of the night, when I got up to use the chamber pot, I heard crying. I peeked in Miss Melman's room. Her back was to me, and she was crying into her pillow. I sat on the side of her bed and softly rubbed her back, like Mama used to do for me.

I said, "Tears are good. Don't try to stop them." I remembered the story Miss Melman had told me under the wagon. I thought about it.

After a while, I said, "It's the man in the gold locket, isn't it." She nodded.

I said, "You're thinking what a fine man he was." She nodded.

I said, "Sometimes, we just have to let go of things we love." She nodded.

I said, "I think Mr. Mikelson is a fine man, too."

She sat up, wiping her eyes. "You do?" I nodded, and we both smiled.

She said, "Me, too." We hugged, and I tiptoed back to bed.

Love,
Teddy

Name_____ Date _____

Persuasive Writing Prompt for the Letter of July 12, 1892
Read and answer the following prompt.

Persuasive Prompt: Miss Melman lost someone very dear to her, and she is crying. Teddy hears her and goes to comfort her. Crying can help you get through the sad feelings of losing someone. In your opinion, is it okay to cry? Is there an age when you are too old to cry? Is it okay for both girls and boys to cry? Give convincing reasons and examples to support your opinion.

_____

_____

_____

_____

_____

_____

_____

_____

_____

_____

_____

_____

_____

_____

_____

_____

_____

_____

_____

July 13, 1892

Dear Martha,

I wish you were here. All this would be easier if you could be with me, too.

Before we left, I stroked Girlie's soft brown hide. She was as sweet as ever. I pictured Mama sitting beside her on the stool, milking. Oh, Mama. How I miss her! I watched Mr. Mikelson hitch Gabriel to the back of the buggy. I pictured Pap sitting on Gabriel, studying the maps and galloping up to the captain. Pap. Would I see him again? The thought of it made me want to get on with my journey as soon as possible.

Mr. Mikelson drove us down to the boat dock. He was gone for a while, making inquiries about where to get tickets, which ship would be leaving the dock, and so forth. He came back with tickets and drove his buggy down to the steamer Daniel and I would be sailing on, The Lady Augustine. "I could get you as far as Ft. Pierce. No one's going farther south than that for three days."

Lots of people, animals, and workers swirled around the dock. Men loaded and unloaded supplies. Mr. Mikelson and Daniel led Gabriel up a ramp to the lower deck to find the animal stalls. While they were gone, Miss Melman gave me instructions.

"Here's some extra money for travel, Teddy. Please keep it safe in your neck pouch. Don't let anyone see you take it out. There's enough for a few night's lodging at a boarding house. When you and Daniel get to the courthouse and all is well, please telegraph me to let me know you are safe. Oh, and here's your suitcase with a change of clothing for each of you. And a clean handkerchief. And here's a hamper of food. That should last you all day and even tonight."

I said, "Thank you, Miss Melman. I'll pay it back. I really will."

She said, "Don't be silly. You already have."

Mr. Mikelson helped Daniel and me find deck chairs. They were long, so we could stretch out our legs and be comfortable. Dogs were allowed, thank goodness, so Ethelbert stretched out between us.

The steam whistle blew. A man shouted, "All ashore that's going ashore."

We waved goodbye to Miss Melman and Mr. Mikelson from our chairs.

The steamer began to chug. The water around the dock vibrated and danced.

Soon, The Lady Augustine was under way, moving south along the coast. The figures of Miss Melman and Mr. Mikelson grew smaller and smaller, until we could no longer see them.

The journey had just begun, but Daniel said, "Let's eat!" That boy must be going through a growing spell because he could eat all day long and then ask for seconds.

We brought out the hamper of food and ate our picnic from the deck chairs. We saw big birds with long yellow beaks with pouches under them. Daniel said, "Pelicans." One of the pelicans dived in the water and came up a moment later with a full pouch. He opened his mouth to let the water drain out. We saw the fish he had caught flipping its silver body back and forth. But before the pelican could close his mouth again and swallow the fish, a seagull swooped in and stole the fish from his mouth!

Daniel said, "Ha! Just like Jimbo Dudd."

After lunch, we lay in the sunshine and watched the scenery go by. We played checkers and told stories and riddles. I remembered we were to dock by sundown, and I wanted to make some sketches before then. While I began a sketch of the pelican and the seagull, Daniel went off on his own to explore the steamer.

It couldn't have been an hour later that he came back, out of breath and looking like he'd seen a ghost.

I said, "What is it? What's wrong."

He said, "You won't believe who's on this ship!"

I said, "Who?"

Daniel said, "Jimbo Dudd!"

Great buckets of butterbeans. It's my worst nightmare.

Love,
Teddy

Reading Multiple Choice Questions for the Letter of July 13, 1892
Circle the letter of the correct answer.

1. Which of the animals were Teddy and Daniel able to take with them on their journey down to Juno?
   A. Only Ethelbert
   B. Ethelbert and Girlie
   C. Girlie and Gabriel
   D. Ethelbert and Gabriel

2. What kind of bird did Teddy and Daniel see dive in the water and come up with a fish?
   A. a seagull
   B. a pelican
   C. a heron
   D. a duck

3. Who did Daniel say was traveling on the same ship down to Ft. Pierce?
   A. Miss Melman and Mr. Mikelson
   B. Suzanna and Massimo
   C. Jimbo Dudd
   D. Mr. Obadiah Lincoln

4. What time was the ship set to dock?
   A. by sundown
   B. the next morning
   C. in three days
   D. in a week

5. What was Teddy doing while Daniel went off to explore the steamer?
   A. playing games
   B. bathing Ethelbert
   C. sketching in her sketchpad
   D. sleeping

6. What did Miss Melman tell Teddy to do once she and Daniel got to the courthouse?
   A. call her and let her know everything was ok
   B. make sure Jimbo Dudd goes to jail
   C. mail her a letter
   D. send her a telegram

7. What did the man shout when the steam whistle blew?
   A. "Time to get off the steam!"
   B. "All aboard!"
   C. "All ashore that's going ashore!"
   D. "Anchors a'weigh!"

July 14, 1892

Dear Martha,

I hated to leave you hanging, but things are so busy, I just write when I can.

I couldn't believe my eyes. Jimbo Dudd lay on a deck chair, in a little alcove, asleep. There were no other passengers around. It was a good thing, because his loud, snuffly snores could have been heard a mile away. In his one hand, he had a thin bottle of whiskey. His other hand was tucked under his head.

Daniel and I tiptoed back, so he wouldn't see us if he woke up.

I said, "That scalawag."

Daniel said, "What's our plan?"

I said, "I bet he's headed right down where we're going. I bet he's got that land deed with him, too."

Daniel said, "Of course he does! We're going to have to get it."

I said, "While he's asleep?" I was filled with dread.

Daniel said, "The thought of facing Jimbo Dudd asleep is a whole lot better than the thought of facing Jimbo Dudd awake."

I said, "You're right about that. But we're going to be docking soon."

Daniel said, "Have you got that extra handkerchief Miss Melman gave you?" I gave it to him.

He said, "Good. Now, you stay back here, and let me get the deed. That way, if he wakes up and chases me, you can get away and get help."

I said, "What are you going to do?"

Daniel said, "I think he's had a few nips of that whiskey. Now, stay here till I come back, okay?"

I agreed. Daniel disappeared into the alcove, and I waited. I waited and waited and waited. What was he doing? What could be taking this long? I pictured Jimbo pinning Daniel down, ripping the deed out of his hands. Suddenly, I noticed the sound of the steamer slowing down. We would be docking soon!

I couldn't stand it any longer. I tiptoed back around to the alcove and peeked inside.

What I saw almost made me jump out of my skin, right on the spot.

Jimbo was lying on his side. His hands were bound together with one of Daniel's long boot laces. Another lace bound his feet. Daniel had stuffed my handkerchief in Jimbo's mouth and had bound his faded blue bandana around Jimbo's head to hold his mouth shut. Jimbo was wide awake and madder than a hornet.

I said, "How did you do all of this by yourself?" My heart was thumping like Sousa's big bass drum.

Daniel said, "I used my noggin, that's how." He smiled, held up the land deed, and sang, "Ta da!"

Jimbo growled and snarled, but the bandana stayed in place.

I looked at his raging face. "You can't have Pap's land."

Daniel said, "Let's go. We're about to dock."

The loud steam engine revved up and began chug-chug-chugging us in toward the dock. The whistle blew. Daniel and I ran back to our deck chairs, gathered up our stuff, and I slipped a leash on Ethelbert's collar.

The dock below was, once again, swarming with people, and I didn't want Ethel to get lost in the turmoil.

Daniel went down to the lower deck to lead Gabriel off. It took a while to get the boat stopped and alongside the dock, get it tied to the pilings, and to lower the gangplank and the ramps. While I was waiting, thoughts of a furious Jimbo Dudd getting loose filled my head. Could we get away in time? Would he continue to come after us?

But there was Daniel, leading Gabriel down the ramp, onto the dock. Ethel and I gathered our bundle and joined him. While everyone else was being greeted by friends and family, while the workers were unloading trunks and suitcases, while children were laughing and crying, we slipped quietly away.

Just as we got to the road, I looked back. My eyes scanned both decks. There was no sign of Jimbo.

Love,
Teddy

Name_____ Date _____

Narrative Writing Prompt for the Letter of July 14, 1892
Read and answer the prompt below.

Narrative Prompt: Teddy and Daniel are determined to get back Pap's land deed. Think of a time when you were determined to do something. This can be from your real life or make believe. Write the story of what you were determined to do, what obstacles you faced, and how you were able to accomplish what you wanted to do. Make sure to add as many details as you can so your reader can form a "mind movie." Read your paper carefully. Share ideas with other writers.

_____

_____

_____

_____

_____

_____

_____

_____

_____

_____

_____

_____

_____

_____

_____

_____

_____

_____

_____

_____

_____

July 15, 1892

Dear Martha,

Do you ever have a day when something totally unexpected knocks the wind out of you?

As Daniel and I rode Gabriel, Ethelbert walked beside us. We needed a place for the night. We found Miss Eileen's Boarding House. It looked inviting with twinkly lights and lace curtains.

We started to go in, but a thought occurred to me.

I said, "Wait, let's not go there."

Daniel said, "What are you thinking?"

I said, "Miss Eileen isn't going to take in dogs or horses. Let's find the stables."

Daniel said, "Good idea. If he got loose in time to come ashore, Jimbo might come here."

The thought of running into Jimbo Dudd after what Daniel had done to him made me shiver.

The stables were run by a kid about our age who had very brown skin and a bright smile. His name was T-Pat. He charged us fifty cents to spend the night. He would have charged us a dollar, but Daniel and I agreed to pitch-out the stall and put down fresh straw. We built it up high, so we would have a soft bed. T-Pat charged us another quarter for Gabriel's food.

Daniel took Gabriel's saddle off while I poured a bucket of oats and some fresh water. When Gabriel finished eating, I brushed him with a currycomb I found in the stables. I stroked his soft face.

Daniel said, "He's a nice horse. Does he belong to your pap?"

I said, "Yeah. Daniel, my pap is a good man. I want you to meet him."

Daniel said, "I want to meet him. He's my kin. I miss my pap. I wish we could all be together."

We shared the rest of our hamper of food with T-Pat, and he was glad to get it, too. It made me wonder when was the last time he had eaten. We saved two apples and two ham biscuits for the next day.

Daniel and I had a fine night on the hay. Ethelbert scratched and dug and made a nest right next to me. Gabriel slept standing on one side of the stall. During the night I heard his breathing, soft and slow. I heard rats running on the wooden beams overhead and a hoot owl outside somewhere in a tree.

Early this morning, Daniel woke me up.

"We better get a move on. We don't know where Jimbo is or what he might be up to."

We worked as quietly as two kids ever worked, saddling Gabriel and leading him out of the stable.

I looked behind to make sure we had left nothing—not even a clue—behind.

We left town just as the sun was coming up. The smell of the sea blew in on the morning breezes. Ethelbert romped and ran alongside. The rising sun was to our left, so I knew we were headed south. We had the road pretty much to ourselves, other than the seagulls that rose and swirled overhead. Gabriel seemed more eager and sure-footed after his long night's rest.

Just before noon, we stopped by a little brook. The water looked fresh enough, so we drank our fill and wet two bandanas for our heads. Ethelbert ran off a little ways, sniffing here and there. All of a sudden, we heard his sharp barks and loud cries. Daniel and I ran to where he was, near a fallen log and some tall brush. We heard the unmistakable sound of rattles, as loud and fierce as an angry swarm of bees.

The snake was poised to strike. Ethel was holding him at bay with growls and barks.

I screamed, "No, Ethel!" but it was too late.

The snake's strike was lightning quick. Ethel jumped back, but the snake struck his thigh. He shrieked in shock and pain.

Daniel yelled, "Teddy, stay back!" I saw that his slingshot was ready to release. He sent the rock flying, quickly reloaded, and fired again. The snake's ugly rattling grew quiet.

Ethel lay in the grass, quivering. I gathered him in my arms and wept.

Oh, Martha. You just can't imagine.

Love,
Teddy

Reading Short Response Questions for the Letter of July 15, 1892
Answer the questions below, and be sure to use complete sentences.

1. Why did Teddy and Daniel decide to stay at the stables instead of the boarding house?

_____

_____

_____

_____

_____

2. Why did T-Pat change his mind about how much he was going to charge Teddy and Daniel to spend the night in the stable?

_____

_____

_____

_____

3. How did Teddy and Daniel take care of Gabriel in the stables?

_____

_____

_____

_____

4. What happened with Ethelbert and the rattlesnake? How could this have been avoided?

_____

_____

_____

_____

July 16, 1892

Dear Martha,

My letters to you are becoming almost like a diary. I hope that's okay. I want to write things down so I won't ever forget them, and I promised you I'd share every detail. I was telling you about the rattlesnake.

Whether Daniel killed the rattlesnake or just stunned it, I don't know, but he picked it up on a stick and carried it far away. He also went to catch Gabriel, who had run away when the rattlesnake struck.

I checked Ethelbert's body to see how bad he was injured. There were definitely two fang marks on his thigh. I didn't know how to treat a snakebite, so I carried Ethel down to the little brook and put his body in the water. I held him on my lap and massaged his leg down and up toward the two punctures. A greenish liquid trickled out into the stream. I knew that would be the poison. I didn't know if I could get it all out this way, but I kept squeezing and massaging, over and over, washing the water over the wound.

When Daniel got back, he tied Gabriel's reins to a tree. Then, he came to the brook. He said, "How bad is it?"

I said, "I don't know. There are two fang marks. I only saw the one bite."

Daniel said, "Well, sometimes big snakes don't release all their poison in the first strike."

I held Ethel in my arms. He whimpered and lay very still.

Daniel said, "We need help. Let's keep going south, Teddy. I can walk. You hold Ethel up on Gabriel." That's what we did. We didn't know what else to do. I felt desperate.

As we rode farther south, I began to feel sick. My head hurt, my stomach was cramping, and I felt achy and miserable. I had to struggle to hold Ethel onto the horse's back with me.

Just when I thought I couldn't go on any farther, that I'd have to tell Daniel to stop, I saw an old man coming toward us. I was sure he was an Indian because of his colorful, patchwork clothes. I didn't know if he spoke English or if he would be friendly or hostile. We must have looked a sight, one kid on a horse, holding a dog with a snakebite, the other kid leading.

Martha, I was so glad to see him. When he got near enough to hear, I called out, "Can you help us?"

The Indian man came very close. I tried to explain that our dog had been bit by a snake. I thought I was speaking out loud, but the Indian man didn't seem to hear me. I turned to ask Daniel if he could hear me, and that's the last thing I remember for a long time.

I woke up in an open Indian hut. It had a thatched roof and was supported by poles. An Indian woman bathed my forehead with a damp cloth. When she saw my eyes open, she said, "Chee-hun-tah-mo."

I tried to sit up, but I was too weak. My stomach was churning, and the Indian woman held my head while I was sick. When I felt better, she held a bowl of water to my mouth. She said, "Okee."

I saw that I was lying on a blanket made of raccoon skins. My Indian nurse sang and chanted songs I had never heard before. She crushed some berries and made a tea. The tea was very bitter, and I made a face. She spooned it into my mouth anyway, one spoonful at a time. I knew it was something to help me, so I drank it.

I whispered, "Where am I?" and made a curious face.

She said, "Chikee." Chikee? I wondered what it meant. She pointed around the hut. "Chikee."

The man I had seen on the road came into the hut.

His skin was brown, and he had lots of wrinkles.

He said, "Chee-hun-tah-mo."

I said, "Where is Daniel?"

The Indian man said, "Nog-no-chee?"

I said, "Daniel? Nog-no-chee?"

He said, "Nog-no-chee," and smiled and nodded.
We were trying to understand each other.

I am relieved. I have no idea where Daniel is, but I feel like he is in good hands.

Love,
Teddy

Chee-hun-tah-mo = *hello*
okee = *water*
chikee = *house*
nog-no-chee = *boy*

Name_____ Date_____

Expository Writing Prompt for the Letter of July 16, 1892
Read and answer the following writing prompt.

Expository Prompt: Today Teddy, Daniel, and Ethel are all suffering from some form of sickness. Think about a time that you or a family member was sick. What was the sickness? Who took care of the sick person? How did the sick person get better? Now explain what it was like for you or your family member to be sick. Be sure to include details, so we'll be able to form a "mind movie" of what you mean. Remember: your paper needs a beginning, a middle, and an ending. After you write, read your expository piece to yourself. Add any improvements you think are necessary. Share your piece with a classmate. Help each other improve.

_____

_____

_____

_____

_____

_____

_____

_____

_____

_____

_____

_____

_____

_____

_____

_____

_____

_____

_____

July 17, 1892

Dear Martha,

I'm trying to keep up my writing even though I'm just now getting strong. I'm still with the Indians.

Through sign language and head nods, I knew Daniel must be alright. That made me feel better.

I said, "Ethelbert?" The Indian man looked at me blankly. I held my hands up in front of my chest like paws and barked. I hoped I looked like a dog.

He said. "Ee-fe."

The woman said, "Eecho Eefe." She made two of her fingers into fangs and pretended to strike.

I said, "Yes! A snake. Where is Eefe? Is he alive?"

She must have understood. She put her hands together and lay her head down on them. At first I thought she meant he was dead. I felt dread. But then she made a snoring sound, and I was hopeful again.

I said, "Is Ee-fe alive?"

She nodded her head. She patted my hand. She must have realized how important Ethel is to me. She said some words in her language.

I said, "Where is Nog-no-chee?"

She made a bowl of one of her hands and used her other hand to "eat" out of the bowl. Her sign language was easy to read.

I said, "Nog-no-chee?"

She smiled and said, "Nog-no-chee impigee-tsabanah."

Daniel was eating! Suddenly, things seemed normal. I felt dizzy and tired but relieved. I lay my head down and went to sleep.

This morning, Daniel came in to see me. I felt much better, much stronger. I said, "I've been sick."

Daniel said, "I was sick, too, but not as sick as you. I think we drank some bad water."

I said, "How is Ethelbert?"

Daniel said, "Lucky to be alive. Not many dogs could live through a rattlesnake bite. Sawni crushed up some purple flower leaves she picked and soaked them in hot water. Then, she put the wet leaves over where the fang marks were. I didn't think he'd pull through, but he's up running around, feeling fine. See?"

Ethel put his paws on the side of my raccoon skin bed. He licked me with his pink tongue as if to say, "It's about time you got up."

I threw my arms around Ethel's neck. Martha, I was so glad to see him I almost danced.

Sawni said something in her language and made hand motions of someone squeezing Ethel's leg where the fang marks are. Then, she swished her hands from side to side. She motioned for Daniel to tell me what she meant.

Daniel said, "Oh yeah. Sawni wants you to know that you helped save Ethel's life when you squeezed his leg in the running water."

I didn't know how to say thank you in her language, so I smiled and gave her a hug.

I said, "Daniel, we've got to get moving. We've got to get to the courthouse in Juno."

Daniel said, "Not yet, Teddy. Nokosi wants to meet with you."

I said, "Who?"

Daniel said, "Nokosi, the old man. While you were sick, he came in and sang some chants for you while Sawni made medicines. Now, he wants to see you before we leave. I think it's something important."

I said, "How will I understand what he is saying?"

Daniel said, "Nokosi's granddaughter, Talisa, speaks some English. She will say his words for you." Everything in me felt impatient. I wanted to jump up and run all the way to Juno by myself. But these people had been kind to us. They had saved Ethelbert's life. All they wanted was to speak to me.

I said, "Alright, I will meet with Nokosi."

Love,
Teddy

Name_____ Date_____

Reading Extended Response Questions for the Letter of July 17, 1892
Answer the questions below. Be sure to use complete sentences, reasons, and details.

1. Describe how Teddy and the Indian woman communicated with each other. Why was it important for Teddy to understand the Indian woman?

_____

_____

_____

_____

_____

_____

_____

_____

_____

_____

2. How did Teddy help to save Ethelbert's life? Who else helped Ethelbert? How?

_____

_____

_____

_____

_____

_____

_____

_____

_____

_____

July 18, 1892

Dear Martha,

That evening, we had a feast in the eating chikee. The whole village gathered for singing, dancing, and a feast of good food. I was hungry for the first time in days. Daniel, as usual, ate like a starving bear.

After the meal, Sawni let me know, through sign language, that it was time for Nokosi to speak with me. I was a little nervous. What was this all about? For some reason, I took my sketchbook with me.

Sawni led me to another hut that had sides. It was darker inside, and my eyes had to adjust to the dim light. Nokosi was sitting with four other Indian men, all smoking pipes. His granddaughter, Talisa, motioned for me to sit across from her grandfather.

Nokosi spoke for a while in his language. Then, Talisa said, "My grandfather welcomes you to his home. This is a great honor. When you were sick, he sang over you. He saw many things."

Then, Nokosi spoke directly to me. Talisa translated his words.

"When you were sick, I sang songs for you and watched the smoke that Sawni spread over you. I saw many things in the smoke. I saw that you are lost, that you have been lost for a long time. I saw a long journey and a grave along the way.

"I saw that you will still have trouble before you find what you are seeking. The trouble will come from a bad man, a man who wears fighting on his face. But you are not to worry. For at the end, when you think all is lost, a woman long dead will come to your rescue. She will offer you the heavens and the ocean, covered with gold."

I was astonished. What did he mean? Who was he talking about, a woman long dead? Was it Mama? How can a man wear fighting on his face? How could anyone offer me the heavens and the ocean, covered in gold?

Talisa said, "Before you leave, he wants to hear your story."

I said, "My story?" Talisa nodded. The men were looking at me intently. Why on earth would these wise men want to hear the story of a kid like me?

But I decided that it would be respectful for me to tell my story the best way I could, slowly, carefully, and with hand gestures and symbols that would help them understand. When I used the drawings in my sketchbook to show things I had seen on the journey, the five men leaned in to get a closer look. I told about the trip by wagon, yellow fever, getting lost from Mama and Pap, and being on my own.

Talisa translated my words. When I was finished, they seemed mystified.

Nokosi stood up. The meeting was over. I was mystified, too.

We slept one more night in the Indian village, I on my raccoon skin blanket and Daniel in another hut. This morning, we gathered our things to leave. I saw a small wooden wagon that looked like it was old and well used. I asked Nokosi, through his granddaughter, Talisa, if he would sell it to us. The wagon would help us travel easier to Juno. I held out twenty dollars Miss Melman had given to me.

Nokosi said some words I couldn't understand. Talisa translated. "My grandfather says he will sell you the wagon, but he wants the gold bracelet you wear on your arm as payment."

I was shocked. I didn't even know he had noticed it. I looked down at Althea Tomlinson's bracelet. I could not part with it for any reason.

"I'm sorry," I said. "I cannot sell this bracelet."

Talisa spoke with Nokosi. "My grandfather wants to know why you cannot sell it."

I said, "Because it gives me courage." Nokosi was watching me. "And because it is not mine to sell."

Nokosi smiled. Talisa translated his words. "He says your answer is an honest one, and he will sell you the wagon for the twenty dollars."

Daniel hitched Gabriel up to the wagon, and Sawni helped us settle our things. Nokosi told Daniel about a trail to Juno that only the Indians know about. It would take us there quicker than the road.

Ethelbert jumped into the wagon. We waved to our friends and left the village.

Love,
Teddy

Grammar Questions for the Letter of July 18, 1892
Circle the letter of the correct answer.

1. What literary device best describes the following sentence?
   Daniel ate like a starving bear.
   A. metaphor
   B. onomatopoeia
   C. simile
   D. transitional phrase

2. What punctuation mark should go at the end of the following sentence?
   "My grandfather wants to know why you cannot sell it"
   A. a question mark
   B. an exclamation point
   C. a semi-colon
   D. a period

3. Which of the following examples has the correct use of commas?
   A. The whole village gathered for singing, dancing, and a feast of good food.
   B. The whole village gathered for, singing, dancing, and a feast of good food.
   C. The whole village gathered for singing dancing and a feast of good food.
   D. The whole village gathered for singing, dancing, and a feast, of good food.

4. In the following sentence, what kind of word is *intently*?
   The men were looking at me intently.
   A. verb
   B. adverb
   C. noun
   D. adjective

5. Which of the following words is spelled incorrectly?
   A. translated
   B. gathered
   C. languege
   D. respectful

6. If Teddy said,
   "Ethelbert is the smartest dog in the whole world,"
   what would this be an example of?
   A. a simile
   B. hyperbole
   C. a comparison
   D. a strong verb

July 19, 1892

Dear Martha,

If I make it through this journey, you and I are going to have to sit down and read about it together!

To get to the Indian trail, we had to veer off the main road to Juno, go through the woods a bit, and find the trail Nokosi had told us about. It wasn't easy, but we found it. The trail was just wide enough for the little wagon. If that wagon had been any bigger, we wouldn't have made it.

The weather was beautiful. The sky was blue with big, fluffy clouds. We were sheltered from the sun by the tall grasses and trees that grew on either side of the trail. Riding in the wagon was actually fun, compared with two of us riding Gabriel or me riding Gabriel while trying to hold Ethelbert.

For a while, we enjoyed the silence. We were happy to be together. We were happy Ethelbert was well. We were happy we were not sick. We were happy to have a wagon to ride in and happy that Sawni had packed a meal for us. Martha, wasn't that kind, after all she's already done for us?

After some time, Daniel said, "So what happened in your meeting with Nokosi?" I think Daniel was a little hurt that he had not been invited to the meeting. I didn't understand why he wasn't invited, either.

I said, "He wanted to hear my story."

Daniel said, "Is that all?"

I said, "Well, not exactly. After I got finished, he wanted to tell me something he had seen."

Daniel said, "What? Where?"

I said, "Well, that's the thing. When I was sick, Sawni spread some smoke over me while they were singing for me to get better. Nokosi saw some things in the smoke. I hope I can remember it all. First, he said he saw that I was lost and had been lost for a long time. He saw a journey and a grave. That has to be our journey from Mississippi and Dylan's grave."

Daniel said, "That makes sense."

I said, "Then, he said I would still have trouble before I find what I am seeking. The trouble will come from a bad man, a man who wears fighting on his face."

Daniel said, "Jimbo Dudd. Jimbo has a scar on his face."

I said, "How did he get that scar?"

Daniel said, "He got it in a fight with Billy Bob Gates, and Billy Bob cut him with a Bowie knife."

I said, "Did you tell Nokosi about Jimbo? About him stealing the land deed?"

Daniel said, "No, I never mentioned Jimbo."

I said, "It's amazing, then, how he knew about a bad man and that his face is marked by fighting."

Daniel said, "Did he say anything else?"

I said, "One more thing, and I can't figure it out. He said that at the end, when I think all is lost, a woman long dead will come to my rescue. She will offer the heavens and the oceans, covered in gold."

Daniel said, "Now, that is just plain weird. A woman long dead? The oceans covered in gold?"

I said, "I don't have a clue, either, as to what it means."

I didn't know if Nokosi was right about all of that, but I did know he was right about the trail. The trail took us straight toward Juno. The trail was marked with rocks that had drawings on them and markings carved into the trunks of trees.

I said, "I wonder who made these markings?"

Daniel said, "Nokosi said for many years, even in his father's time, the Indians have had to run from soldiers and men who took their lands. The soldiers wanted them to leave the state and go to Indian land in Oklahoma. The Indians made special trails that were known only to them, so they could travel and hide at the same time."

I was grateful Nokosi had shown us the secret trail. He trusted us. Now, I will trust him.

Love,
Teddy

Writing Questions for the Letter of July 19, 1892
Circle the letter of the correct answer.

1. Read the following sentence from Teddy's letter today:
    For a while, we enjoyed the silence.
    The words *For a while* are an example of what good writing skill?
    A. dialogue
    B. metaphor
    C. transitional phrase
    D. persuasive writing

2. Read the following sentence from Teddy's letter today:
    **The trail was marked with rocks that had drawings on them and markings
    carved into the trunks of trees.**
    What does the author use that we should use in our own writing?
    A. details you can picture
    B. persuasive writing
    C. metaphors
    D. juicy color words

3. Read the following sentence from Teddy's letter today:
    I was grateful Nokosi had shown us the secret trail. He trusted us. Now, I will trust him.
    These sentences are examples of what good writing skill?
    A. juicy color words
    B. metaphors
    C. sentence variety
    D. persuasive writing

4. Read the following sentence from Teddy's letter today:
    We were happy to be together.
    This sentence has an example of what good writing skill?
    A. juicy color word
    B. specific emotion word
    C. sentence variety
    D. metaphor

5. If the author had wanted to emphasize the knife fight that Jimbo had with Billy Bob Gates, she could
    have used the word **"Slaaaaash!"** to describe the sound of Jimbo getting cut. The word *Slaaaaash!*
    would be an example of what type of good writing skill?
    A. metaphor
    B. juicy color word
    C. onomatopoeia
    D. simile

July 20, 1892

Dear Martha,

If I can't have you to travel with, Daniel is the next best thing!

He and I followed the trail all day yesterday. When the sun was beginning to set, we came to an empty chikee.

Daniel said, "Nokosi told me about this chikee. We can spend the night here. He said the water is safe to drink."

I said, "I don't see any water."

Daniel said, "He said there's a stream. It has to be here somewhere."

The stream wasn't hard to find. Ethelbert lapped thirstily. We took Gabriel out of the wagon harness and led him to the stream. He drank and drank. Then, he looked at me like, "Boy, that was good water."

Daniel made a campfire while I laid out the meal Sawni had prepared for us. It was some sort of meat that had been cooked over the fire and then wrapped in banana leaves. She sent two coconut halves, two roasted sweet potatoes, and two pounded corn cakes. We shared our meal with Ethel and staked Gabriel out in a patch of grass. Martha, do you remember that I used to be a picky eater? Well, not anymore.

Daniel said, "Tomorrow, we'll be in Juno, Teddy."

I said, "That's right. I don't know what will happen."

Daniel said, "Well, no matter what, I'm on your side."

We slept in the open hut, under the stars. As we lay on our backs on our pallets of palm fronds and grass, I pointed out the Big Dipper, the Little Dipper, and the North Star. It reminded me of sleeping outside with Mama and Pap, doing the same thing. Thinking about them made me wonder, are they alive? Are they together? Have they been looking for me? Do they even know I'm alive? Could they be somewhere right this minute, looking at the North Star, remembering the night our family slept under the stars so long ago?

I thought of Daniel, all alone. At least I have a family that loves me. At least I have parents who take care of me and make sure I get schooling and plenty of food and a safe home to live in. I thought of him growing up without his mama and being left alone with Verna when his pap died. I thought of him living out in the woods just to get away from her cruelties. Martha, Daniel is so happy he has a cousin—anyone—to call family. He came on this long journey with me and is always by my side. Isn't that what FAMILY is all about?

I said, "Daniel, I want you to know that I'm glad you're my cousin. I'm glad we're both Bodains. I never knew you before, but now we belong together." I hoped he didn't think I was corny.

I waited for him to say something back, but he was snoring, that rascal! Here I had opened my soul to him, and he was sleeping.

The next morning, I wrote some more on my letter to you. Then, we broke camp. We doused the fire with water, hitched Gabriel to the little wagon, filled our canteens with water, and set off for Juno.

It took another long day of traveling, but we pulled into Juno late that afternoon. We stopped at the post office, so I could ask where the courthouse was. I also asked if there was any letter waiting for Teddy or Theodosia Bodain. There wasn't. I was disappointed. I had hoped Mama and Pap would try to get in touch with me by sending a letter. Of course, they had no way of knowing that I would come on down here, so it made sense, but I was still sad about it. Vexation.

We drove to the courthouse. My heart was pounding. Would Jimbo Dudd be there, waiting to leap out and steal the deed back, again?

I asked the lady at the front desk where the Land Deed Office was. She said it was there, but it was closed. "The courthouse is open till five," she said, "but the Land Deed Office closes at three o'clock. Come back tomorrow morning at nine."

Vehement vexation!

Love,
Teddy

Name_____ Date_____

Persuasive Writing Prompt for the Letter of July 20, 1892
Read and answer the following prompt.

Persuasive Prompt: Teddy and Daniel are family. They stick together through thick and thin. Think of your best friend or a close family member you enjoy being with. What kinds of activities do you enjoy doing together? How do you get through tough times with this special person? Convince your reader that this person is the perfect person to help you in tough situations instead of going through those times alone. Give examples with plenty of details. Make some up, if you'd like to. Read your paper carefully and add any details you may have forgotten.

_____

_____

_____

_____

_____

_____

_____

_____

_____

_____

_____

_____

_____

_____

_____

_____

_____

_____

July 21, 1892

Dear Martha,

Once again, trouble has reared its ugly head.

Yesterday evening, Daniel and I found a stable for our wagon and Gabriel. I paid the man a little extra to let Ethelbert stay there, too. Daniel watered and fed Gabriel while I went to the general store. I bought some meat for Ethel's supper and a big ham bone to last him through the night.

We found rooms at Molly Baden's Bed and Breakfast. Both of us looked forward to sleeping in a real bed for a change. Molly was very nice and told us we were welcome to use her indoor bathroom. An INDOOR bathroom! Can you imagine?

For supper, we went to The Liberty Bell, a restaurant here in Juno. We were starving, and we have a little money left from Miss Melman. I don't know why, but the town of Juno is filled with people right now, and they all seemed to want to eat at The Liberty Bell. The restaurant was full, and there was a crowd of people sitting and standing outside. Daniel and I put our names in for a table and waited with everyone else. We had to wait almost an hour, but it wasn't too boring because The Liberty Bell has a big fish pond out front with pretty goldfish in it. I wanted you to be there with me to see them.

When we finally got our table, they brought us more food than you could shake a stick at! They brought platters of ribs, corn on the cob, collard greens, swamp cabbage, cinnamon apples, potato salad, sliced tomatoes, sliced pickles, and three kinds of pie. Daniel and I started laughing. With the two of us, it's either feast or famine, as Mama used to say. Remember when she used to say that to us?

During the meal, though, a big fight broke out right outside of the restaurant. Two or three men were beating each other up and yelling insults. Suddenly, they came through the door of the restaurant. We all kind of scooted our chairs back and jumped out of the way. After a few moments, though, the fight broke up and the men left. We went back to our chairs.

Daniel thought the fight was great fun and excitement. He kept saying things like, "Did you see that roundhouse? He took that uppercut like he was made of iron!"

As for me, I just wanted to eat. And that's what we did, until we could hardly move.

When I went to pay our bill, I noticed my neck pouch was hanging outside my shirt, not under the shirt where it usually lay covered. I thought, that's odd. I counted out the money we needed for our meal and handed it to the girl who waited on our table. As I was putting the neck pouch back, a scary thought occurred to me. I opened the pouch to make sure everything was there. The land deed was gone!

I jumped up from my chair and shouted, "Daniel, it's gone! The land deed was here. Now, it's gone."

He said, "Maybe you dropped it on the floor when you took the money out." He helped me search the floor around our table. Folks were beginning to stare and murmur. Daniel faced the restaurant of people and said, "Has anyone seen a folded paper on the floor? It's very important!" Everyone began to look.

Someone yelled, "I'll check outside." Martha, I was so nervous, my palms were sweating.

No one had seen the paper.

An older lady called me over to her chair. She motioned for me to lean down. She whispered, "There was a man standing behind you just as the fight broke out. I thought it was odd because he was so close. I happened to glance up and saw him pulling on something you had around your neck."

I felt like my heart might stop. I said, "What did he look like?"

She said, "Well, I don't want to be unkind, but his face had a scar."

I sunk down to my feet and put my head in my hands. Jimbo Dudd has brought the trouble Nokosi warned me about. Martha, what will I do now?

Love,
Teddy

Reading Multiple Choice Questions for the Letter of July 21, 1892
Circle the letter of the correct answer.

1. When Teddy and Daniel went to The Liberty Bell for supper, there was a long wait. What did they do to pass the time?
   A. They played marbles.
   B. They went to the general store to buy colored pencils.
   C. They sat and watched the goldfish in the pond in front of the restaurant.
   D. They played hopscotch in the street with some other children.

2. What happened while Teddy and Daniel were eating at the restaurant?
   A. a woman fainted
   B. the waitress spilled water down Daniel's back
   C. Teddy felt sick to her stomach again
   D. a fight broke out

3. How did Teddy lose the land deed again?
   A. Jimbo Dudd stole it from around her neck during the fight.
   B. It fell out of her pouch and blew away while she was outside the restaurant.
   C. Daniel spilled a chocolate milkshake all over it.
   D. She dropped it in the pond out in front of the restaurant.

4. What did Teddy find to be so special about Molly Baden's Bed and Breakfast?
   A. Daniel and she stayed on the top floor and had an excellent view of the city.
   B. It had an indoor bathroom.
   C. There was a special room just for pets where Ethel was able to stay.
   D. Molly Baden serves her guests breakfast in bed.

5. What did Teddy buy at the general store to get Ethel through the night?
   A. a warm blanket
   B. some jerky
   C. a ham bone
   D. a fluffy pillow

6. When did Teddy notice that something was amiss with her neck pouch?
   A. when she went to pay their bill
   B. while they were eating dessert
   C. in the middle of the fight
   D. after they had gone back to the bed and breakfast

7. Who had warned Teddy about more trouble with Jimbo Dudd?
   A. Mama and Pap
   B. Wanda Watson
   C. Verna Dudd
   D. Nokosi

July 23, 1892

Dear Martha,

It's tempting to wish I was back in Mississippi with you, playing, but I keep pressing on. Mama and Pap would be proud that I'm not a quitter.

First of all, Daniel was not able to go to the Land Deed Office with me. Rats! When we got up this morning, Molly Baden fixed a nice breakfast. But when she was serving us, she forgot she had left the pan of bacon grease on the stove. It caused a small fire in her kitchen, and the fire brigade had to come. She turned to us and said, "Please, would you watch my children while I try to deal with this?" Without waiting for an answer, she handed us three small children and went back into the house.

Daniel looked at me, helpless. I said, "I'll be alright. Come to the Land Deed Office when you can."

I didn't want to take the time to harness Gabriel to the wagon, so I ran all the way to the courthouse.

The clock on the front of the clock tower said a quarter past nine. I was just sick that I hadn't been there at the stroke of nine. I went into the courthouse, and the same woman who had helped me the day before was there. She said, "The Land Deed Office is open. Down this hall and to the left."

That walk to the Land Deed Office was like walking through quicksand. I opened the door and went in. Just as I had feared, there stood Jimbo Dudd. He was being helped by the clerk behind the counter. The clerk had spread out an enormous map and was going over it with Jimbo.

He said, "This would be your 40 acres right—here. See? Your land borders this spring. That will be vital for irrigation."

Jimbo said, "Where do I sign?" He still had not seen me.

The clerk said, "You must be in a hurry. Well, Mr. Bodain, I'll get the papers in order, and we can—"

The way Jimbo was standing it was hard for the man to see me. I shouted to get his attention.

"Stop! It's a lie! That man is not Mr. Bodain."

Jimbo turned around in surprise. Then, he spoke in a harsh voice. "You better get out of here. I warned you about not causing any trouble." Martha, he was so scary I nearly backed down. I had to summon all my courage.

I looked him right in the face and said in a loud voice, "And I warned you that you can't steal what my pap has worked so hard for." I spoke to the man behind the counter. "Mister, you'd be making a big mistake if you turn our land over to this man. He's a liar and a thief. My pap is Dalton Bodain. This man stole his land deed." I was shaking by the time I finished talking.

The clerk behind the counter said, "Come forward. I want to see who is talking."

As I tried to get around Jimbo, he hissed, "You are making a big mistake."

I walked to the counter. I said, "My name is Theodosia Bodain. I came from Mississippi in a covered wagon with my parents, Grace and Dalton Bodain. My little brother, Dylan, died in the yellow fever epidemic up near Gainesville. I was separated from my parents. I've been keeping this land deed for my pap. This man, Jimbo Dudd, from Micanopy, stole it because he wants the land for himself."

The clerk snatched the land deed off the counter. He said, "If this is true, then you, sir, could be put in jail for attempting to steal property that doesn't belong to you. This is a matter for the court to decide. His Honor will be presiding tomorrow afternoon in court. We'll let him settle this matter."

Jimbo's face turned dark red. He said, "This is a lie, and I'll have none of it! I want that land."

The clerk said, "I'm afraid it's too late for that. You may have made a false and illegal claim. I'm sure the constable will want you to be his guest at the jailhouse until this matter can be settled tomorrow afternoon at two o'clock. If you are proven innocent, all the proper apologies will be made."

Jimbo turned to me in a rage. "Look at the trouble you've gone and made for me! You'll pay for this! And I ain't going to no jailhouse."

He turned to leave. The constable stood in the doorway with two other men. The constable said, "Sir, you can come willingly—or unwillingly. The choice is yours."

Martha, it's not every day that you get to see a man led off to jail.

Love,
Teddy

Name_____ Date_____

Narrative Writing for the Letter of July 23, 1892
Read and answer the writing prompt below.

Narrative Prompt: It took a lot of courage for Teddy to tell the Land Deed Office clerk, right in front of Jimbo, that Jimbo was a liar and thief. Think of a time you had to be very courageous. Maybe you were courageous when you helped a friend. Maybe you felt courageous when you were alone. You might have even been courageous with a group of other people. Now write the story of what happened, and be sure to tell how being courageous helped you. Add details and examples, so we understand how you felt. If you need more room to write, use an additional piece of paper. When you've finished, read your story to yourself. Are there any important details you left out? If so, add them in. Now share your story with a classmate.

_____

_____

_____

_____

_____

_____

_____

_____

_____

_____

_____

_____

_____

_____

_____

_____

_____

_____

_____

_____

July 24, 1892

Dear Martha,

I bet every time you open one of my letters you ask yourself, "What next?" The saga continues....

After the big ruckus with Jimbo Dudd at the courthouse, I went to find Daniel because he hadn't shown up yet. They had put out the fire, which didn't do too much damage. When I got there, Molly Baden was just thanking Daniel for watching her children and keeping them safe.

I told Daniel all about seeing Jimbo and the fuss he had made. Daniel said, "Oh man, I missed it."

I told him he'd get to see the real excitement tomorrow afternoon at two o'clock in front of the judge. We talked about that, wondering what would happen and if the judge would believe me or Jimbo.

In the meantime, we decided to telegraph Miss Melman to let her know we had finally arrived in Juno and were staying at a nice place. I have never sent a telegram before, so the operator at the telegraph office showed me how to word it. You pay by the word, so you have to keep your message short.

My telegram said, "Arrived Juno. Staying Molly Baden's Bed & Breakfast. Court tomorrow at two o'clock about land deed. Jimbo Dudd in jail. Teddy"

I paid the fee, and Daniel and I watched the telegraph operator tap out our message. It seems a miracle that you can be in one place, miles away from someone you want to send a message to, and in just a few minutes, your message arrives on their end.

Daniel and I went to the drugstore to have an ice-cream soda, and afterward, we came back to the telegraph office. The operator said, "You have a telegram." Daniel and I were thrilled to receive an answer.

Miss Melman wrote: "Happy you are safe. John Mikelson investigating your parents. May have a lead. Cassie Melman."

I felt my heart beating faster and faster. I sent another telegram. "Are my parents alive?" We waited. There was no answer.

Daniel and Ethelbert and I walked around the town of Juno and fed some ducks down at the pond.

When we checked later, there was another telegram. "Located the Larks. May have news."

I felt all fluttery inside. I thought of Travis Lark and what good friends we had become. I wondered if his parents had any news of my parents.

We got a third telegram. "Larks claim heard Dalton Bodain alive back in May. Mikelson telegraphing U.S. Health Office."

Pap! Pap might be alive. I had an idea.

I asked the operator, "Can I send a telegram to Micanopy?"

He said, "Of course."

My telegram was to the postmistress. It said, "Did Dalton Bodain pick up letter left for him? Theodosia Bodain."

The answer arrived fifteen minutes later. "Letter still here." My heart sank.

But one hour later, the telegraph operator found us at The Liberty Bell. He said, "Teddy, another telegram arrived for you."

This telegram was from Miss Melman. "John received telegram from post office, Ft. Pierce. Bodain family living Miss Eileen's Boarding House."

I was stunned. Bodain family? Does it mean Mama and Pap? Does it mean the other Bodain family we met on the wagon train? Daniel and I had stood right outside of Miss Eileen's Boarding House when we were in Ft. Pierce! Were Mama and Pap there at the same time?

I didn't know the answers, but I had to take a chance.

I sent another telegram to Miss Melman. "Telegraph Bodains. Come to Juno Courthouse tomorrow two o'clock. Emergency." Martha, I can tell you that my knees were knocking when I sent that message.

Daniel said, "Well, tomorrow we will know for sure."

My eyes filled with tears, but they weren't tears of sadness. They were tears of hope.

Love,
Teddy

Name_____ Date_____

Reading Short Response Questions for the Letter of July 24, 1892

Answer the questions below, and be sure to use complete sentences.

1. Teddy went to send her first telegram. Explain why the telegraph operator told Teddy that in sending a telegram, she should keep her message short.

_____

_____

_____

_____

2. Describe the things that Teddy, Daniel, and Ethelbert did while waiting for the telegrams to arrive.

_____

_____

_____

_____

3. Teddy received a telegram from Miss Melman about the Bodain family. Where did she say they were living? How did Teddy feel about this?

_____

_____

_____

_____

4. Explain what Teddy meant when she said, **"My eyes filled with tears, but they weren't tears of sadness. They were tears of hope."**

_____

_____

_____

_____

_____

July 25, 1892

Dear Martha,

Today is a day that will be burned into my memory, like the inscription etched inside Althea Tomlinson's gold bracelet. I would give anything if you had been here to share it with me.

At a quarter till two, Daniel and I took a seat in the courtroom. The clerk said, "Miss Bodain, the judge has a few matters to preside over at two o'clock. We'll get to your situation as he has time."

The judge was just like you would imagine: a large man with white hair. He wore a big, black robe. He rapped on the table with his wooden gavel, and things began.

The judge listened to a case about a man who bought a sow from another farmer. She was supposed to have piglets, and she didn't. He then listened to a case about a shipment of sugar cane that had fermented before it was delivered. He listened to another case of a man who bought some land and found a moonshine still on it. After three more cases, the constable brought Jimbo Dudd into the courtroom.

When it was our turn, the clerk from the Land Deed Office told the judge that Jimbo had claimed 40 acres with a deed that might not be his.

The judge asked that Jimbo be brought up front. He said, "State your name."

Jimbo said, "My name is Dalton Bodain."

I said in a loud voice, "It is not! That man is Jimbo Dudd."

There was a commotion in the back of the courtroom. Some men were coming forward. The judge hammered on the table and said, "What is this?"

The court clerk said, "Your Honor, this man also claims to be Dalton Bodain."

The whole courtroom turned to see Pap, standing right in the aisle. I thought my heart would jump out of my chest.

The judge said, "Come forward, please, Sir. You claim to be Dalton Bodain?"

Pap said, "I am Dalton Bodain."

The judge said, "Is there anyone who can verify that you are Dalton Bodain?"

I couldn't keep quiet any longer. I shouted, "I can! That's my father, Dalton Bodain." I pointed toward Pap.

The judge said, "Come forward please, son."

I went close to the judge. I said, "I am not a boy. I'm dressed like a boy. My hair is cut like a boy, but I'm a girl. There's a reason for that, but I'll have to tell you later. My name is Theodosia Bodain."

Martha, the strangeness of it all almost seemed funny.

The judge said, "Can you prove this man is Dalton Bodain?"

The courtroom was so quiet you could have heard a pin drop.

I thought for a second. I said, "No, sir, but you can."

The judge said, "How can I do that?"

I took Pap's father's watch from the pouch around my neck. I handed it to the judge. I said, "This watch belonged to my grandfather, who was also Dalton Bodain. It was given to him by his wife, Isabelle."

Jimbo practically screamed, "That's my watch! She stole it from me! Give it here!"

I'll have to continue this tomorrow. There's just too much to tell for now, and my hand is killing me.

Love,
Teddy

Name_____ Date_____

Expository Writing Prompt for the Letter of July 25, 1892
Read and answer the following writing prompt.

Expository Prompt: In the courtroom, Teddy had to prove that Dalton Bodain was really, in fact, her pap. Think of your own life. Have you been absolutely right about something, yet others weren't so sure? Now explain what you did to stand up for yourself and what the outcome was of this. Be sure to include details and examples, so your reader will be able to form a "mind movie" of what you mean. Remember your paper needs a beginning, a middle, and an ending. After you write, read your piece to yourself. Add any improvements you might need. Share your expository piece with a classmate.

_____

_____

_____

_____

_____

_____

_____

_____

_____

_____

_____

_____

_____

_____

_____

_____

_____

_____

_____

July 26, 1892

Dear Martha,

I know you're waiting to hear what happened, so I'll get right to it. I'm writing as fast as I can.

In the courtroom, Jimbo looked like he was about to explode with anger. He said again, "This girl is a thief. She stole this watch from me. I've worn it every day for years."

The judge said, "Theodosia, tell me how this watch can prove that your father is Dalton Bodain."

I said, "Your Honor, there is an inscription written on the inside. The real Dalton Bodain will know what it says." For the first time, I turned to look at Pap. How handsome he looked. How strong. His eyes smiled at me. I thought my heart would burst.

The judge turned to Jimbo. He said, "Sir, if you've worn this watch every day for years, I'm sure you've read the inscription many times. Please, tell us what it says."

Jimbo's face turned white. He looked down at his shoes and had nothing to say.

The judge turned to Pap. He said, "Sir, can you tell us what the inscription says?"

Pap cleared his throat. Then, he said, "This watch was given to my father by his wife, Teddy's grandmother, long dead. The inscription says, 'To my beloved Dalton: I love you more than the stars are bright, more than the moon is round, more than the ocean is deep. Isabelle'"

As the judge closed the gold watch cover, I remembered Nokosi's words!

The courtroom buzzed with excitement. The judge rapped his gavel on the table. "I think that about settles it, folks. Clyde, take Mr. Bodain and his daughter down to the Land Deed Office, and help them file their deed. Welcome to Florida, Mr. Bodain. Constable Biddle, take Mr. Jimbo Dudd to jail."

The constable stepped forward and led Jimbo away.

When we got outside of the courtroom, Pap gave me a bear hug. He looked at me like he couldn't believe his eyes. Neither one of us said anything for a long, long time.

Then, Pap said, "I thought you were dead."

I said, "I wondered if you were dead, too. Where's Mama? I mean, is Mama—"

Pap said, "Teddy, your mama was very sick. The doctors tried everything they could to save her. She was very weak and almost didn't make it, but she did. She's in Ft. Pierce with—well, she'll want to tell you about that." That sounded like a mystery, but I was just so happy to know that Mama is alive. Martha, I let out my breath in a sigh of relief. A big smile spread over my face.

But that reminded me. I said, "Pap, there's someone I want you to meet." I found Daniel sitting on a bench in the hallway. I motioned for him to come over.

I said, "Pap, this is Daniel Bodain, our cousin!"

Pap stared for a moment, obviously in shock. He said, "Well, I'll be. You must be Daniel's boy."

Daniel said, "My pap's dead. He died eight months ago of pneumonia."

Pap said, "I'm sorry, son. Do you have family?"

Daniel said, "My mama died when I was little. I don't have any other family."

I said, "He's all alone, Pap."

Pap said, "Daniel, I lost a son awhile back. I sure would love to have another one. A boy ought not to be alone. Would you consider being a part of our family?"

Daniel said, "That would mean a whole heap to me."

Pap said, "Then, it's settled." He looked at me. "We're still the Bodains." He looked at Daniel. "We're ALL Bodains."

Martha, I was so proud, so relieved, so happy. My journey is almost at an end.

Pap took my hand in one of his and Daniel's hand in the other.

We left the courthouse with 40 acres of land and a new family member.

Love,
Teddy

Name_____ Date_____

Reading Extended Response Questions for the Letter of July 26, 1892
Answer the questions below. Be sure to use complete sentences, reasons, and details.

1. Teddy used Pap's watch as proof that Dalton Bodain was her father. Explain how using Pap's watch proved that he was her father.

_____

_____

_____

_____

_____

_____

_____

_____

_____

2. Teddy just introduced Daniel to Pap. Explain how Pap reacted to the news that Daniel is his cousin.

_____

_____

_____

_____

_____

_____

_____

_____

_____

July 27, 1892

Dear Martha,

I can't remember ever being as happy as when I wrote you yesterday. What a day! What a victory! All this, and we don't have to worry about Jimbo Dudd anymore.

Pap, Daniel, and I had a celebration dinner at The Liberty Bell. They served us a fine meal. We did a lot of smiling and hugging and staring at each other in wonderment. But none of us felt like talking much, really. There are too many stories to tell. All that will come later. We are just glad to be together.

Pap said, "It's going to take some getting used to that you are alive, Teddy. For months now, your mama and I thought you were dead. It about killed us to think that we had lost two children in just one month. We have missed you—more than you can imagine."

I said, "But why, Pap? Why did you think I was dead?"

Pap said, "Your mama was bad off sick. So was I, for a while. But when I got to where I could stand and walk again, I started searching all over to find you. I searched every quarantine station. When I got to the last one, the one run by Mrs. Plum, she was gone, so I didn't get to talk to her directly. But I did find Miss Essie Mae Pitts. I asked her if she had seen you, and she said, "Oh, Dalton. I have the saddest news to tell you. Your little Teddy is gone. A few nights ago, she died. They came and took her body in the night."

I said, "Miss Essie Mae told you that?" I was stunned. Puzzled. Maybe Miss Essie Mae just assumed I had died, or maybe she was confused from the fever. Or, for some reason, maybe the girl who had helped me told her I had died.

Pap said, "It liked to have killed me to hear that, and the worst part was telling your mama. She was already grieving so over Dylan. Telling her about you almost did her in. She even gave up the will to live."

I said, "So that's why you didn't come looking for me. I wondered about that a lot."

Pap said, "Did you have any word of our whereabouts?"

I said, "At Mrs. Plum's quarantine station, the head soldier told me that Mr. and Mrs. Bodain had died. I refused to believe him. I looked for you and Mama for days. I went to every quarantine station, every hospital. I felt so lost and alone."

Pap said, "I'm sure you did. We at least had each other, but you were all alone."

I said, "I was until Daniel found me. I didn't want to believe it at first, but we eventually realized we were cousins."

Pap grinned. "Daniel, I didn't mean to stare so when I met you, but seeing you at this age is like looking at myself. I'll show you a picture I have of me, and you won't believe it's not you you'll be seeing."

After supper, Pap wanted to send a telegram to Mama, so she wouldn't be so shocked at seeing me in person. I said, "Does she know I'm alive?"

Pap said, "No. The telegram we received just said, 'Bodains come to Juno Courthouse tomorrow two o'clock. Emergency.' It didn't say anything about you, Teddy."

I smiled. "Then, the first you knew of me was when you saw me standing there in front of the judge?"

Pap smiled. "Great day in the morning! I didn't know what to think. All of a sudden, a boy I didn't even recognize stands up and shouts, 'I can! That's my father, Dalton Bodain.' My eyes almost popped out of my head, I was so surprised. You'd cut off all your hair! Then, I heard that scrappy little voice of yours telling everybody what-for, and I knew it was you. It's a wonder I didn't keel over dead from the shock of it all."

We spent the night at Miss Molly Baden's Bed and Breakfast. I could hardly sleep because I was thinking about 100 things at once, so I spent the time writing to you.

I felt the gold bracelet on my arm. It always makes me feel good, like I own something precious. I was holding onto that bracelet when I finally quit thinking and fell asleep.

Love,
Teddy

Name_____ Date_____

Grammar Questions for the Letter of July 27, 1892
Circle the letter of the correct answer.

1. What kind of word is *gold* in the following sentence?
   I felt the gold bracelet on my arm.
   A. noun
   B. verb
   C. adverb
   D. adjective

2. What kind of punctuation mark should go at the end of the following sentence?
   Great day in the morning
   A. a question mark
   B. a quotation mark
   C. an exclamation point
   D. a semi-colon

3. Which of the following words is spelled correctly?
   A. celebration
   B. recieved
   C. beleive
   D. directley

4. What does the word *keel* mean when used in the following sentence?
   It's a wonder I didn't keel over dead from the shock of it all.
   A. throw up
   B. fall over
   C. run away
   D. bend from side to side

5. In the following sentence, what is the subject?
   Maybe Miss Essie Mae just assumed I had died.
   A. Maybe
   B. Miss
   C. Miss Essie Mae
   D. I

6. Which of these should be capitalized?
   A. miss essie mae pitts
   B. the liberty bell
   C. teddy
   D. all of the above

7. What is the subject of the following sentence?
   My eyes almost popped out of my head.
   A. My
   B. eyes
   C. almost
   D. head

July 28, 1892

Dear Martha,

Pap was delighted to see Gabriel.

He said, "I had no idea I'd ever see you again, old boy."

I said, "Miss Melman has been keeping him for you. She has Girlie, too."

Pap said, "That Miss Melman is a good soul. Your mama will be glad to hear news of Girlie."

He was also glad to see Ethelbert, who jumped in his lap and tried to lick his face.

Pap said, "Ethel, I do believe you are happy to see me. Don't you look healthy and nice."

Pap, Daniel, and I took a steamer, The Southern Odyssey, from Juno Beach up to Ft. Pierce. Daniel led Gabriel up the ramp to the lower deck and tied him in a stall.

The three of us and Ethelbert sat in deck chairs. Miss Molly had sent a hamper of food: tomatoes, ham sandwiches, sliced watermelon, deviled eggs, celery sticks, and chocolate cake.

Pap said, "It's a feast, don't you think, Daniel?"

Daniel said, "Yes, sir, it's a feast alright."

The three of us enjoyed our meal as the steamer chugged steadily northward. We had sent Mama a second telegram telling her the boat would dock at Ft. Pierce sometime around four o'clock.

I said, "Pap, why are you and Mama in Ft. Pierce?"

He said, "The Carters are going to be buying a place somewhere near there, and their relatives own a big, roomy boarding house. They let the Carters room there while they're waiting on everything to fall into place. Mrs. Carter stayed to help with the fever victims, so we found each other again when your mama was healing. They asked us to stay with them until we can get our feet back under us, so to speak."

I said to Daniel, "You'll love the Carters."

The steam engine started slowing, and the captain turned the bow of the boat toward the shore. Lots of people stood together in groups on the dock, waving. As we got closer, I saw Martin Carter and then Miss Emily. I saw Mr. and Mrs. Carter, and then, there was Mama. She had a smile as big as Texas.

My heart was thumping something terrible. I had looked forward to this day forever. Sometimes, I didn't know if I would ever see Mama's face again. Almost before they got the gangplank in place, I was running toward her.

We both burst out crying at the same time, hugging each other like we would never let go. There was so much to tell, so much to say, I felt like it all wanted to burst out at the same time. We gripped each other like that for a long time.

Then, Mama looked at my face. She said, "Teddy, you've come back to me. I thought I had lost you forever—but what happened to your hair?"

I laughed. "It's a long story. I've been a boy, and Daniel's been a girl."

Suddenly, I remembered Daniel. I said, "Mama! There's someone you've got to meet. This is Daniel. Daniel Bodain. He's our cousin. His parents are dead, and he was all alone, but now he's with us."

Mama looked at Daniel. She said, "I know you! I've got a picture of Dalton that could be your twin brother." She wrapped her arms around him and said, "Welcome, Daniel. Welcome to the family."

Daniel was too shy to say anything, but he hugged her back real hard.

Then, Mama said, "Teddy, now I have someone I want you to meet." Mama turned to Mrs. Carter, and she put a bundle in Mama's arms. Mama then turned to me and opened the blanket.

Inside was the most adorable little baby girl I've ever seen. She had soft brown curls and huge brown eyes. When she saw me, she laughed and kicked her feet. She reached her arms out to me, and I took her.

Mama said, "This is a day of surprises and love and new family members. Meet your baby sister."

Love,
Teddy

Writing Questions for the Letter of July 28, 1892
Circle the letter of the correct answer.

1. Read the following sentence from Teddy's letter today:
   She had soft brown curls and huge brown eyes.
   The author could have chosen to use the terms *auburn* and *hazel* instead of brown.
   The words *auburn* and *hazel* are examples of what kind of good writing skill?
   A. similes
   B. juicy color words
   C. metaphors
   D. onomatopoeia

2. Read the following sentence from Teddy's letter today:
   She had a smile as big as Texas.
   The words *as big as Texas* are an example of what kind of good writing skill?
   A. simile
   B. juicy color words
   C. metaphor
   D. onomatopoeia

3. Read the following sentence from Teddy's letter today:
   Miss Molly had sent a hamper of food: tomatoes, ham sandwiches, sliced watermelon, deviled eggs, celery sticks, and chocolate cake.
   This sentence is a good example of what type of writing skill?
   A. persuasive writing
   B. descriptive writing
   C. transitional phrases
   D. dialogue

4. Read the following sentence from Teddy's letter today:
   We gripped each other like that for a long time.
   The word *gripped* is an example of what type of good writing skill?
   A. dialogue
   B. simile
   C. strong verb
   D. transitional word

5. Read the following sentence from Teddy's letter today:
   The three of us enjoyed our meal as the steamer chugged steadily northward.
   The word *chugged* is an example of what kind of good writing skill?
   A. dialogue
   B. simile
   C. onomatopoeia
   D. transitional word

July 29, 1892

Dear Martha,

When Mama said, "Meet your baby sister," I was stupefied. How could this be? I knew Mama was not expecting a baby when the yellow fever struck us, and this baby is almost a year old!

I said, "Mama, where did she come from?"

Mama said, "She's a flower that grew in the garden of sickness and death."

Pap said, "Why don't we save all our stories for later, when we've got time to tell all the details. We've got a lot of catching up to do."

We went back to the Carters' house. It was good to see Miss Emily and Martin and their baby, Lucy. Daniel helped the men find a place for Gabriel and our little wagon. Mama put the new baby in the playpen with Lucy, and the two babies played happily. I helped Mama, Miss Emily, and Mrs. Carter fix supper. We were all exploding, wanting to ask each other questions, but Pap reminded us to wait till after supper, so we could all hear things together.

We gathered around Mrs. Carter's big table. We held hands, and Mr. Carter asked the blessing. Before he was done, he said, "Lord, thank you for bringing these wayward lambs back into the fellowship of their family." Mama squeezed my hand. I squeezed hers back, and I also squeezed Daniel's.

We had a jolly supper, but it didn't last too long. Everyone was waiting to get to the living room, so the talking could begin. I wish you could have heard it all in person instead of just reading it in a letter.

When we were all seated, I burst out, "Tell me about the baby!"

Mama smiled. Pap said, "Your mother was terribly ill with yellow fever. She was weak."

Mrs. Carter said, "Near death. That's the truth of it."

Pap said, "She was already heartbroken over losing Dylan, and then, when the news came along about you, Teddy…." Pap put his hand over his eyes.

Mrs. Carter said, "The news that you were dead was the last straw. I think Grace was about ready to just lay down and die right then."

Mama said, "I was." She took over telling the story.

"There was a woman in the next bed who was very sick with the fever. She had already lost her husband, two sons, and a daughter. She had no other relatives. Her baby daughter was sick, too, and lay on the bed beside her mother. I could barely hold my head up myself, but we would talk a little bit."

"One night, the woman said, 'Grace, would you take my baby if anything happens to me?'"

"I said, 'Oh, Honey, you're going to make it.' But in the morning, I saw that she had not. Her baby was wet, soaked through, and so weak she could hardly cry. She was snuggled against her mother on the pallet next to mine. When I opened my eyes and looked at her, she reached out for me. I didn't even know her name. But I knew I had to take her. She didn't have anyone else to care for her, and I wasn't going to let her go to an orphanage, not when I had lost two children of my own."

"So I pulled her over with me, changed her, and helped her to get well. No one at the quarantine station even noticed. They had so many people dying and so many new ones coming in, they just took the mother away, and that was it. I never knew her name, either."

I said, "She's beautiful, Mama." I picked up the baby. She lay her head on my shoulder. I squeezed her tight.

Mama said, "Isn't she?"

I said, "What did you name her?"

Mama said, "When Dylan died, you gave him your most precious possession, so he wouldn't be all alone. Now, here I was all alone and another woman had given me her most precious possession. I thought about your gift to Dylan, and the name seemed perfect. I named her Veronica."

Martha, why is it that when we're the happiest, we cry?

Love,
Teddy

Name_____ Date_____

Persuasive Writing for the Letter of July 29, 1892
Read and answer the following prompt.

Persuasive Prompt: Teddy was just told how Mama received a new baby. Mama explained how the baby's mother died, and she took the baby. She didn't go through an adoption agency or any other official way of legally adopting the baby. Do you think she did the right thing? Do you think she did the wrong thing? Decide what you think. Now write your opinion so that you convince us that your decision is right. Be sure to bring out convincing reasons, emotions, and examples.

_____

_____

_____

_____

_____

_____

_____

_____

_____

_____

_____

_____

_____

_____

_____

_____

_____

_____

_____

July 30, 1892

Dear Martha,

I hope you've been well. I'll be glad when I receive YOUR letters. I was telling you about being reunited with Mama. It felt strange to sleep in the same house with her and Pap, but it was wonderful. This morning, we woke up to a house full of people and a delicious breakfast. I'm so glad I'm not out on my own anymore. I had some great adventures and some fun times with Daniel, but it's good to just be a kid again with parents to take care of me.

One thing I enjoy is playing with Veronica. She's younger than Dylan was, but she does some of the same baby things he used to do. My heart still hurts when I think of Dylan, but Veronica is helping us all heal. She is so happy! I wish you could hear her trying to talk.

If all goes well, we're leaving this week to drive down to where our land is. Today, Pap is expecting our covered wagon to arrive. He and Mama made a claim at the government office weeks ago before they left Gainesville, and it's taken this long to sort out all the paperwork. Pap would have had to pay a man $100 to drive the wagon down from Gainesville to Ft. Pierce, but they agreed that the government would pay.

So with a little bit of luck, our wagon will be here today. We are hoping that all of our household goods and staples will still be there. Mama is not worried because she said she never expected to see the wagon again, and anything we get back will be a blessing.

Pap and Mr. Carter and Martin went last week to pick up Jeb and January from Captain Walsh. So our two oxen are in the stable here with Gabriel. We're just missing Girlie, but we're hoping to find a way to get her from Miss Melman. Mama says it would be nice to have a milk cow, with a baby in the house again.

Because we were able to file our land deed, the bank gave Pap a special loan for us to build a house and a barn. So Pap and Mama sketched out our new house. It will have a porch on the front. It will also have a main room for living, a bedroom for Pap and Mama, a bedroom for me and Veronica, and a loft for Daniel. It will have a kitchen that has running water, a pantry, a back porch, and an outhouse. Mama lit up like the Fourth of July when she and Pap worked out all the plans.

We went shopping this afternoon to buy all the building materials we will need to put up our new house. Until the house is ready, Daniel and Pap will sleep outside under the wagon, and Mama, Veronica, and I will sleep in the wagon.

At the lumberyard, Pap and the man who is in charge went over the plans that Pap and Mama made. They did lots of ciphering and made measurements and did a lot of figuring about how much lumber we will need, how many window panes, how many doors, and things like that.

At the catalogue store, Mama picked out a sofa and two chairs, a rocking chair, a bed for her and Pap, a bed each for Veronica, Daniel, and me, and a few other pieces of furniture we will need. Mama and I are so excited! We've never owned new furniture before.

At the dry goods store, we picked out fabric for curtains, tablecloths, and bed linens. Mama picked fabric for some new dresses for me and gowns for Veronica. She picked out overalls and jeans for Daniel, shirts, a belt, and new shoes. Martha, I wish you could have seen him! He was overjoyed with new things.

We will wait to see what all comes in the wagon, if it arrives. If the wagon comes, and our goods are undisturbed, we should have food supplies. Mama will make other purchases before we leave Ft. Pierce.

All of the new purchases will be delivered to the land that is now officially ours. Pap had to pay extra to have everything delivered because our wagon would never hold it all.

Martha, I feel strange. For weeks and weeks I was alone. I didn't know if I had a future or not. I didn't know if we would ever own our own land. I didn't know for sure if I would see Mama and Pap again. Now, that it's all coming true, I am happy, but there are times I feel like crying, too. I don't know why I would cry, but at times, life just overwhelms me. Do you ever feel that way, too?

Love,
Teddy

Reading Multiple Choice Questions for the Letter of July 30, 1892
Circle the letter of the correct answer.

1. What did Mama name the new baby?
   A. Veronica
   B. Theodosia
   C. Cassie
   D. Essie Mae

2. Where are the Bodains currently staying until they move down to their new land?
   A. Gainesville
   B. St. Augustine
   C. Ft. Pierce
   D. Sarasota

3. Which of the Bodain's animals is still missing from the family?
   A. Gabriel
   B. Girlie
   C. Jeb and January
   D. Ethelbert

4. Where will Teddy, Mama, and Veronica sleep while their new home is being built?
   A. in the wagon
   B. outside under the wagon
   C. in Ft. Pierce at the Carters'
   D. in St. Augustine with Miss Melman

5. Why does Teddy say at the end of her letter that she feels like crying?
   A. she misses Miss Melman
   B. she is still upset about Dylan's death
   C. her new life is overwhelming to her
   D. she doesn't want to leave the Carters

6. Why does Mama say it would be nice to have Girlie back?
   A. because Girlie is Mama's beloved pet
   B. because Girlie can help with the field labor at the new house
   C. because then the whole family will be complete again
   D. because Girlie could provide milk for Baby Veronica

7. What is an outhouse?
   A. a doll house
   B. a separate kitchen
   C. an outdoor bathroom
   D. a toolshed

July 31, 1892

Dear Martha,

Our wagon arrived! Everything is fine—nothing broken and all of our food supplies are in good order. Seeing the wagon again made us happy and sad at the same time. It reminded us of all the good memories of our trip. But it also made us sad that we weren't able to finish the journey with the rest of the wagon train. It made us cry to see Dylan's little seat, his playpen, and his tiny clothes and toys.

But it was like coming home! The wagon helped me feel like I am in the right place and that I belong again. Just the smell of it—the linseed oil on the canvas— the smell of the wood—the smell of the kegs of supplies—the food barrels—were friendly, homey smells.

Today, Daniel and I helped Mama and Pap pull everything out of the wagon. We set our supplies and bedding out on the ground. Then, we swept the inside of the wagon until there wasn't a grain of dirt or sand anywhere. Mama and I oiled the canvas with linseed oil. Pap and Daniel loaded all of the compartments and buckets with animal feed, fresh water, and kindling for starting fires. We reloaded everything back into the wagon, so tomorrow, we'll be able to start driving down to our new land.

The plan is that in two weeks, all of the Carters will come down and help us build part of the house. Then, the rest of the building will have to be up to Pap, Daniel, and me. Our lumber and crates of furniture should be delivered to our new land sometime next week. Oh, Martha! We are so excited.

Daniel said, "My pap was a carpenter. I learned a lot from him, so I can help you build."

Pap said, "It will be a fine thing to have you helping me. I need another set of strong arms."

I don't think Pap could have said anything that would have made Daniel happier. He is still shy because he is not used to being part of a family. Even when his pap was alive, it was just the two of them, and they didn't even eat regular meals. I talked to Mama about it, and she said that a boy like Daniel will have to work his way into feeling comfortable in our family. I think the new house will be good for us all. It will be a fresh start, so all the memories we make, all the adventures we have, will be new.

The stories I want to tell my family haven't all come out at once, like I expected them to. But sometimes, they come out when I least expect them. This afternoon we went fishing with the Carters. While we were waiting for the fish to bite, I told the story of staying with Wanda Watson and going fishing with her. Mama and Pap were fascinated that she was so old in years and yet so spry.

Mama said, "How did you get to her house, Teddy?"

I told her about walking from where Joe, the cotton farmer, left us off at the end of the road.

Pap said, "And you two left her place in what kind of a boat?"

Daniel said, "A jon boat. It's like a rowboat but with a flatter bottom. We poled down the spring and up the river for a few days."

Mama said, "Teddy, what an adventure."

I said, "Mama, since I saw you last, I rode across the sky in a big, big balloon."

Mama said, "You didn't!"

I said, "Daniel and I rescued Ethelbert from Dr. Zoren again."

Pap said, "The scoundrel who makes the elixir?"

I said, "And we rode elephants."

Daniel said, "And we marched in the Fourth of July parade with John Phillip Sousa!"

Mama said, "You met John Phillip Sousa?"

Daniel said, "He gave us each a silver dollar."

The truth is, Martha, that I have had incredible experiences these last few months. Good or bad, those memories have become a part of me and now, a part of you, too, because of my letters.

Love,
Teddy

Name_____   Date_____

Narrative Writing for the Letter of July 31, 1892
Read and answer the writing prompt below.

Narrative Prompt: Teddy has been through many adventures. Think about an adventure you would like to have. Your adventure could happen anywhere in the world. Think about the details of the adventure: Where would you go? How would you get there? What kinds of people would you meet? What happens? After you've thought of these details, write the story. Be sure to include many outlandish and fun details, so we can form "mind movies" of your experience. When you've finished, read your story to yourself. Are there any important details you may have missed? Now, share your adventuresome piece with a friend. Enjoy!

_____

_____

_____

_____

_____

_____

_____

_____

_____

_____

_____

_____

_____

_____

_____

_____

_____

_____

_____

_____

August 1, 1892

Dear Martha,

Today was another one of those days when I wish you could have been with me. It was a good day. Martha, why do we have to live so far away from each other?

We are headed to our new land! Pap has a map that was given to him by the man at the Land Deed Office in Juno. It shows exactly where our new land will be.

Mama is driving the wagon. Veronica is sitting beside her in the little chair Pap made for Dylan. Pap is riding Gabriel, and Daniel is riding Swift. Oh, I forgot to tell you about Swift. Pap bought a beautiful new horse from Mr. Ampole, a man in Ft. Pierce. She's just two years old, and she is gorgeous.

Pap took me with him to buy her. He said, "Teddy, this being part of a family is new for Daniel. He's been on his own for a long time. I think he needs something of his own, something that is all his, something he can take care of. Do you think he would like to have a horse?"

I could see where Pap was going with this. Part of me was envious. I'll admit I would have loved to own a horse of my own. Hadn't I been away from my parents, out on my own? Didn't I deserve something special for all I'd been through?

But I could also see what Pap was trying to do for Daniel. I knew that this was right. I swallowed hard to keep my disappointment down.

I said, "I think a horse would be the perfect gift for Daniel."

Pap let me pick her out. Well, that wasn't hard. She was the best looking horse in the lot and very gentle and obedient. Pap checked her out carefully. He looked at each of her hooves and at her teeth. He ran his hand over her withers and watched her gait. When he was satisfied, he paid Mr. Ampole, tied her behind the little wagon we had come in, and we drove the wagon home.

I wanted to name her! I had all kinds of great names picked out. Pap said, "Well now, you could do that. We could give Daniel a horse that you've already named. Do you think he'd like that?"

Rats. Why do I always have to do the right thing? I said, "You're right. He'd probably like to name her himself."

When we got home, Daniel, Mama, Veronica, and the Carters came out to the stable to see her.

Daniel said, "That is the prettiest horse I've ever seen." Everyone agreed.

Pap said, "I asked Teddy to pick her out. She did a good job, didn't she?"

Daniel said, "Teddy, you are one lucky duck."

I said, "Well, this horse isn't for me. It's for another lucky duck."

Daniel didn't get it. He said, "Who's that?"

I said, "Start quacking." He stared at me. "It's you, silly. We picked her out for you."

Daniel said, "For me? Nuh-uh. Whose is she, really?"

Pap said, "She's for you, Daniel. You'll need a horse to ride on our new property. She's yours."

I watched Daniel's face as he tried to understand that this exquisite new horse was for him. I looked at Pap's face, too, and he winked at me. The happiness I felt for Daniel almost made up for the fact that the horse was for him and not me.

Daniel said, "Does she have a name?"

Pap said, "No, that's for you to decide."

Daniel said, "Me? I don't know what to name her. Teddy, will you help me name her?"

We spent the rest of the afternoon thinking up names. We finally decided on "Swift."

Daniel said, "I like that name. It's short, and it means faster than fast."

It always feels good when you do the right thing.

Love,
Teddy

Name_____ Date_____

Reading Short Response Questions for the Letter of August 1, 1892
Answer the questions below, and be sure to use complete sentences.

1. Pap bought Daniel a special gift. Describe the various emotions Teddy felt about this gift.

_____

_____

_____

_____

2. When Pap purchased the horse, he did several things before deciding to take her home. What did he do?

_____

_____

_____

_____

3. Teddy said, **"Well, this horse isn't for me. It's for another lucky duck."** What did she mean by this statement? How did Daniel react?

_____

_____

_____

_____

4. How did Teddy and Daniel go about naming the horse? Describe the name they chose.

_____

_____

_____

_____

_____

August 2, 1892

Dear Martha,

Today, on our way to our new place, we stopped to see Lake Okeechobee. I never knew a lake could be so big. We all walked up on the levee to see it. Martha, the lake stretches as far as you can see. It's not very deep, about 12 feet in the deepest parts, but Pap said he heard it's teeming with fish.

Mama said, "How could anyone ever starve in country like this?"

Pap said to me and Daniel, "How about the three of us come back sometime and go fishing?"

We agreed that would be a bushel load of fun. I would love any adventure that involves Pap and Daniel. Of course, it would be even better if you could be with us, too. I'm still hoping you can visit.

We drove for a few more hours and then, we were here!

Pap said, "According to this map, this is it. This is our land."

Mama stood on the wagon seat and shaded her eyes. She looked all around. Then, she said, "Dalton Bodain, I do believe we are home."

Home. This will be our new home. It doesn't feel like home yet, but that will come later.

We drove all around the property. We have 40 acres, and a spring runs along the eastern side of our land. The land is pretty scruffy, but there are a few large oak trees clustered near the spring.

Mama said, "Dalton, let's put the wagon here, so we can make use of the shade. The spring will be nice for cooking and bathing."

Pap said, "It's big enough to swim in. What do you think, children? Want to try it out later?"

We cheered and Ethelbert ran around in circles.

Daniel and Pap unhitched the oxen and watered the animals.

Mama said, "Teddy, we have an extra canvas. Remember when your pap tied it up so that Girlie wouldn't get wet in the rain? Well, we can make an awning that will give us more shade and keep a bigger space dry if it rains."

I found the canvas. Daniel and I shook it out while Pap raked the ground where Mama wanted to stretch the canvas. While Pap and Daniel cut branches and stripped the leaves and bark, Mama and I painted the tarp with linseed oil.

She said, "We're getting pretty good at this, don't you think, Teddy?" I love the familiar smell of the linseed oil. I'd slept so many nights under that smell, I felt like it had become a part of me.

By late afternoon, we had the wagon parked under the oaks, a patch of ground cleared of rocks and sticks and raked smooth, and a canvas awning stretched out from the side of the wagon to four tall wood poles. It was pretty good for a half a day's work.

Pap said, "What do you say we go swimming in the spring?"

Mama said, "With all this work to do, you want to go swimming?"

Pap said, "Yes, I do, and I want my wife and children to go with me."

Mama smiled. "Alright then. Let me get on some old clothes and get the baby ready."

We splashed and played in the spring for at least an hour. It felt wonderful! I didn't realize how hot and sweaty we all were until we were cooling off in the clear flowing water of the spring. Our spring. We own land. We own trees. We own a spring. It seems hard to believe. This place is OURS.

Daniel made a campfire, a good one. Pap said, "Son, somebody taught you well. That is about as fine a campfire as I've seen."

Daniel said, "My pap taught me."

Pap said, "I'm sure I would have liked him. Too bad I didn't get to meet him. But I'll get to know him through you, Daniel."

Mama and I fixed dinner and guess what? Our jerky is still good! Can you believe it?

Love,
Teddy

Name_____ Date_____

Expository Writing Prompt for the Letter of August 2, 1892
Read and answer the following writing prompt.

Expository Prompt: In the story today, the family feels a sense of accomplishment because they have finally arrived on their own land after a long, long journey. Their lives are going to be different from their lives in Mississippi and from their lives on the wagon train. Explain how the Bodains' lives will be different. Include as many specific details and creative reasons as you can. Remember, your paper needs a beginning, a middle, and an ending. After you write, read your piece to yourself. Think of ways to improve, and add those improvements to your writing. Now share your piece with another writer and exchange ideas.

_____

_____

_____

_____

_____

_____

_____

_____

_____

_____

_____

_____

_____

_____

_____

_____

_____

_____

August 26, 1892

Dear Martha,

I haven't had time to write because we've had so much to do. It reminds me of when Daniel and I first joined the circus. We were so tired our hands ached at night. Well, it's been like that around here.

I have a lot of good things to tell you. The best thing is, we had a house raising. Our lumber was delivered here a few days ago. We were expecting the Carters to come because Pap and Mr. Carter and Martin talked about it before we left Ft. Pierce. Since we filed our land deed first, we need a home first. They agreed to come help us build it. Then, when they get their land, which should be pretty soon, we'll go help them build their house.

As I said, we were expecting the Carters. But we were not expecting all the other folks who came, too. Mrs. Carter and Miss Emily telegraphed everyone they could think of, and folks came from miles and miles away. Captain Walsh came and brought his two grown sons. The Larks came. I had no idea they were here, but suddenly a voice behind me said, "What will it be, Bodain, marbles or slingshots?"

It was Travis! I was so glad to see him I almost gave him a bear hug. Almost.

The Goods came, so I got to see Minnie and Hallie. Jasper Lowe's father died of the fever, but Jasper and his mother came. The Porters came, too. Remember the family whose wagon rolled down the hill?

Mrs. Lowe said, "Grace, I knew you'd need someone to help with the cooking."

First, Pap introduced Daniel and told a little bit about how he came to live with us. Then, he held up Veronica and told the story of how she came to be his second Bodain daughter. Folks cheered for them both.

People parked their covered wagons in a circle under the stand of oaks. The men set up sawhorses, saws, planes, woodworking tools, and put on overalls and boots.

The women set up all the house doors on extra sawhorses end to end, so we had one long, long, long eating table. The women made an outdoor stove near the spring. They set up all the tripods, and the entire time, I don't think I ever looked over there that there wasn't a big pot of something boiling and bubbling.

Travis and Daniel and Jasper were in charge of hunting up small game for some of our meals. They brought home quail, squirrel, and rabbits. And didn't they think they were so big and important!

The men laid the floor first, sanding and smoothing it with planes, just so. Then, the walls went up. The walls made it very exciting because we could see what it was going to look like as a house. There were so many people working that they were finished with the house in about a week. But right in the middle of things, we had another HUGE surprise.

Miss Melman and Mr. Mikelson arrived! Their excuse was that they were bringing Girlie, but I really think Miss Melman wanted to be with everyone again and to introduce her beau. Folks were so happy to see her. All the kids came running! The women hugged her neck, but what they were really interested in was finding out about Mr. Mikelson. They pestered her with questions right and left. She just grinned!

Everyone worked hard during the day. The men and some of the women helped build the house. Other women cooked, and a few watched the babies and little children. Most of the time all of us kids swam and played in the spring.

After a week, when the house was finished, Martin Carter said, "I think we could get this barn up in four days. Maybe three. What do you say, folks?" Pap and Mama didn't want to impose on our friends.

Pap said, "This is enough. We'll get the barn."

But Mr. Mikelson said, "Bodain, the house was almost finished when I got here. You're not going to cheat me out of a barn." Pap shook his head and smiled.

When we kids heard that we had a few more days together, we went berserk! Travis yelled, "Last one in the swimming hole is a rotten egg!"

I hope I hear from you soon. I miss you bunches and bunches!

Love,
Teddy

Name_____ Date_____

Reading Extended Response Questions for the Letter of August 26, 1892
Answer the questions below. Be sure to use complete sentences, reasons, and details.

1. Teddy and her family are having a house raising. Explain what a house raising is. What happens during a house raising?

_____

_____

_____

_____

_____

_____

_____

_____

_____

_____

_____

2. What did Mr. Mikelson mean when he said, **"You're not going to cheat me out of a barn"**? How did the kids react when Mr. Mikelson said this? Why?

_____

_____

_____

_____

_____

_____

_____

_____

_____

_____

August 29, 1892

Dear Martha,

I wish you could see this place! It's been transformed from a wilderness to a—homestead. A house. A home.

The barn is almost up. But the real news is, today our furniture arrived! None of the ladies, including Mama, has ever had store-bought furniture. Oh, maybe Miss Melman has, but if she has, she didn't let on. She "ooed" and "aahed" along with everyone else.

The furniture arrived, and the ladies went right to work. They set up beds, put the sheets and blankets on the mattresses, hung quilts, arranged furniture, put books on shelves, hung clothes in wardrobes, and hung the portrait our family had taken at Mr. L.H. LeGrand's Photographic Studio in Meridian. When we saw Dylan in the picture, all of us cried, but not for too long. He will always be a part of our family.

But it gets even better. One last big box arrived with the furniture, but Pap told us not to open it. That afternoon, when all of the furniture was arranged and looking beautiful, Pap asked Daniel and Travis to help him unwrap the special box. He wouldn't let anyone else, including me, in there. When it was in place, he covered it with one of Mama's quilts.

We had a big dinner together, and then folks gathered by our front porch. Miss Melman had cut a grapevine from the woods and fashioned it into a wreath for the front door. She wove wildflowers into it, and it was just the prettiest thing you ever saw.

When we were gathered, Pap asked Mr. Mikelson to pray a prayer of dedication on our house. His words were full of thanksgiving that no one had been hurt in building this house. He must not have known about the big splinter I got in my toe. He ended the prayer by saying, "Bless this house, oh Lord, we pray. Make it safe by night and day."

Then, Pap stood on the porch. He took his hat off and held it in his hands. He said, "None of this could be possible without the love and support of good friends and family. None of this would be possible without a good woman standing by my side and precious children to bring happiness and laughter."

Then, he did something that shocked us all! He picked Mama up in his arms and said, "Grace, I want to carry you over the threshold of your new house," and he carried her inside! Everyone laughed about that, like Pap and Mama were newlyweds. I saw Mr. Mikelson look at Miss Melman and raise his eyebrows.

But the surprises weren't over yet. Folks crowded inside the house and admired all the furniture. Then, Mr. Carter said, in a loud voice, "Dalton, what's this here?"

Pap said, "One more thing, then I promise you folks can go to bed." Mama looked at him curiously. "My wife left Mississippi without complaining. She endured a long trip down here and many hardships along the way. This is my thank you present to her."

While we all looked on, Pap and Mr. Carter took the quilt off, and there was a beautiful piano!

Mama was so astounded that she didn't know what to say! She put her hands on her cheeks.

The look on Pap's face was priceless. He was so proud. I was happy for him and Mama.

Mama said, "This is almost the best present I've ever received."

Pap was feeling his oats. He said, "Almost the best present? What could be a better present than a brand-spanking-new piano?" You could tell he was joking, but people waited to hear what Mama would say.

She motioned for me and Daniel to come to her. She took Veronica from Miss Emily. Mama held us tight. She said, "This."

I heard sniffling, and some folks wiped their eyes with their handkerchiefs.

Mama said, "Miss Melman, would you please play this new piano for us?"

Miss Melman said, "We would love to hear YOU play it, Grace. I think you're ready."

And Martha, I don't even have to tell you what song Mama played.

Pap's gift to Mama was the piano, but Mama's gift to us all was her beautiful playing.

Ethelbert came and lay his head in my lap. My heart was so full of happiness I felt like I could fly off into the night.

Love,
Teddy

Grammar Questions for the Letter of August 29, 1892
Circle the letter of the correct answer.

1. What would you call the following example?
   The look on Pap's face was priceless.
   A. simile
   B. onomatopoeia
   C. transitional phrase
   D. metaphor

2. Which of the following sentences has the correct use of commas?
   A. He wouldn't let anyone else, including me, in there.
   B. He wouldn't let anyone else including me in there.
   C. He wouldn't let anyone else, including me in there.
   D. He wouldn't let anyone else including me, in there.

3. Which of the following words is spelled incorrectly?
   A. Mississippi
   B. newlyweds
   C. somthing
   D. handkerchiefs

4. Where do the quotation marks go in the following sentence?
   A. "Mama said, Miss Melman, would you please play this new piano for us?"
   B. Mama said, "Miss Melman would you please play this new piano for us?
   C. Mama said, "Miss Melman, would you please play this new piano for us?"
   D. Mama said, Miss Melman, would you please play this new piano for us?"

5. Which of the following examples has the correct use of capitalization?
   A. She took Veronica from miss Emily.
   B. She took Veronica from Miss Emily.
   C. She took veronica from miss emily.
   D. She Took Veronica from Miss Emily.

6. Where does the comma go in this compound sentence?
   You could tell he was joking but people waited to hear what Mama would say.
   A. after *Mama*
   B. after *joking*
   C. after *waited*
   D. after *tell*

7. What is this sentence missing?
   She took veronica from miss emily.
   A. three commas
   B. three nouns
   C. three capital letters
   D. end punctuation

August 30, 1892

Dear Martha,

This morning, the men finished the barn. Everything is complete.

Captain Walsh drove to the trading post and bought a wagonload of bedding straw and some hay for the animals. Travis, Daniel, Minnie, Hallie, Jasper, and I spread it out in the barn for Jeb and January, Gabriel, Girlie, and Swift.

The sad thing is that everyone left today. We hated to see them leave. We were mourning about it, being sad and all, but Minnie reminded us that we'll probably be together again when the Carters get their land in a few weeks. That made saying goodbye a little easier.

Before she left, Miss Melman said, "Teddy, it was good to see you. Promise me you'll come for a visit."

I smiled and said, "Would there be any 'special occasion' that might be coming up that I would want to attend?"

She pinched the tip of my nose and said, "Maybe." She blushed. She and Mr. Mikelson seem very fond of each other. I want her to be happy.

Miss Emily said, "I made you a few dresses before I came. They're hanging in your wardrobe."

Minnie said, "Promise to write, Teddy. I'll miss you."

Travis whispered, "You look like a boy, Bodain. Grow out your hair, so you'll be pretty again."

I said, "Hush up, Travis." Oh, that boy!

Hallie said, "Let me see your gold bracelet one more time. Ooooo."

Jasper said, "I hope I get to come back sometime."

Mr. Mikelson said, "I haven't had this much fun since I was a kid. Come see us, Daniel and Teddy."

We watched their wagons leave, waving and calling our goodbyes.

And then it was just us, the Bodains, standing on the porch. It was a strange feeling. I felt happy about a lot of things: a new house, a new barn, a new sister—but I felt sad at the same time. Sad down to my bones.

That night, none of us talked much. I guess we were each lost in our own thoughts, as Mama says.

When Veronica finally went to sleep, Mama came to me with a lantern. She said, "Want to go to the spring with me to bathe tonight?"

I said, "Sure." Bathing in the spring sounded like fun.

Mama had her French soap, a hairbrush, two big towels, and our nightgowns.

The lantern lit our way. The spring water was just right. We bathed with the French soap, and Mama washed my hair. It felt luxurious. I remembered how she had washed it months ago when we were on the wagon train. She brushed it with her brush and said, "Soon, you'll look like a girl again."

When we finished, we walked back to the house and sat in the swing on the front porch. The swing was Miss Melman's gift to us for our new house. We sat side by side. Mama put her arm around me and drew me to her. I put my head on her shoulder. I said, "Mama, I'm so happy. I want you to know that. But sometimes I feel like crying. Why is that?"

Mama put her hand on my cheek. She said, "That's just life, Teddy. We love people. We lose some people along the way. People share their lives with us, they share their love with us. And sometimes our hearts get so full of it all, we don't know whether to laugh or cry."

It made sense when Mama said that. Sitting next to her again was a dream come true.

Then, Mama said, "But the good thing is, we're home. Finally, finally, finally, we're home."

I said, "How do you know, Mama? How do you know this is really home?"

Mama smiled. "Because just this morning, as the sun was peeking up over the horizon, I heard the redbird sing his cheery little song. And as he was singing, I knew he was saying, 'Welcome home.'"

Love,
Teddy

Name_____ Date _____

Writing Questions for the Letter of August 30, 1892
Circle the letter of the correct answer.

1. Read the following phrase from Teddy's letter today:
   But I felt sad at the same time.
   The word *sad* is an example of what kind of good writing skill?
   A. juicy color word
   B. simile
   C. specific emotion word
   D. transitional word

2. Read the following sentences from Teddy's letter today:
   Travis whispered, "You look like a boy, Bodain. Grow out your hair, so you'll be pretty again."
   These sentences are examples of what kind of good writing skill?
   A. juicy color words
   B. dialogue
   C. metaphor
   D. transitional sentences

3. Read the following sentences from Teddy's letter today:
   Travis whispered, "You look like a boy, Bodain. Grow out your hair, so you'll be pretty again."
   The words *look like a boy* are an example of what kind of good writing skill?
   A. onomatopoeia
   B. metaphor
   C. simile
   D. juicy color word

4. Read the following sentence from Teddy's letter today:
   Mama had her French soap, a hairbrush, two big towels, and our nightgowns.
   This sentence is an example of what kind of good writing skill?
   A. details you can picture
   B. dialogue
   C. transitional phrase
   D. persuasive writing

5. Read the following sentence from Teddy's letter today:
   It felt luxurious.
   The word *luxurious* is an example of what kind of good writing skill?
   A. specific emotion word
   B. specific sensory word
   C. a metaphor
   D. simile

September 3, 1892

Dear Martha,

After I talked with Mama, I needed to get off by myself and figure out what was making me feel like my shoes were on the wrong foot. I asked myself, what is it? This is everything I've hoped for: Mama and Pap are alive, we're on our own land, Daniel is part of our family, we have a new baby, and she's adorable. So why do I feel like something still needs to be done? I puzzled about those things for a long time. There's a big, flat rock that's near the spring not too far from the house. It is the perfect place to be by myself.

After a while, I figured it out, and coming up with the answer was like scratching an itch that I could finally reach. I had come through a journey, but it was not complete. I had met people along the way that had taken me in or helped me in some way. Those people meant something to me even though I might have just known them for a little while. I wanted to let them know that I had found Mama and Pap. I needed to let them know. For some reason, my life felt like a circle that was still open and needed closing.

Wanda Watson had said, "I'd love to know you got to where you're going."

That was it! I needed to let folks know that I was finally home with my family.

I spent the last three days writing letters and drawing pictures.

I wrote to Mrs. Plum and thanked her for taking care of me while I was sick. I said I was sorry I had to run away, but I was afraid of being put in an orphanage and never seeing Mama and Pap again. I told her that I finally found Mama and Pap alive. I sent the letter to Mrs. Plum's Quarantine Station, Gainesville, Florida.

I wrote to Dr. Winklepleck and thanked her for letting me sleep in her brother's feed store and for the balloon ride. I included a drawing of the balloon with me, Ethel, and her in the gondola. I didn't know where else to send it, so I sent it to the feed store in care of her brother, Carl Winklepleck.

I wrote to Carlene Green and her family. I thanked Mrs. Green for taking me in and making me feel welcome and for the pretty pink dress with the white pinafore. I told them about Verna and Jimbo and how I had to run away. That was the longest letter because I had to tell them just about everything up until now. I drew a picture of me and Carlene bathing Freddy and Ethelbert. I asked Carlene to be my Florida pen pal. I hope she writes back.

I wrote to Wanda Watson and thanked her for being so kind to me and Daniel. I thanked her for the delicious fried fish and for the story about the firefly and for the clothes and the boat. I told her that of all the people I met, I loved her most of all. I drew a picture of her, me, and Daniel fishing in her creek. I asked her to please tell Joe that we thank him for helping us get away in his cotton wagon. I sent it to Wanda Watson, General Delivery, Orange Springs. I am crossing my fingers that it gets to her.

I wrote to Suzanna and Massimo and thanked them for letting Daniel and me help take care of the elephants. I told them we would never have made it without their help. I asked them to thank Marie and Elmer and Carl Ringling. I sent them a drawing of Suzanna riding Babbette at the front of the parade. I told them that someday, if Mama and Pap would allow it, Daniel and I might like to come back and work with them again. I sent their letter to Baraboo, Wisconsin, the home of the Ringling Circus.

I wrote to John Phillip Sousa and sent a drawing of him giving me and Daniel the silver dollars. I told him that I thought his marching band was the best band ever. I sent his letter to Washington, D.C.

I wrote to Miss Melman and thanked her for taking us in and for the tickets for the steamer and the extra money and the clothes. I told her that I thought she was the best teacher and friend. I told her to please thank Mr. Mikelson for me. I said, P.S. Do you have something you want to tell me yet? Ha ha! Love, Teddy

It took me days to write all the letters and do the drawings. But as I wrote, I felt the circle closing, little by little. I began to feel like the old me. That's a good thing.

Now, there is just one more thing I have to do. I don't want to do it, but I have to.

Love,
Teddy

Name_____ Date_____

Persuasive Writing for the Letter of September 3, 1892
Read and answer the following prompt.

Persuasive Prompt: Throughout our lives, we meet amazing people who willingly give us special gifts they already have inside of them. When we are fortunate enough to receive these gifts from others, they help us to become the people we are. Think of the many gifts you have that you could have offered to Teddy if you were someone she met on her journey. It might be the gift of bravery. It might be the gift of patience. It might be the gift of being a hard worker. Maybe you are good with directions. Now choose one of these gifts or one of your own choosing, and convince us that your gift would have helped Teddy in some big way. Be sure to use convincing arguments, examples, and great description.

_____

_____

_____

_____

_____

_____

_____

_____

_____

_____

_____

_____

_____

_____

_____

_____

_____

_____

_____

October 18, 1892

Dear Martha,

I got your letters! They made me miss you even more. You will always be my best friend. I feel like you've been on this entire journey with me.

Yes, school started for us, too. We have a brand new school. There are nine families who own land near us, and all of the children, including me and Daniel, go to The North Dade Rural School. We are all together, and our teacher is a man! I was shocked on the first day of school. He is nice, though, and I think he's a good teacher. His name is Amos Weathers, but we call him Mr. Weathers.

Daniel about died when he had to go to school. He didn't want to go. He's used to being on his own, I guess. I thought it was going to be a big problem, but Mama had a talk with him. I don't know what all she said because I wasn't with them, but he told me later that she said, "I'll make a deal with you. The first day you don't learn something at school, you don't have to go anymore."

Well, that did it. Daniel is an excellent student, and you should hear him read. Mr. Weathers said he is a very intelligent student. Daniel and I ride Swift to school every morning and back home in the evening.

The best thing happened. Mr. Weathers allowed the two of us to go to the Carters' house raising. We had to miss a week of school, but Mama told Mr. Weathers we would finish all of our lessons.

We packed the little wagon Daniel and I bought from Nokosi with all of Pap's woodworking tools and extra food supplies. We packed our big wagon that still has the canvas on it, with everything we would need to sleep outdoors for a week. We tied Girlie behind because we couldn't leave her home alone, and Pap rode Gabriel. Daniel let me ride Swift. He said for me to take a turn, and he'd drive for Mama.

Mama said, "You sure are a blessing, Daniel Bodain. I think I might keep you."

As we pulled out, Pap said, "We've got enough stuff to be heading out on another journey."

The week at the Carters' house raising was as much fun as I was hoping it would be. Most of the same families came to help out, so once again, we had a huge circle of wagons. I got to see Minnie and Hallie, Jasper Lowe, the Porters, Captain Walsh and his sons, Miss Melman, Mr. Mikelson, Miss Emily and her husband, Martin.

Someone came up behind me and said, "I got your letter, Bodain."

It was Travis Lark! I said, "Yeah? And are you ready, Lark, or are you scared? I'll let you back out if you don't think you're up to it."

He said, "I ain't scared of you. I beat you last time, and I'm going to CREAM you this time. You don't stand a chance. Your kite is MINE!"

I said, "You're on."

In between all the work and the chores and the running errands for our parents and the laughter and the games, Travis and I each found the time to make a kite. Minnie and Hallie helped me, and Jasper and Daniel helped Travis. This time we were ready for them! Our kite was beautiful, with pelicans and waves and a setting sun. We named it The Florida Belle Two. We coated our string with glue and glass dust and let it dry overnight. Two can play at this string cutting game.

The next day, the crowd gathered to watch. As I expected, the boys' kite was ugly. They named it The Kite Killer. Minnie held my kite while I ran with the string. Daniel held Travis's kite while Travis ran with the string. Soon, both kites were launched high in the air. I crossed Travis's line with my line. I sawed my line. He sawed his line. The crowd screamed. The tension grew. Suddenly, The Florida Belle Two was cut free and sailed away, disappearing into the sky. Everyone cheered, and Travis took a dramatic bow.

I screamed, "How did you do that, you rapscallion, you? Rats! Rats! And DOUBLE RATS!"

He said, "That's just it: I used a double string!" He laughed like only Travis Lark can laugh.

Vexation! Vehement vociferous vexation! I'll get him back. I swear I will.

I'll write more soon, I promise.

Love,
Teddy

Name_____ Date_____

Reading Multiple Choice Questions for the Letter of October 18, 1892
Circle the letter of the correct answer.

1. How many families live near Teddy and have children who attend her school?
   A. three
   B. eleven
   C. nine
   D. eight

2. What is the name of the school that Teddy attends?
   A. The North Dade Rural School
   B. Dade Elementary School
   C. North Dade Circuit School
   D. Juno Elementary School

3. What is the name of Teddy's new teacher?
   A. Mr. John Mikelson
   B. Mr. Amos Weathers
   C. Mr. Matt Damon
   D. Mr. Dalton Bodain

4. What shocked Teddy the most about her new teacher?
   A. He was single.
   B. He was so young.
   C. He was so old.
   D. He was a man.

5. Teddy and her family helped which person or family with their house raising?
   A. Miss Melman and Mr. Mikelson
   B. Wanda Watson
   C. the Carters
   D. Althea Tomlinson

6. What did Teddy name her new kite?
   A. The Kite Killer
   B. The Florida Belle Two
   C. Girlie Takes Flight
   D. Ethelbert Nevin

7. What is the relationship between Teddy and Travis?
   A. They are friends.
   B. They are close friends.
   C. They are boyfriend/girlfriend.
   D. They don't really like each other.

October 28, 1892

Dear Martha,

I've been reading your letters every chance I get. We are two writing maniacs, aren't we? Please don't ever stop writing me.

I still can't believe you are going to get to come for a visit over the holidays. What a dream come true. And yes, I'll introduce you to everyone I've been talking about all these months. Daniel, especially, wants to meet you. He's seen me writing so many letters to you, and he's dying to know what you look like.

School is going well. Another school, North Dade Circuit School, came to spend two days with our school. We are pen pals with them, so we finally got to meet our pen pals. Their school is 12 miles away. On Friday, we had a spelling bee, and I won with the word "consternation."

Mr. Weathers gave Daniel a book to read, and guess what it is! The Adventures of Tom Sawyer. So every minute he's not riding Swift or doing some chore for Pap, he's got his nose in the book. I never got to finish the story, so when he's through, I'm going to read it, too.

I have a surprise to tell you. I got a package in the mail yesterday, and there was a letter with the package. Rather than my telling you about it, I'm going to copy the letter here. You'll know why.

Dear Teddy,

You can't imagine my surprise upon receiving the package you sent that contained my gold bracelet. I sat in astonishment for a long while, staring, unbelieving. I was looking at a treasure that had been lost some 25 years earlier on an outing to Fanning Springs. Foolishly, I wore the bracelet while swimming, and it slipped off my arm and was lost to me. While we looked and looked, it could not be found in the sand at the bottom. I left the springs heartbroken, this special gift lost forever, I thought.

That bracelet represents something very dear to me. My husband, the love of my life, had the bracelet inscribed and gave it to me for my 35th birthday, August 13, in 1862. As I'm sure you know, the inscription reads: "To Althea Tomlinson from her loving husband, Joseph. How do I love thee? Let me count the ways."

My Joseph was lost in The War Between the States, at the battle of Vicksburg, in 1863. I miss him to this day. And so, when I held the gold bracelet again, it brought back many wonderful memories of a thoughtful and gentle man who died at such a young age.

Thank you for sharing the wonderful story of how you "fanned" for treasure at Fanning Springs. If I'd known about "fanning" years ago, perhaps I would have found my bracelet and pirate treasure, as well!

Thank you for sharing the incredible story of your journey, Teddy, all the way from Mississippi to south Florida. I was again astonished to learn of the twists and turns your path took before you were reunited with your parents.

My daughter, Alice Tomlinson Edisto, told me of meeting you at the yellow fever quarantine station outside of Gainesville. She and I have discussed the bracelet, and she agrees with my decision. My bracelet, like my dear husband, was lost to me years ago. A gold bracelet was found by an enterprising girl who was looking for treasure. This brave girl wore it on her journey through losing her baby brother, succumbing to yellow fever, being separated from her parents, having to live on her own, and surviving by her wits. The gold bracelet was a source of comfort to her, a reminder of just what you can find if you look hard enough.

And so, dear Teddy, it would give me great pleasure to know that you are still wearing the bracelet as you go through life. Please receive it as my gift to you.

Your friend,
Althea Tomlinson

Martha, I'm wearing the bracelet now. I'm never going to take it off. Once, I felt like I lost myself. But now, I feel like I've found the old Teddy Bodain again.

Love,
Teddy

Name_____ Date_____

Narrative Writing for the Letter of October 28, 1892
Read and answer the writing prompt.

Narrative Prompt: Someone special would be visiting Teddy over the holidays. Her best friend, Martha, from Mississippi! Think of a time someone special came to see you. Think about the details of that visit: Who came to see you? What made the visit so wonderful? Why were you happy to have this person come see you? After you've thought of these details, write the story of your visit. Add details, so we can form "mind movies" of your experience. When you've finished, read your story to yourself. Are there important details you've left out? If so, add them in.

_____

_____

_____

_____

_____

_____

_____

_____

_____

_____

_____

_____

_____

_____

_____

_____

_____

_____

_____

_____

Author's Note

Teddy Bodain is an imaginary girl I made up in order to tell this story. Although she is fiction, there were hundreds, if not thousands of girls just like her who came to Florida during the late 1800s. Each girl would have had her own creative story to tell. My own grandmother, Rebecca Lenora Nix, crossed into primitive Florida in a covered wagon just about the same time as my fictional character, Teddy Bodain. She, too, lost her little brother and watched her father and the other men bury him across a creek on the bank of a little island. It was a scene she was never to forget in all her 97 years.

When she grew up, my grandmother had eight children of her own and many grandchildren. She told detailed stories of her life in early Florida. Some of the very things she did, some of her adventures, some of her heartbreaks, and even a few of her recipes are woven throughout this story.

As a kid, I loved to read. It's been said many times before, but reading a great book is like stepping into someone else's life for a while. We cease to be ourselves, and suddenly, we meet up with new locations, friends, villains, and heroes. Now, as an adult, I love to write the kinds of stories I enjoyed reading when I was growing up.

Some will ask, "How did you come up with this story?" The idea of a novel about a girl crossing Florida in a covered wagon and getting separated from her parents rushed into my mind all at once. I had a general idea where things were headed. But the specific plot details developed each day as I was writing. Teddy told her own story in my imagination. I saw it like a movie and wrote down what I saw. I hope you have enjoyed reading her adventure.

Historical Note

In 1892, much of the state of Florida was a wild, undeveloped wilderness. The beaches had few houses or hotels. Many of them were pristine stretches of sand, sand dunes, and sea oats. The state of Florida was happy to welcome pioneer families, and land, even beachfront property, was cheap. The governor and legislature were eager to see agriculture flourish and progress arrive.

At the time of this story, the railroad had not yet made its way down into Florida farther than Daytona Beach and Tampa. The development of Henry Flagler's elaborate hotels and resorts, and the staging of the Spanish American War a few years later, changed that. By the end of the century, Florida had a structure of railroads and highways, making progress inevitable.

Great care went into the research for this book. I have tried to strive for accuracy. If there are discrepancies, they are unintentional. Certain encounters, such as Teddy's meeting with the great entrepeneur, Carl Ringling, and world-famous composer, John Phillip Sousa, are simply fiction. I have attempted to recreate what life was like for pioneer families who migrated to the state of Florida during the last part of the nineteenth century.

Writing Style

I am a writing teacher. Therefore, I have tried the impossible: to write from a child's point of view, in an 11-year-old child's letter writing style, and yet be as faithful as possible to the techniques of good writing. There are few instances, such as not underlining or italicizing book titles, using sentence fragments, repeating the word and instead of using commas in a series, that I felt were more authentic and faithful to how children really write when they are just writing to a friend.

However, this book is meant to be a teaching tool for kids, so, at the same time I have tried to keep a standard of excellence and incorporate as many writing skills and literary devices as possible into Teddy's letters. It is my sincere desire that her story, and the accompanying lessons, will lead children to look forward to the next day's lesson with great anticipation.

Recipes

Hush Puppies
2 cups sifted fine stone ground white cornmeal
1 tablespoon sugar
2 teaspoons baking soda
2 teaspoons salt
1 tablespoon minced yellow onion
1 egg
1 cup buttermilk
4 to 5 tablespoons cold water

- Scoop batter up with a tablespoon.
- Drop into hot oil.
- Fry until light brown.

Mama's Macaroni and Cheese
4 cups cooked elbow macaroni, drained
2 cups grated colby cheese
4 oz. cream cheese, cut in cubes
3 eggs, beaten
½ cup sour cream
4 tablespoons butter, cut into pieces
½ teaspoon salt
1 cup milk

- Preheat oven to 350°F degrees.
- Cook and drain the macaroni in salted water.
- Pour the cooked, drained macaroni in a large bowl while it's still hot.
- Add the grated cheese and the cream cheese.
- In a separate bowl, combine the remaining ingredients and add to the macaroni mixture.
- Spray a casserole dish with non-stick baking spray.
- Pour in the macaroni mixture.
- Bake for 30 to 45 minutes.

Johnny Cake
2 cups yellow cornmeal
1 cup flour
1 cup milk
½ cup melted butter
1 egg
½ cup sugar
2 tablespoons baking powder
pinch of salt

- Mix all ingredients together and pour into greased skillet or pan.
- Bake at 375°F for 20-25 minutes.

Blackberry Cobbler
½ cup butter
2 cups self-rising flour
2 cups white sugar
2 cups milk
3½ cups blackberries

- Preheat oven to 350°F degrees.
- Melt butter in a 9"x 13" baking pan.
- Stir together the flour, sugar, and milk; batter will be slightly lumpy.
- Pour mixture on top of melted butter in baking pan.
- Do not mix butter and mixture together.
- Drop the blackberries into the batter.
- Bake for one hour or until golden brown.

Beef Jerky
¼ cup soy sauce
¼ cup balsamic vinegar
¼ cup worcestershire sauce
2 teaspoons liquid smoke flavoring
1½ tablespoons steak seasoning rub
1 London broil roast, thiny sliced along the grain

- Combine everything but the London broil in a saucepan and bring to a boil.
- Reduce heat to low, and simmer for ten minutes.
- Remove from heat, and set aside to cool.
- Pour the marinade into a covered plastic container.
- Add the meat slices, and stir to coat.
- Refrigerate for two days, turning occasionally.
- Arrange the beef strips on a wire rack set over a baking sheet.
- Bake for 60 to 90 minutes at 175°F, until dry but still pliable.
- Store in an airtight container in the refrigerator.
- Enjoy this tasty treat!

Teddy's Breakfast Grits
4 cups water   2 tablespoons butter
1½ teaspoons salt   1 cup quick grits (not instant)

- Bring water, butter, grits, and salt to a boil, stirring as the water heats. Reduce to a simmer. Cook with the top on, stirring occasionally, for five to eight minutes.

Recipes

Miss Essie Mae's Pound Cake

2 sticks of butter
3 cups sugar
3 cups plain flour
6 eggs
1 cup sour cream
¼ teaspoon baking powder
¼ teaspoon baking soda
1 tablespoon vanilla

- Preheat oven to 325°F.
- Cream butter and sugar together until light and fluffy.
- Add eggs one at a time.
- Add vanilla and sour cream to mixer.
- In a separate bowl, sift together dry ingredients.
- Slowly add dry ingredients to the egg mixture.
- Grease and flour a hollow tube pan.
- Pour in mixture.
- Bake for 1½ hours or until golden brown.
- Cool in pan for one hour, then remove to a plate.
- Serve and enjoy!

Deviled Eggs

1 dozen hard cooked eggs, chilled
mayonnaise
2 teaspoons yellow mustard
paprika

- Peel the eggs. Wash the outside to make sure there are no shells left.
- Slice the eggs in half lengthwise.
- Gently remove the yolks with a spoon and place in a bowl.
- Grate the yolks or mash them with a fork to get the lumps out.
- Add the mustard to the yolks and mix together.
- Add mayonnaise 2 tablespoons at a time until the mixture is smooth and thick.
- Spoon this mixture back into the egg white.
- Place deviled eggs on a plate or container.
- Cover the eggs and store in the refrigerator.

Cucumber Salad

3 large cucumbers, peeled and thinly sliced
1 cup white vinegar
¾ cup water
¾ cup sugar
1 teaspoon salt
6 grinds of pepper

- Combine all ingredients except cucumbers.
- Heat until sugar melts.
- Pour warm mixture over cucumbers.
- Store in refrigerator.

Skillet Biscuits

¼ cup butter
Seasoning salt
Garlic salt
Paprika
2 cups Bisquick baking mix
½ cup water

- Melt butter in 9" or 10" skillet.
- Sprinkle butter with seasoning salt, garlic salt, and paprika.
- Mix Bisquick and water with fork to a soft dough.
- Knead five times on lightly floured surface.
- Roll or pat dough ½" thick.
- Cut ten biscuits with a biscuit cutter.
- Arrange biscuits in skillet, turning to coat both sides with seasoned butter.
- Cover skillet with heavy duty aluminum foil.
- Place on grill 4" from hot coals.
- Cook ten minutes.
- Lift foil to be sure biscuits are not burning.
- Cook five minutes longer or until biscuits are done.
- Turn skillet over and dump biscuits onto serving plate.

Glossary

Adventure – an exciting experience

Ailments – sicknesses

Alcove – a little cubbyhole or small room

Anhinga – a water bird known for its diving skill for catching fish

Antiseptic – a substance to prevent infection

Apprentice – a person in training

Architecture – the look or character of a building

Awning – a canvas covering, like a tent without sides, that makes a shady area

Baby pram – a baby carriage or stroller

Balconies – the second floor of a building that overlooks the first floor

Bamboo – a plant that grows very quickly, and the stalks can be used for fishing poles

Banana spider – a large, harmless spider whose body is banana-shaped

Bandana – a colorful handkerchief

Banjo – a stringed instrument similar to a mandolin

Bathing costume – swimsuit

Batten down the hatches – sea-faring term that means to close all the hatches, and prepare for rough weather

Bawling – crying

Bear hug – to grip or hug someone very tightly like a bear

Beat the band – excessive, as in someone who sings louder than the band

Beau – a boyfriend

Bedding straw – the straw used in stables for animals to sleep on

Beet red – a reddish color associated with a beet, which is a vegetable

Berserk – crazy, out of control

Big Dipper – a group of stars, or constellation, in the shape of a water dipper

Bindings – wrappings of cloth

Bloodline – a blood vein running along a fish's backbone

Bloomers – loose-fitting pants, gathered at the knee, usually for ladies

Bluegill – a small freshwater fish

Boarding house – a small hotel where people eat their meals family style

Bodacious – outrageous or incredible

Bogus – false or untrue

Boil – the part of a spring where the water comes out from underground

Bow – the front of a ship or boat

Bowie knife – a very large fixed-blade knife named after Jim Bowie, of Alamo fame

Bow-legged – a person's legs that bend outward

Bream – a small freshwater fish

Brine – salty water

Broth – a flavored soup without any solid foods

Budge – to move just a tiny bit

Burlap – a very coarse cloth

Butcher – someone who cuts up meat for a living

Butterbeans – an idiom for lima beans

Cabana – a tent-like structure on the beach in which people change their clothes

Calico – an inexpensive cotton cloth

Canning jar – a glass jar used to make preservatives of fruit, vegetables, or meat

Cannon fire – when a cannon goes off

Canteens – containers for holding water

Canvas – coarse cloth

Caravan – a group traveling together

Cardinal – a red songbird, also known as a redbird

Cartographer – a maker of maps

Cat's cradle – a game played with string that is passed back and forth between children

Cat's pajamas – a slang term for wonderful

Cat's-eye shooter – a marble that looks like a cat's eye

Centipede – a small predatory insect supposedly with 100 legs

Chaos – confusion or disorganization

Chaplain – a minister in the military

Checkers – a board game for two players where they "jump over" or take each other's pieces or checkers. Last one with checkers remaining wins.

Chee-hun-tah-mo – the Miccosukee word for a friendly greeting like "hello"

Cheesecloth – a cotton cloth with small holes in it for air and liquids to pass through

Chikee – the Miccosukee word for a dwelling

China – porcelain or ceramic material used for plates, cups, and saucers

Chow – food

Chow line – the line where the men get fed, like a cafeteria line

Chow wagon – the wagon where the supplies are stored for food preparation

Ciphering – calculating or using arithmetic to solve problems

Clustered – grouped together

Coals – the remains of a fire that are still burning hot and glowing

Cobbler – a man who makes and repairs shoes

Cobwebs – spider webs

Collard greens – cabbage-like, large, green leaves that are cooked and eaten

Commoners – non-royalty, ordinary folks

Commotion – a disturbance or disruption

Conductor – the official in charge of a train

Confounded – confused

Constable – a law officer similar to a sheriff or policeman

Consternation – fear or alarm that comes from a sense of danger

Cornhusks – the outside of an ear of corn

Coneflower – purplish blue coneflowers are a source of medicine

Cornmeal – flour made from corn

Corral – a fenced place to put livestock

Crack of dawn – the time of day just as the sun rises

Cross spar – a cross bar or beam

Currycomb – a comb with very short teeth used to groom animals like horses

Cypress knees – growths from cypress trees that stick up out of the water

Dedication – to set aside for a special purpose

Deed – a legal document that shows ownership

Deviled eggs – fancy hard-boiled eggs

Disguise – to make one look different either with clothing, makeup, or haircuts

Dime novel – cheap paperback books of the late 1800s

Doubletree – a crossbar on a wagon to which the harnesses are attached

Doubloon – an old Spanish coin of gold, popular with pirates

Drought – a season with a lack of rainwater

Dry goods store – a store that sold cloth, food, clothing, and other products

Dumplings – dough balls that are cooked in meat or fruit stew

Dyspepsia – upset stomach or poor digestion

Eefe – a Miccosukee word for dog

Elegant – fancy or refined

Elixir – a liquid mixture, sometimes with supposed or claimed medicinal powers

Enterprising – a resourceful person who undertakes a difficult task

Entrails – the guts or insides of an animal

Epidemic – a sickness that happens to many people at the same time

Expired – to die or pass away

Famine – a season or time when there is not enough food to eat

Farrier – an individual who works on horses' feet and hooves

Fate – luck

Feed store – a store that sells food for animals

Feeling his oats – when someone acts puffed up, frisky, or smarty

Felly rim – the part of the wheel into which the spokes are fitted

Felt – a soft fabric

Festivities – celebrations

Fiddle – another term for a violin

First-of-Mays – a circus term for newly hired boys and men

Fistfuls – handfuls

Flabbergasted – completely taken by surprise and shocked

Flute – a small instrument played by mouth

Foolishment – cutting up or acting like fools

Frontiers – unknown or previously unvisited areas

Fuddy-duddy – someone who is "out of touch" with the current young generation

Fuss – overreacting to a situation

Gait – how a horse walks or trots

Gangplank – a long wooden or metal ramp used for getting people on or off a ship

Gavel – the official wooden hammer of a judge that he uses to keep order in the court

Gentry – wealthy people

Gingham – checkered cotton cloth

Ginned cotton – cotton that has been separated from the seeds

Gondola – a basket that hangs under a hot-air balloon

Good Book – the Bible

Goose down – the soft, downy feathers from a goose that are stuffed into a blanket-like covering

Gout – a painful joint disease caused by poor diet

Grudge – a personal problem with someone else that you, or they, don't forget

Hammock – a sling bed made of blankets or rope and hung between two points

Hamper – a basket-like container with a lid

Harmonica – a reed/wind instrument that you play with your mouth

Heirlooms – valuable family possessions passed from generation to generation

Herbivores – plant-eating animals

Hickory – a hardwood tree whose wood is very strong and good for making bows and slingshots

Hogwash – worthless, something of no value, garbage, water left from washing hogs

Hoist – to lift up in the air

Hornbooks – early schoolbooks on wooden paddles, covered in thin layers of cow horn

Hornswoggler – a deceiver or cheater

Hostile – a reaction like that of an enemy

Hotcakes – pancakes

House raising – where a group of family and friends gather to build a new house in a few days

Huffy – arrogant or mad

Hummingbird – a very tiny bird that eats nectar from plants

Impounded – belongings that are taken into custody by officials for safekeeping

Inscription – the words that are engraved on a piece of jewelry or in stone

Iron tonic – a liquid mixture, in this case containing an important nutrient, iron

Irrigation – a method to bring water to crops in the field

Jaundice – a liver condition where the skin color turns yellow

Jerky – meat strips that have been dried to prevent spoiling

Johnny cake – a small cornmeal bread

Jon boat – a flat-bottomed boat that can be propelled by poling or rowing

Jostling – to move around violently

Jubilation – a joyous celebration

Kapok – the fiber from a tropical tree used as stuffing for pillows, dolls, and mattresses

Keel over – to fall over or turn over

Kegs – barrel-like containers, typically made of wood with metal bands

Kinfolk – relatives or family

Lag – a term in marbles where the players try to get their marble closest to a line drawn on the ground. The player whose marble is closest has "won the lag" and goes first.

Lago Maggiore – a lake in Northern Italy just north of Milan

Land Deed Office – an official place where they record, file, and store all the land deeds

Lard – hog fat

Lashed – tied down

Latrines – primitive bathrooms

Leap year – occurs every fourth year when February has 29 days in the month

Levee – a dam to hold back a lake or a river

Lifeline – a rope thrown from a boat to save a drowning person in the water

Limestone – rock that is very soft and easily worn away by water

Liniment – a lotion rubbed on the skin for healing sore muscles

Linseed oil – oil extracted from the flax plant, used as waterproofing

Little Dipper – a group of stars that look like a water scoop, contains the North Star in the handle or tail

Livelihood – a job, or how someone makes his or her living

Livery stables – a place for horses to be housed and cared for

Lurches – moves abruptly

Mahogany – a beautiful reddish-brown wood

Malaise – the general feeling of being unhealthy, sickly

Manatee – a large, aquatic, plant-eating mammal found in sub-tropical areas

Mandolin – a stringed instrument like a guitar

Mantis – a predatory insect whose front legs look like it's praying

Matinee – a show that is offered in the afternoon

Midway – an area of a circus or fair where there are games to play and foods to eat

Militia – a military-like group made of ordinary citizens rather than professional soldiers

Milkweed – a wild plant that when squeezed, produces a milky-white liquid

Millinery – related to the making or selling of hats

Mold – a form of fungus that grows on some foods

Mongrel – a dog of several unknown breeds

Mortar and pestle – old time medicinal vessels made of heavy porcelain. The mortar is the container, and the pestle is the hand-held grinder.

Mourning – a time of sadness or grief

Mugs – drinking glasses with handles

Murmur – to whisper or mutter so no one can understand what is being said

Muslin – a fine cotton fabric

Narcissus – a beautiful flower and also the title of a song written by Ethelbert Nevin

Ne'er-do-well – a shortened term for never-do-well, a bad person or villain

Nip – small sips or drinks of a beverage

Noggin – slang for your head

Nog-no-chee impigee-tsabanah – Miccosukee words for "boy wants to eat"

Nook and cranny – little spaces

North Star – the star at the tail of the Little Dipper, also called Polaris

Nubs – very short pieces of something

Odyssey – a journey or long trip

Oilcloth – a waterproof cloth

Okee – Miccosukee word for "water," as in Lake Okeechobee (chobee means "big")

Old maid – an older unmarried woman

Onion grass – a plant that has an onion flavor to it

Opera – a musical play that has only singing

Operator – the individual who sends and receives messages by telegraph. They know how to use Morse code on the telegraph key that clicks out the signals.

Operettas – similar to an opera but there is singing and speaking, usually humorous

Orphan – a child with no parents

Orphanage – a place where children with no parents live

Osprey – a large bird of prey, referred to as a fish eagle

Outhouse – a primitive bathroom located outside

Overalls – clothes that combine jeans with an upper portion that is held up by suspenders

Pace – the speed of something

Pallet – a small bed

Pantalettes – undergarments for girls and ladies similar to frilly pants

Panther – large wild predator, member of the big-cat family with lions and tigers

Pantry – a cupboard in the kitchen, typically for storing canned and dry foods

Pattern books – books that contain dress patterns for sewing

Peddler – a salesman

Philistines – ancient, fierce, war-like people to which the giant, Goliath, belonged; the enemy

Piccolo – a small instrument similar to a flute

Pinafore – a sleeveless, decorative garment worn as an apron over a dress

Pistachios – hard-shell, green nuts from trees in Iran and Afghanistan

Plane – a woodworking tool for smoothing out lumber

Plantations – large farms

Plumes – large clouds of smoke or ornate, tall feathers on a headdress or costume

Pneumonia – a sickness of the lungs that makes it very difficult to breathe

Porcelain – material made from clay that is heated in an oven to make it hard

Porter – the person on a train or ship who helps with the luggage

Possession – something you own or personal belongings

Postmaster – the official in charge of the post office

Postmistress – the woman official in charge of the post office

Pound cake – a cake traditionally made up of a pound each of butter, flour, and sugar

Pulleys – mechanical devices with round disks on which ropes or chains are placed to multiply pulling strength

Quack – someone who practices medicine with no training

Quarantine – to isolate or separate from others

Quicksand – a mixture of sand and water in the ground that can trap people or animals and cause them to drown

Quilts – a blanket made up of pieces of cloth sewn together

Rafters – the support beams for a roof

Rancid – when fat goes bad and smells

Rapscallion – a rascal, a trickster, a kid who pulls pranks

Redd up – an old term for cleaning up

Regenerative – able to restore to health

Reinforce – to make stronger

Remedy – a medical cure

Rhubarb – a vegetable with long, red stalks that is cooked and sweetened before eating

Ride shotgun – a term for someone who rides next to the driver, as in a stagecoach

Ringmaster – the official announcer of the circus inside the "Big Top" tent

Roll-out – the morning time when everyone gets out of bed and begins their day

Roundhouse – a boxing term for a punch that starts behind the body and comes all the way around to the front

Ruckus – a disturbance or commotion

Rump – the rear end of an animal

Rustlers – criminals who steal livestock

Sack – a bag

Sacking – a primitive form of a sleeping bag

Saltwater taffy – candy that originated in Atlantic City, New Jersey

Sand dunes – large mounds of sand that typically line a beach area

Sawdust – the fine shavings of wood leftover from sawing

Sawhorses – the wooden supports that are used in carpentry to hold pieces of lumber for sawing

Scalawag – a bad person, a ne'er-do-well, a scoundrel

Scoundrel – someone who is no good, a villain

Scout – someone who goes in advance of others to see what is ahead

Scrounged – gathered from a variety of places

Scruffy – not tidy or overgrown with weeds

Sea cow – another term for a manatee

Sea glass – glass from broken bottles and jars that wash up on the shore, but due to wave action and the sand, the glass gets very smooth and frosty

Shingle-rot – what happens to the shingles of a roof when they decompose or rot

Showoff – someone who draws attention to himself

Shut-eye – sleep

Shutters – the protective or decorative covers for windows

Sign language – gestures or movements of the hands that mean words or phrases

Silhouette – the outline of someone

Silver dollar – a silver coin worth $1.00

Sixth sense – a feeling someone gets beyond the five senses of taste, touch, smell, sight, or hearing, usually a warning

Skeeters – a slang term for mosquitoes

Skillet – a large kitchen frying pan

Skimp – use too little of

Skink – a small lizard

Slate – a sheet of flat rock used for chalkboards in old schools

Slingshot – a Y-shaped branch and a rubber sling that shoots rocks or marbles

Soft spot – the heart

Spangles – shiny, decorative beads or sequins

Spanish colonial style – a form of architecture in an old style

Spec – a circus term, meaning the grand entrance of the performers and animals into the Big Top

Spine – a backbone

Splint – a flat piece of wood to keep a broken arm or leg stiff or unbending

Splinter – a sliver or sharp piece of wood that gets embedded in the skin

Spry – very active or lively, nimble

Stakes – the wooden sticks hammered into the ground to which ropes are tied

Stand of oaks – a group or cluster of oak trees

Starched – clothes that have been treated with cornstarch to make them stiff

Steam engine – a train locomotive powered by steam from burning wood or coal

Steamer – a steamship that operates on steam

Stellar – outstanding

Stew – a very thick, soup-like food with vegetables and meat

Stockade – a fenced area used for keeping livestock contained

Strongbox – a protective box for storing valuables

Stubs – short remains or pieces of something

Stupefied – utterly amazed, confused, or in shock

Sundries – various or miscellaneous supplies

Swamp cabbage – the center of the palm tree that is edible

Sweetheart – someone you are in love with

Swindled – to be cheated by someone

Swooning vapors – passing out or becoming unconscious

Syrup – a thick liquid

Talons – the very powerful claws on an osprey's feet

Tassels – fancy, stringy decorations bound together at one end but loose at the other

Tattles – tells or informs on someone

Teeming – overflowing or excessive numbers

Telegraph – a signal that is sent by wires in a code (Morse) and decoded elsewhere into words

Territory – a large piece of land

Threshold – the entrance to, a doorway

Tidbit – a small piece

Timpani – large, kettle-shaped drums

Tin plate – a thin dinner plate made of a cheap metal

Tincture – a liquid medicine in alcohol

Tizzy – uproar or confused state

Tomboy – a girl who plays or does a lot of "boy" things

Tonics – liquid medicines

Translate – to interpret or talk from one language to another

Trapezes – the swings that are above the circus floor on which performers swing

Tripod – a three-legged stand

Troll – an evil creature of fantasy or folklore

Trombone – a large horn with a sliding piece that creates the different notes

Trout – a freshwater fish known for its excellent flavor

Trumpet – a brass horn that has three valves for making different notes

Trunk – a large, box-like piece of luggage, or an elephant's long nose

Tuba – a very large horn that wraps around the body and makes low notes

Turbans – strips of cloth that are wrapped around the head like a hat

Turpentine – a liquid that is made from pine tree sap and used to clean paintbrushes

Undertaker – a mortician, one who prepares a body for burial

Uppercut – a boxing term meaning to strike upward with the fist

Varmints – a slang term for predatory animals

Vehement – intense feeling, usually of disgust

Venison – meat from a deer

Vexation – trouble

Vittles – food

Vociferous – loud, blatant, strident

Waltzing – an old-style elegant dance from the 1700s done in ¾ music time

War Between the States – another term for the American Civil War

Wardrobe – a piece of furniture for hanging clothes, takes the place of a closet

Warmouth perch – a small freshwater fish

Washtub – a large, metal tub used for laundry

Wheelwright – the person who builds and repairs wooden wheels

Whereabouts – a term for "where you are located"

Whey – the watery part of milk after solids are taken out, as in the making of butter or cheese

Whippersnapper – a term for a smarty-acting child or someone who is unimportant but acts important

Whippoorwill – a songbird whose call sounds like "whip-poor-will"

Whirlwind – a swirling wind, similar to a tornado

Whitewash – a mixture of lime and water used to whiten a surface

Whiz – a smart person for his or her age

Whoop-de-doo – a noisy celebration, dance, or party

Wicks – the waxed strings in the centers of candles that you light with matches

Willies – the "creeps" or something scary

Willow trees – trees that grow by water and have long, thin branches

Withers – the highest point of the back, behind the neck of a horse

Wooden stays – the wooden supports on a wagon that hold the canvas in place

Wreath – a large, decorative circle of vines or branches that is hung on a door or wall

Xylophone – percussion instrument with wooden plates that, when struck, plays notes

Yellow fever – a sickness that is carried by mosquitoes and causes very high fevers

Yoke – a wooden bar that attaches two animals together

"Teddy Bee" Questions
Now that you've finished the story, test your knowledge of
The Astonishing Journey of Teddy Bodain with a "Teddy Bee."
This game is for fun, only!

1. What town in Mississippi did Teddy come from?
2. What is the name of her Mississippi school teacher?
3. Where did Miss Melman grow up?
4. What is the name of the Indian woman who nursed Teddy back to health?
5. What are the names of the two elephant trainers?
6. What is Mr. Obadiah Lincoln's son's name?
7. What is a Spec?
8. What is the poem that tells us whether your snake is a coral snake or not?
9. What is the name of Miss Emily Carter's baby?
10. What is the name of Miss Melman's new school?
11. What kind of snake bit Miss Emily Carter?
12. What is Mr. Mikelson's first name?
13. Who was the man in Miss Melman's locket?
14. What kind of meat did Mama and Teddy use to make jerky?
15. What was Teddy's grandmother's name?
16. What type of transportation did Teddy use to get to the Greens' farm?
17. What kept Baby Dylan from falling out of the wagon?
18. To what operetta did Miss Melman take Teddy and Mama?
19. What is the name of the two rivers in Florida that share the same name?
20. What does a farrier do?
21. Who bought Jester and Jingo?
22. What song did Mama want to learn to play on the piano?
23. What is the name of Verna Dudd's oldest daughter?
24. What did Mr. Green do for a living?
25. What two things did Mr. Green suggest would bring in money for Pap?
26. What did Mama paint on the canvas of the wagon?
27. How did Jimbo Dudd get the scar on his face?
28. What did Travis Lark win away from Teddy?
29. Who did Pap work for in Mississippi?
30. What object helped Teddy prove who was the real Dalton Bodain?
31. What is Mama's first name?
32. Where did Pap sleep most nights?
33. How did Travis and Jasper cut Teddy's kite string?
34. What cool drink does Teddy fix for Mama?
35. What instruments does Pap play?
36. What is the party called when the two wagon trains get together?
37. What is the name of Mama's milk cow?
38. What is Miss Melman's first name?
39. Who is Travis Lark's best friend?
40. What instrument does Miss Melman play?
41. What is the name of Pap's horse?
42. What is the name of Captain Walsh's horse?

43. What is the name of Travis Lark's horse?
44. What is the name of Daniel Bodain's horse?
45. What kind of dolls do Minnie and Hallie own?
46. Whose hair was first on Veronica?
47. Whose hair was finally on Veronica?
48. What was the name of the product Dr. Zoren sold?
49. From what country did Dr. Zoren claim his Elixir of Life came?
50. What is the name of Teddy's baby brother?
51. Who is Dr. Zoren's assistant?
52. In what town did they attend the operetta?
53. What did Dylan say when the camera flash went off?
54. Who winked at Teddy?
55. What did the pirate drop in Teddy's lap?
56. What kind of skirts did Miss Melman wear?
57. When was Teddy's birthday?
58. How old was Teddy on her birthday?
59. What word did Teddy miss in the first spelling bee?
60. How much was Teddy tipped to deliver a loaf of fresh bread?
61. How many miles was Teddy's original journey from Mississippi to Florida?
62. What did Travis Lark make for Teddy and teach her how to use?
63. What were the fishing poles made out of that Pap and Teddy fished with?
64. What did Dylan always beg to play with?
65. What did Mr. Carter paint on Hallie's arm bandage to keep it stiff?
66. What did Captain Walsh give Hallie because she broke her arm?
67. How did Mama dry out Pap's feet?
68. What did Mama rub on Pap's feet?
69. What book did Miss Melman read to the wagon train class?
70. What does Tom Sawyer trick his friends into doing?
71. What does Mama agree to teach Miss Melman?
72. Who gave Ethelbert to Teddy?
73. What happened to the sheriff's kitty when she drank Dr. Zoren's elixir?
74. What three things did Pap point out to Teddy in the night sky?
75. What does Teddy repeat to get her directions during the day?
76. In what town did the Bodains buy their oxen?
77. What sad news does Martha write to Teddy?
78. What do you say to get an oxen team to turn left?
79. What do you say to get an oxen team to turn right?
80. What does Teddy pick behind Verna's house?
81. Where did Teddy and Daniel have to first sleep when they joined the circus?
82. After they became elephant performers, where did Teddy and Daniel get to sleep?
83. What is Mama's favorite songbird?
84. When Travis made a burlap troll, what was it used for?
85. What trick did Miss Melman play on April Fools' Day?
86. What sound did the soldier hear when he tried to go into the Bodains' wagon at night?
87. What did Mama ask Teddy to put in the buckets of dirty clothes?
88. What reptile bit Ethelbert's thigh?
89. What is Dr. Zoren's first name?

90. What large bird did Captain Walsh point out when they visited the swamp?
91. What little brown animals were swimming in the swamp among the cypress knees?
92. Who was the first person to dive in with the manatee?
93. What three things did Pap keep in the secret compartment?
94. Who gave Pap's watch to him?
95. How many acres of land did Mr. Albritton give to Pap?
96. How did the wagon train cross the Apalachicola River?
97. What did Travis accidentally drop in the river?
98. Who made new clothes for Veronica after she was ruined?
99. What dish did the women ask Mama to bring to the whoop-de-doo?
100. What beautiful items had Mama made that Jasper told about in his interview?
101. What did Teddy and Pap use for bait?
102. Who washed Teddy's hair when she was with the wagon train?
103. Who cut Teddy's hair?
104. What did Daniel write on the riverbank?
105. What was the name of the boys' first kite?
106. What was the name of the girls' first kite?
107. What was the name of the boys' second kite?
108. What was the name of the girls' second kite?
109. Whose wagon tumbled down the hill?
110. What epidemic hit the wagon train that killed some of the people?
111. What did Captain Walsh tell Travis that would be fun to do in the spring?
112. Whose bloomers did Teddy see in the spring?
113. What did Travis and Teddy use to fan the sand?
114. Whose bracelet did Teddy find in the spring?
115. What was inscribed inside Althea Tomlinson's bracelet?
116. What caused the scars on Mr. Obadiah Lincoln's back?
117. Who was Miss Melman crying for in the middle of the night?
118. What did Lucas Lincoln say was fit for a king and a queen?
119. What was the name of the lady at the quarantine station who took care of Teddy?
120. Who helped scrounge food so Teddy could escape from the quarantine station?
121. Where did Teddy sleep the first night after she left the quarantine station?
122. What mean poem did Teddy say to Althea Tomlinson's daughter?
123. Who told Pap that Teddy had died?
124. What was Miss Essie Mae Pitts known for?
125. What is the date on the inside of the bracelet Teddy found?
126. Who had originally given the bracelet to Althea Tomlinson?
127. What was in the brown paper sack the baker gave Teddy?
128. Where was Ethelbert hiding the night that Teddy snuck into her family's wagon?
129. What book did Teddy use to hide the light in the impounded wagon?
130. Who owned the hot-air balloon Teddy rode in?
131. What was Carlene Green's dog's name?
132. What was Dr. Winklepleck's first name?
133. What did Mrs. Green make for dinner that impressed Dr. Winklepleck?
134. Which one of Verna Dudd's children throws things at animals?
135. What is the name of the steamer that takes Daniel and Teddy down to Ft. Pierce?
136. What does the judge rap on the wooden table?

137. What happened to Daniel's father?
138. What did Mrs. Carter's mother teach her when she was a girl?
139. What did Mama do so that they could always recognize their own wagon?
140. What did Pap say he had never done as a child?
141. What two things did Teddy do to disguise Daniel's hair?
142. What was the name of the matriarch elephant who was in charge of all the other elephants?
143. What kind of people did Teddy meet from the circus midway?
144. Who was the first person to spot the manatee at Fanning Springs?
145. What did Miss Melman say is another name for a manatee?
146. What was the name of the canvas house that Teddy used to change in at the beach?
147. What kind of boat did Wanda Watson give to Teddy and Daniel?
148. What did Dr. Winklepleck call the basket that hung underneath her balloon?
149. What animal jumped onto Ethelbert's back at the circus?
150. What new last name did Massimo give Teddy and Daniel?
151. What was the name of the bed and breakfast that Teddy stayed at in Juno?
152. What was the name of Nokosi's granddaughter?
153. Why did everyone come to the Bodains' new land at the end of the story?
154. How many sons did Captain Walsh have?
155. What happened to Captain Walsh's wife?
156. Where did Pap hide the land deed?
157. What hung underneath the Bodains' wagon?
158. What was Baby Dylan's middle name?
159. What was the name of Martha's kitty who died?
160. What does Massimo call out to make the elephants spin in a circle?
161. What is the first name of Massimo's brother who owned the Italian restaurant?
162. What is one of the dishes that was served to Teddy at the Italian restaurant?
163. What color did Teddy dye Daniel's hair?
164. What jumped onto Dr. Zoren's face that allowed Ethelbert to escape from him?
165. What was the book that Miss Melman chose as "the girls' book"?
166. What special sweet treat did Miss Melman give the students?
167. What did Mama buy for Miss Emily to thank her for keeping Dylan?
168. Who went to the dentist to have a tooth pulled in Dothan?
169. What did Teddy do to Ethel's leg when he was bit by the rattlesnake?
170. What did Miss Melman say she collects, the day they went to the seashore?
171. What story did Teddy read aloud to Mama?
172. Who did Teddy say reminded her of Tom Sawyer?
173. Who did the pocketknife belong to that Wanda Watson gave to Teddy?
174. What was in the box that Pap said not to open, at the end of the story?
175. Who played "Narcissus" in the Bodains' new home at the end of the story?
176. Why did Mama say she chose the name Veronica for the new baby?
177. What made Mama leap into the water on the day the wagons were to cross the river?
178. Which character did Teddy say was her favorite in *Little Women*?
179. Which character did Mama say was her favorite in *Little Women*?
180. Who got to keep Mrs. Althea Tomlinson's bracelet at the end of the story?
181. What are the names of the two Good sisters?

"Teddy Bee" Answer Key

1. Salter's Grove
2. Miss Pedigrew
3. Charleston, South Carolina
4. Sawni
5. Suzanna and Massimo
6. Lucas Lincoln
7. The grand entrance into the Big Top at the start of the circus
8. Red on yellow, kill a fellow. Red on black, won't harm Jack.
9. Lucy
10. The Sheridan School for Girls
11. Scarlet king snake
12. John
13. Her sweetheart, Edward James Hudson
14. Venison or deer meat
15. Isabelle Bodain
16. Hot-air balloon
17. His playpen or the little seat Pap made for him to ride "shotgun"
18. *The Pirates of Penzance*
19. Withlacoochee
20. Checks horses hooves and puts shoes on horses
21. The dentist in Dothan, Alabama
22. "Narcissus"
23. Sissy
24. He was a farmer
25. Cattle and tomatoes
26. Flowers
27. A knife fight with Billy Bob Gates
28. Marbles
29. Mr. Albritton
30. Pap's pocket watch
31. Grace
32. Outside underneath the wagon
33. They put glue and crushed glass on their line and sawed their string against Teddy's.
34. Lemonade
35. Harmonica and fiddle
36. A whoop-de-doo
37. Girlie
38. Cassie
39. Jasper Lowe or Teddy Bodain
40. Piano
41. Gabriel
42. Highlander
43. Dixie
44. Swift
45. Cornhusk dolls
46. Martha's (Martha Lyndall's)
47. Travis Lark's
48. Dr. Zoren's Elixir of Life
49. Rambonia
50. Dylan
51. Flavia
52. Meridian, Mississippi
53. "Boom!"
54. A pirate (an actor in *The Pirates of Penzance*)
55. A pink rose
56. Starched white skirts
57. June 4th
58. 11 years old
59. Jostling
60. 2 cents
61. 1,000 miles
62. A slingshot
63. Bamboo
64. Teddy's doll, Veronica
65. A thick coat of wax
66. A silver dollar
67. She lit a fire in a washtub up in the wagon and propped Pap's feet up over it.
68. Lard
69. *Tom Sawyer*
70. Whitewashing Aunt Polly's fence
71. To cook
72. The constable
73. The kitty got drunk.
74. The Big Dipper, the Little Dipper, and the North Star
75. The sun rises in the east and sets in the west.
76. Dothan, Alabama
77. That her kitty, Bernice, died
78. "Haw"
79. "Gee"
80. Blackberries
81. The "possum belly," a storage shelf under the wagons
82. In the costume wagon
83. The redbird or cardinal
84. Target practice for the slingshots
85. The fake rattlesnake fangs trick (with a rubber band and paperclip in an envelope)
86. "Z-z-z-z-z-z!!!" He thought it was a rattlesnake.
87. Rocks from the river
88. A rattlesnake
89. Xavier
90. Osprey
91. Otters
92. Miss Melman

93. His land deed, money, and his pocket watch
94. His father
95. 40 acres
96. By ferryboat
97. Teddy's doll, Veronica
98. Miss Emily Carter
99. Macaroni and cheese
100. Quilts
101. Crickets
102. Mama
103. Daniel
104. DANIEL BODAIN
105. The Destroyer
106. The Florida Belle
107. The Kite Killer
108. The Florida Belle Two
109. The Porters
110. Yellow fever
111. Swimming and fanning for treasure
112. Miss Melman's
113. A piece of slate
114. Althea Tomlinson's
115. To Althea Tomlinson from her loving husband, Joseph. How do I love thee? Let me count the ways. August 13, 1862.
116. He was whipped when he was a slave.
117. Her first sweetheart, Edward James Hudson
118. Teddy's biscuits
119. Mrs. Plum
120. She was a young girl who had also been sick. Teddy never knew her name.
121. In a hammock in the backyard of a house on the edge of town
122. "Finders keepers, losers weepers."
123. Miss Essie Mae Pitts
124. Her delicious pound cake
125. August 13, 1862
126. Her husband, Joseph
127. Three jelly doughnuts
128. Inside the hammock beneath the wagon
129. *Little Women*
130. Dr. Winklepleck
131. Freddy
132. Amanda
133. Fried chicken
134. Georgie
135. The Lady Augustine
136. His gavel
137. He got pneumonia and died.
138. Which plants were good for different ailments

139. She painted flowers on it.
140. Written a letter
141. Cut and dye it
142. Babbette
143. Performers like a fire eater, a man who swallows swords, a woman whose neck is ten inches long and covered in brass coils, Lena, the alligator woman, and a man whose entire body is covered in hair
144. Debbie Goguen
145. Sea cow
146. A cabana
147. A jon boat
148. A gondola
149. A monkey
150. Tornecki
151. Molly Baden's Bed and Breakfast
152. Talisa
153. To help with the house raising
154. Two
155. She died years ago.
156. In the secret compartment underneath the wagon
157. A hammock that Mama made for Teddy
158. Luke
159. Bernice
160. "Around the World!"
161. Stefano
162. Sausages, peppers, fish, meats, cheeses, octopus
163. Black
164. A banana spider
165. *Alice's Adventures in Wonderland*
166. Peppermint sticks
167. Lemon drops
168. Mama
169. She squeezed out the poison by massaging his leg in the river.
170. Sea glass
171. *Little Women*
172. Travis Lark
173. Wanda's son, Samuel
174. A piano
175. Mama
176. Because Teddy gave up her most prized possession for Dylan, and the baby's mother had given up her most prized possession to Mama.
177. She thought Dylan was in the water drowning.
178. Jo
179. Beth
180. Teddy
181. Minnie and Hallie

Lesson Answer Key — Grammar Questions

Day 6
1. A.
2. B.
3. D.
4. C.
5. A.
6. D.

Day 14
1. C.
2. A.
3. C.
4. D.
5. B.
6. B.

Day 22
1. A.
2. C.
3. D.
4. B.
5. C.
6. A.
7. C.

Day 30
1. D.
2. B.
3. C.
4. A.
5. D.
6. A.
7. C.

Day 38
1. D.
2. B.
3. C.
4. A.
5. C.
6. A.
7. C.

Day 46
1. D.
2. C.
3. A.
4. C.
5. B.
6. C.
7. A.

Day 54
1. A.
2. D.
3. B.
4. C.
5. A.
6. A.

Day 62
1. D.
2. B.
3. C.
4. A.
5. C.
6. B.
7. A.

Day 70
1. D.
2. A.
3. C.
4. A.
5. C.
6. A.
7. B.

Day 78
1. D.
2. B.
3. A.
4. B.
5. D.
6. B.

Day 86
1. D
2. B.
3. C.
4. A.
5. C.
6. A.
7. D.

Day 94
1. B.
2. D.
3. C.
4. B.
5. A.
6. C.

Day 102
1. B.
2. D.
3. A.
4. C.
5. D.
6. A.
7. B.

Day 110
1. C.
2. D.
3. A.
4. B.
5. C.
6. B.

Day 118
1. D.
2. C.
3. A.
4. B.
5. C.
6. D.
7. B.

Day 126
1. D.
2. A.
3. C.
4. C.
5. B.
6. B.
7. C.

Lesson Answer Key — Reading Multiple Choice Questions

Day 1
1. C.
2. D.
3. B.
4. C.
5. A.
6. B.
7. A.

Day 9
1. C.
2. A.
3. B.
4. A.
5. C.
6. B.

Day 17
1. D.
2. B.
3. C.
4. A.
5. C.
6. D.
7. C.

Day 25
1. C.
2. B.
3. D.
4. A.
5. B.
6. D.
7. A.

Day 33
1. D.
2. B.
3. C.
4. A.
5. C.
6. D.
7. B.

Day 41
1. D.
2. B.
3. C.
4. A.
5. C.
6. D.
7. A.

Day 49
1. D.
2. B.
3. C.
4. A.
5. C.
6. D.
7. B.

Day 58
1. D.
2. B.
3. C.
4. A.
5. C.
6. D.
7. B.

Day 65
1. D.
2. B.
3. C.
4. A.
5. C.
6. D.
7. B.

Day 73
1. D.
2. B.
3. C.
4. D.
5. C.
6. D.
7. A.

Day 81
1. C.
2. A.
3. D.
4. B.
5. A.
6. D.
7. C.

Day 89
1. C.
2. A.
3. B.
4. D.
5. A.
6. D.
7. A.

Day 97
1. D.
2. B.
3. C.
4. A.
5. C.
6. D.
7. B.

Day 105
1. D.
2. B.
3. C.
4. A.
5. C.
6. D.
7. C.

Day 113
1. C.
2. D.
3. A.
4. B.
5. C.
6. A.
7. D.

Day 121
1. A.
2. C.
3. B.
4. A.
5. C.
6. D.
7. C.

Day 129
1. C.
2. A.
3. B.
4. D.
5. C.
6. B.
7. B.

Lesson Answer Key — Writing Questions

Day 7
1. C.
2. B.
3. C.
4. B.
5. D.

Day 15
1. C.
2. A.
3. D.
4. C.
5. B.

Day 23
1. D.
2. A.
3. C.
4. B.
5. C.

Day 31
1. C.
2. C.
3. B.
4. B.
5. B.

Day 39
1. C.
2. B.
3. A.
4. B.
5. D.

Day 47
1. B.
2. A.
3. B.
4. B.
5. B.

Day 56
1. D.
2. B.
3. C.
4. D.
5. D.

Day 63
1. C.
2. A.
3. C.
4. D.
5. B.

Day 71
1. B.
2. B.
3. C.
4. D.
5. A.

Day 79
1. B.
2. D.
3. B.
4. C.
5. B.

Day 87
1. B.
2. D.
3. C.
4. B.
5. D.

Day 95
1. A.
2. B.
3. A.
4. B.
5. C.

Day 103
1. A.
2. B.
3. C.
4. B.
5. D.

Day 111
1. C.
2. A.
3. C.
4. B.
5. C.

Day 119
1. B.
2. A.
3. B.
4. C.
5. C.

Day 127
1. C
2. B.
3. C.
4. A.
5. B

Resources for Lessons

There are two major resources for the language arts lessons in
The Astonishing Journey of Teddy Bodain:

Forney, Melissa. (2001). *Razzle Dazzle Writing: Achieving Excellence Through 50 Target Skills.* Gainesville: Maupin House.

Forney, Melissa. (2008). *Writing Superstars: How to Score More Than Ever Before.* Orange City: Buttery Moon Multimedia, Inc. (This is the Florida Edition).

Here is a recommended list of other books that aid in the teaching of persuasive writing:

DePaola, Tomie. (1979). *Oliver Button is a Sissy.* New York: Harcourt Brace Jovanovich.

Diamond, Mark. (2006). *6 Tricks to Persuasive Writing.* Anyone Can Write Books.

Hoose, Phillip. (1998). *Hey, Little Ant.* Berkley: Tricycle Press.

Lane, Barry and Bernabei, Gretchen. (2001). *Why We Must Run With Scissors.* Discover Writing Press.

Lutrario, Chris. *Activities for Teaching Persuasive Writing for Ages 9-11.* New York: Scholastic.

McCarthy, Tara. (1999). *Persuasive Writing.* New York: Scholastic.

Orloff, Karen Kaufman. (2004). *I Wanna Iguana.* New York: Putnam.

Powel, Jillian. (2003). *Activities for Teaching Persuasive Writing for Ages 7-9.* New York: Scholastic.

Rozmiarek, Rebecca. (2004). *Persuasive Writing, Grades 3-5.* Teacher Created Resources.

Rozmiarek, Rebecca. (2004). *Persuasive Writing, Grades 6-8.* Teacher Created Resources.

Viorst, Judith. (1993). *Earrings.* New York: Aladin Books.

How to Use the Following Daily Writing Resources:

Writing Superstars: How to Score More Than Ever Before and *Razzle Dazzle Writing* offer many lessons on specific writing skills. Only you, the classroom teacher, will know the exact needs of your students. Your writers might be proficient in some skills and lacking in others. The lessons that go with *The Astonishing Journey of Teddy Bodain* start on Day 1 and go through Day 130. Some days have writing prompts, some days have reading, writing, or grammar questions. We have listed individual pages in both resource books that speak to specific skills. You may choose lessons and practice pages your students need in either book.

Some teachers may choose to start at the beginning of one of the resource books and work their way ahead as their students continue to read Teddy's story. Others may prefer to pick and choose specific lessons and readers theater plays out of order. Whatever works for you and your students is fine!

Writing Superstars

Narrative Writing Prompts
    pp. 26, 28-30, 33-37, 56, 63-65, 68-69, 101, 107, 156-159, 166, 172-179, 200-203

Expository Writing Prompts
    pp. 27-28, 31-35, 38-39, 63-66, 98-99, 106, 160-163, 168-170, 180-181, 197-199

Grammar Questions
    pp. 116-152

Writing Questions
    pp. 24, 44-49, 52, 57, 79, 83-85, 91-93, 95, 97-107

Razzle Dazzle Writing

Narrative Writing Prompts
    pp. 46-50, 58-87

Expository Writing Prompts
    pp. 48-50, 90-115

Grammar Questions
    pp. 126, 132, 143, 148-157

Writing Questions
    pp. 16-23, 26-45, 64-66, 74-75, 78-79, 93-95, 99-102, 121, 130-132

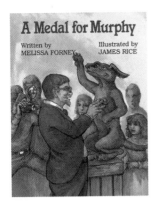

A Medal for Murphy
Written by MELISSA FORNEY
Illustrated by JAMES RICE

OONAWASSEE SUMMER
Melissa Forney

TO SHAPE A LIFE
A tribute to teachers
by Melissa Forney
Illustrated by Judy Richardson

RAZZLE DAZZLE WRITING
Achieving Excellence Through 50 Target Skills
MELISSA FORNEY

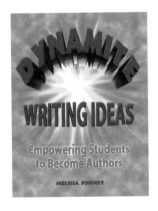

DYNAMITE WRITING IDEAS
Empowering Students to Become Authors
MELISSA FORNEY

Melissa Forney's PICTURE SPELLER FOR YOUNG WRITERS
Written by Melissa Forney
Illustrated by John Bianchi

THE WRITING MENU
Ensuring Success for Every Student
MELISSA FORNEY

Writing Superstars
How to Score More Than Ever Before
MELISSA FORNEY

THE ASTONISHING JOURNEY OF TEDDY BODAIN
Written by Melissa Forney
Illustrated by Dave Olson

THE ASTONISHING JOURNEY OF TEDDY BODAIN
TEACHER EDITION
Written by Melissa Forney • Illustrated by Dave Olson

TEDDY BODAIN'S ADVENTURE QUEST
Written by Melissa Forney • Illustrated by Dave Olson

MELISSA FORNEY'S WRITING CAMP
A READER'S THEATER ADVENTURE FOR YOUNG WRITERS
Written by Melissa Forney • Illustrated by Dave Olson

Primary PIZZAZZ Writing
Melissa Forney

PIZZAZZ! Songs for the Writing Classroom

www.melissaforney.com
800-500-8176

Author, teacher, and educational writing consultant Melissa Forney holds a Masters of Fine Arts in Writing for Children from Vermont College. Her dynamic **writing seminars, young authors conferences,** and humorous, motivational **keynote speeches** have delighted audiences for years. She is a popular speaker and trainer at state, regional, national, and international educational conferences. Schools using her writing books and training have achieved the highest writing assessment scores, revolutionized teaching strategies, and produced innovative, creative student writers. Her hands-on, energetic teacher training and writing workshops consistently receive the highest evaluations.